"BIDDING FAREWELL TO MAGISTRATE FONG"
HYUNG YANG

WE BID FAREWELL TO EACH OTHER ON AN
    AUTUMN DAY.
BEYOND THE DOCK LIE A THOUSAND MILES
    OF LONG ROAD.
THE CARRIAGE STOPS AT THE GLOW OF
    SUNSET.
THE RHYTHM OF A ZITHER HASTENS THE
    FAREWELL DRINKS.
THE TREES OF THE GARDEN ARE
    TINTED WITH THE EVENING SUN.
EVEN BEFORE THE PARTING WORDS ARE
    SPOKEN,
TEARS ROLL DOWN AND WET MY SLEEVES.

TIME AND AGAIN

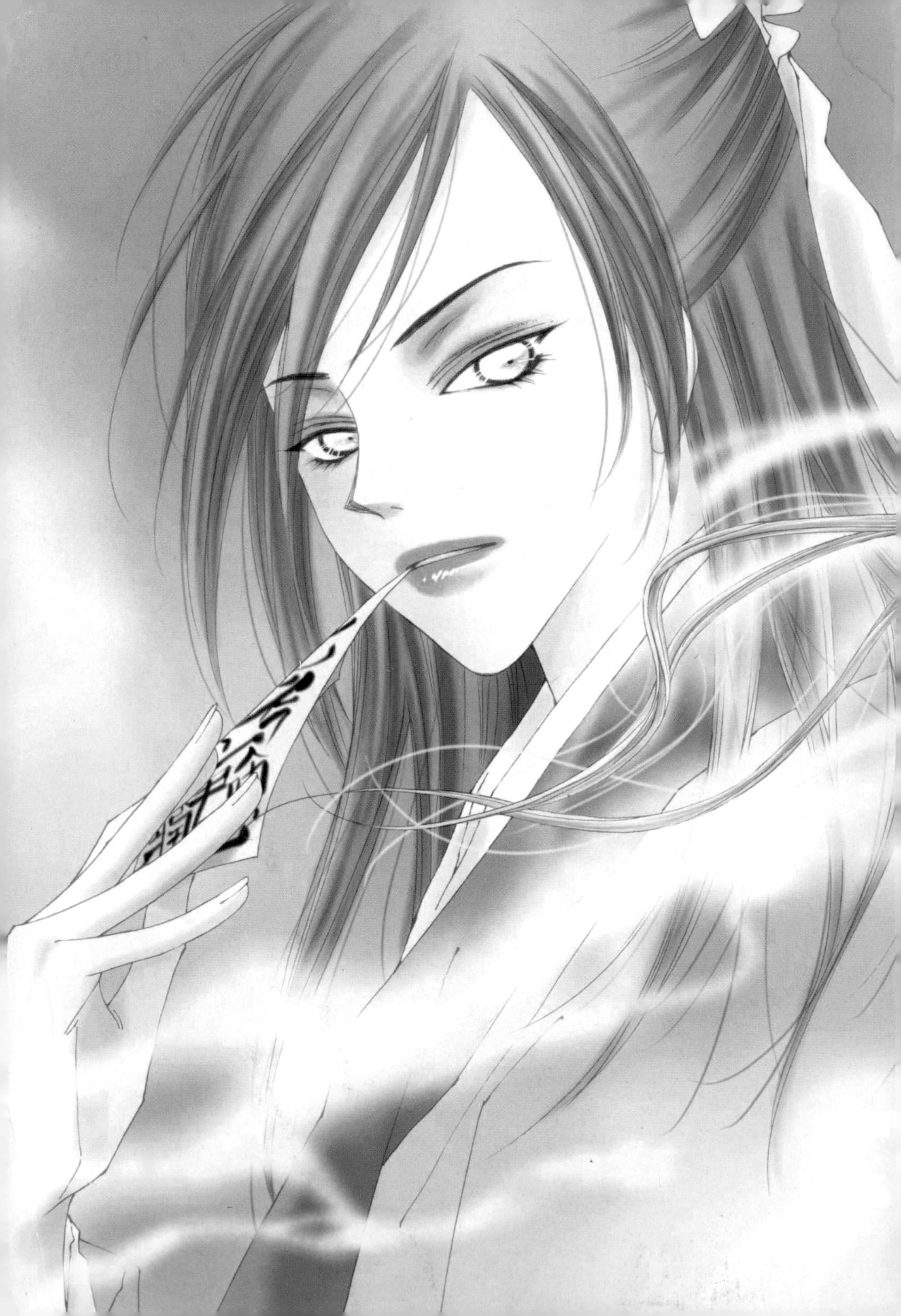

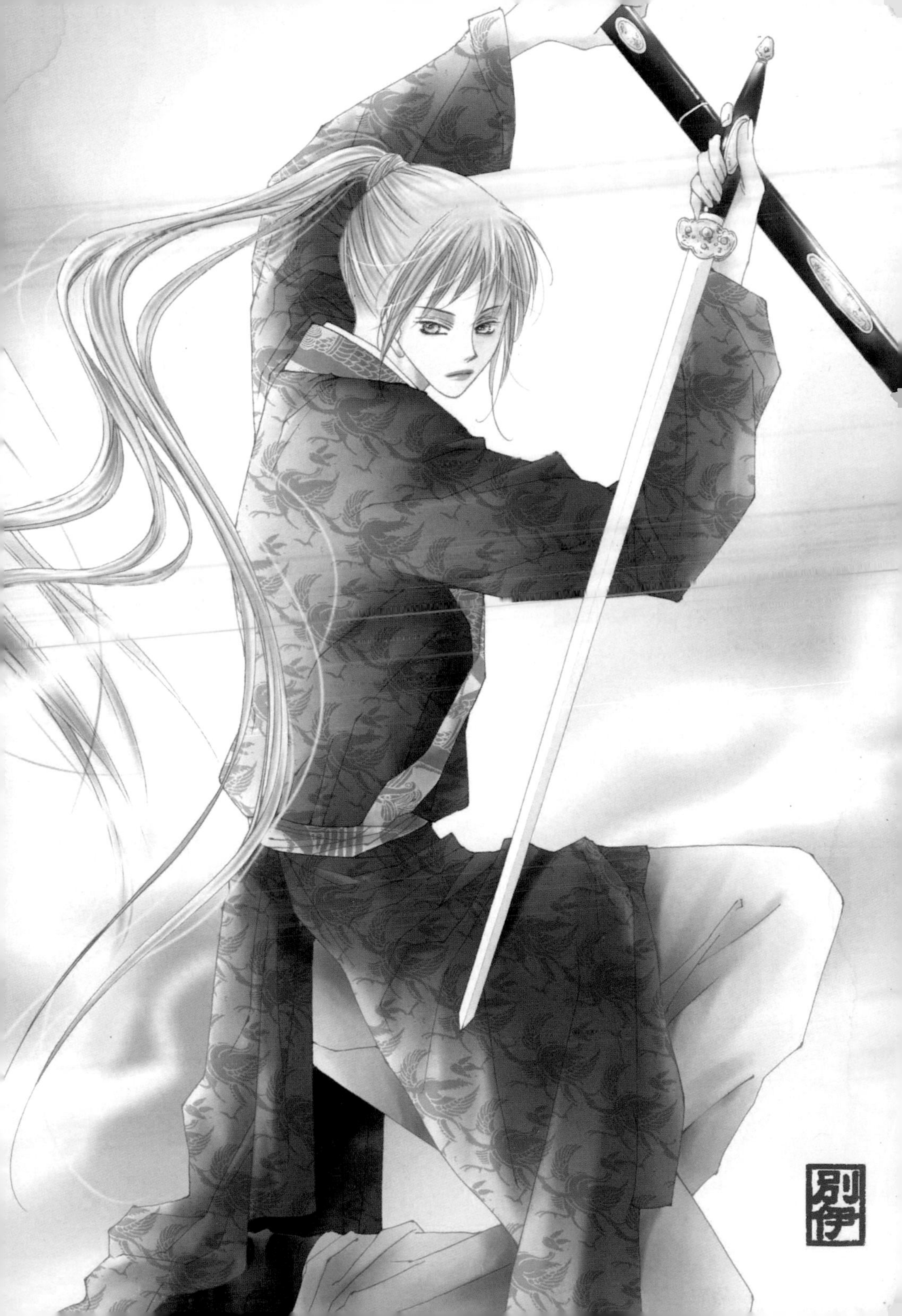
別伊

CONTENTS

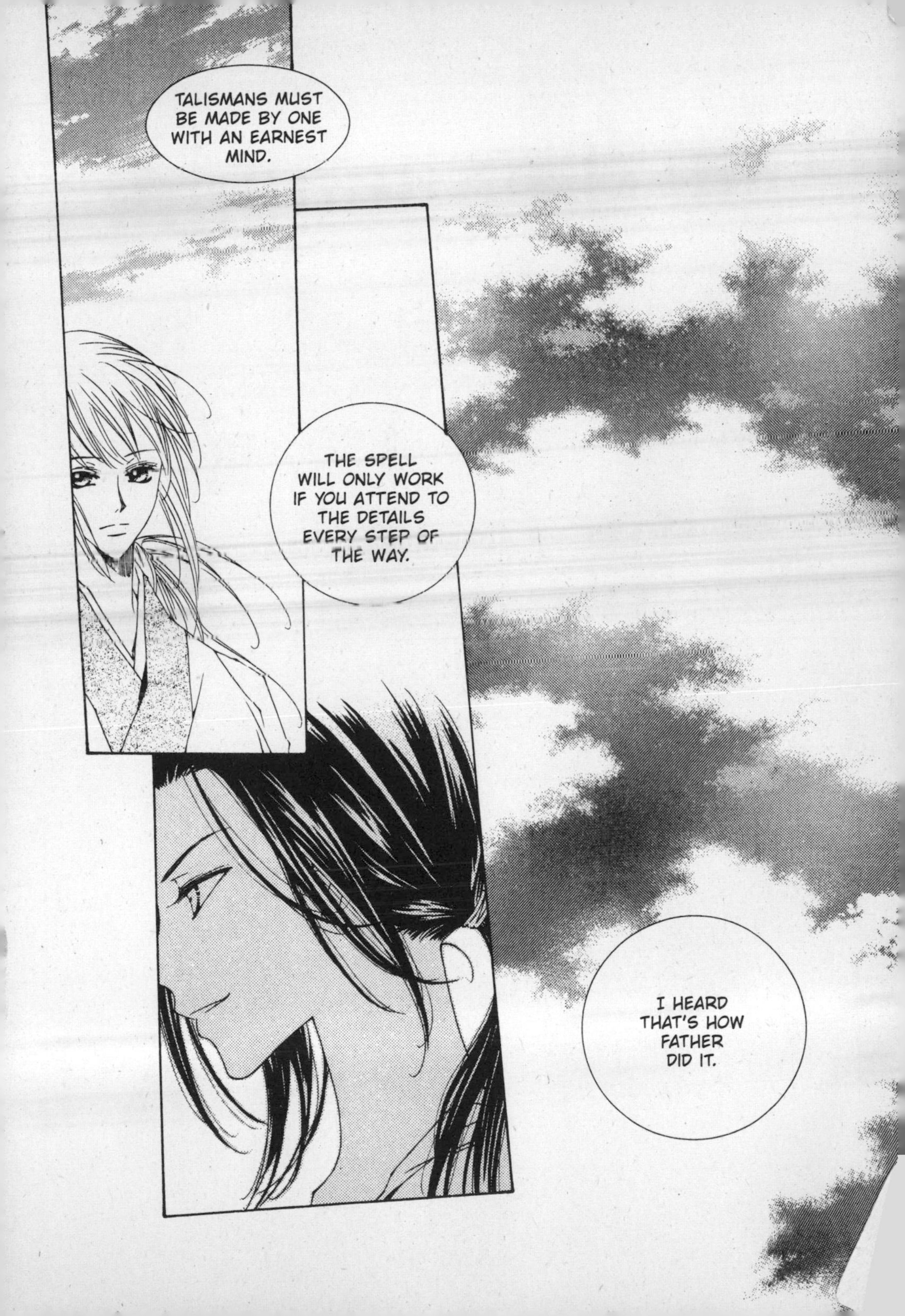
TALISMANS MUST BE MADE BY ONE WITH AN EARNEST MIND.
THE SPELL WILL ONLY WORK IF YOU ATTEND TO THE DETAILS EVERY STEP OF THE WAY.
I HEARD THAT'S HOW FATHER DID IT.

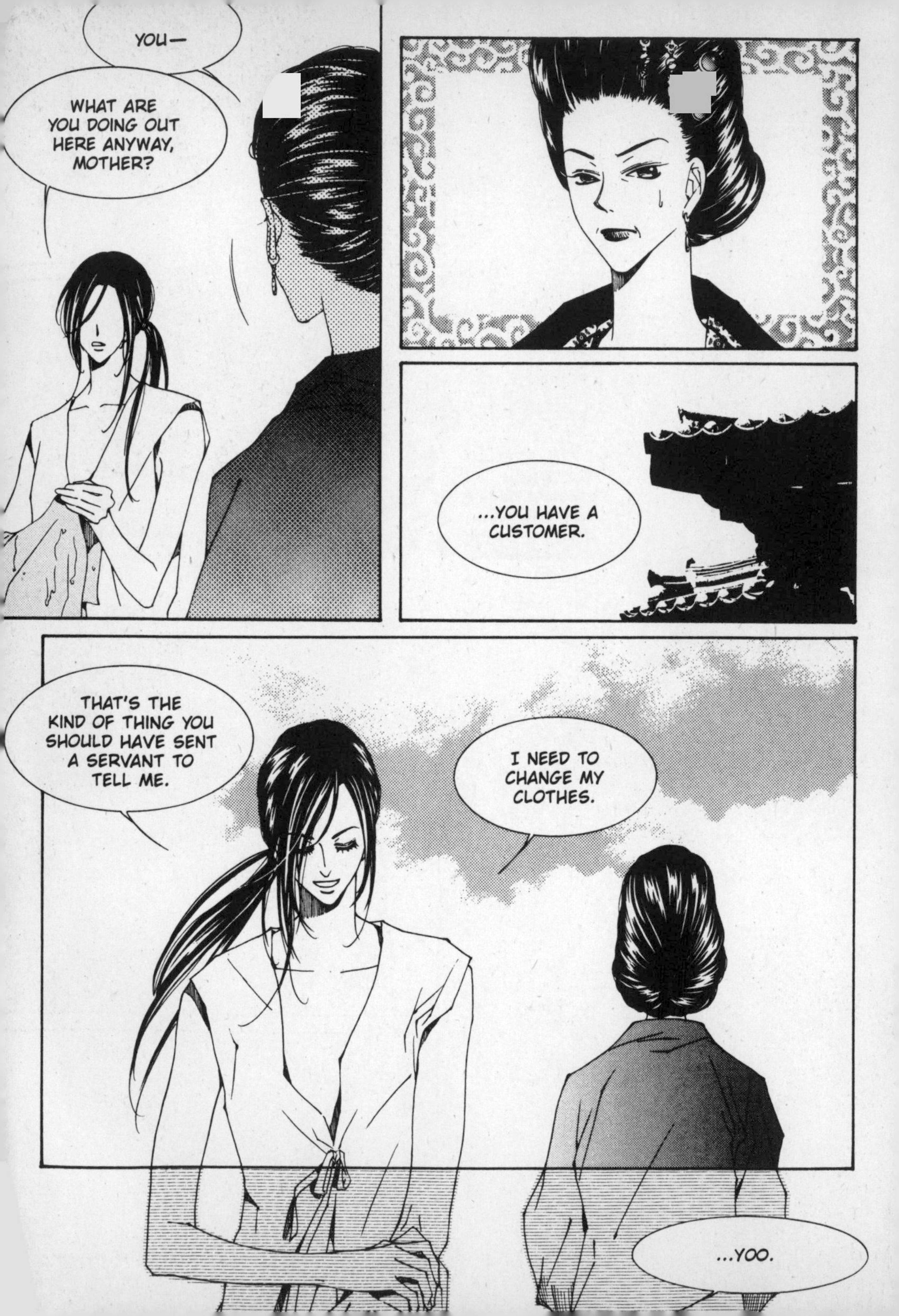
YOU—
WHAT ARE YOU DOING OUT HERE ANYWAY, MOTHER?
...YOU HAVE A CUSTOMER.
THAT'S THE KIND OF THING YOU SHOULD HAVE SENT A SERVANT TO TELL ME.
I NEED TO CHANGE MY CLOTHES.
...YOO.

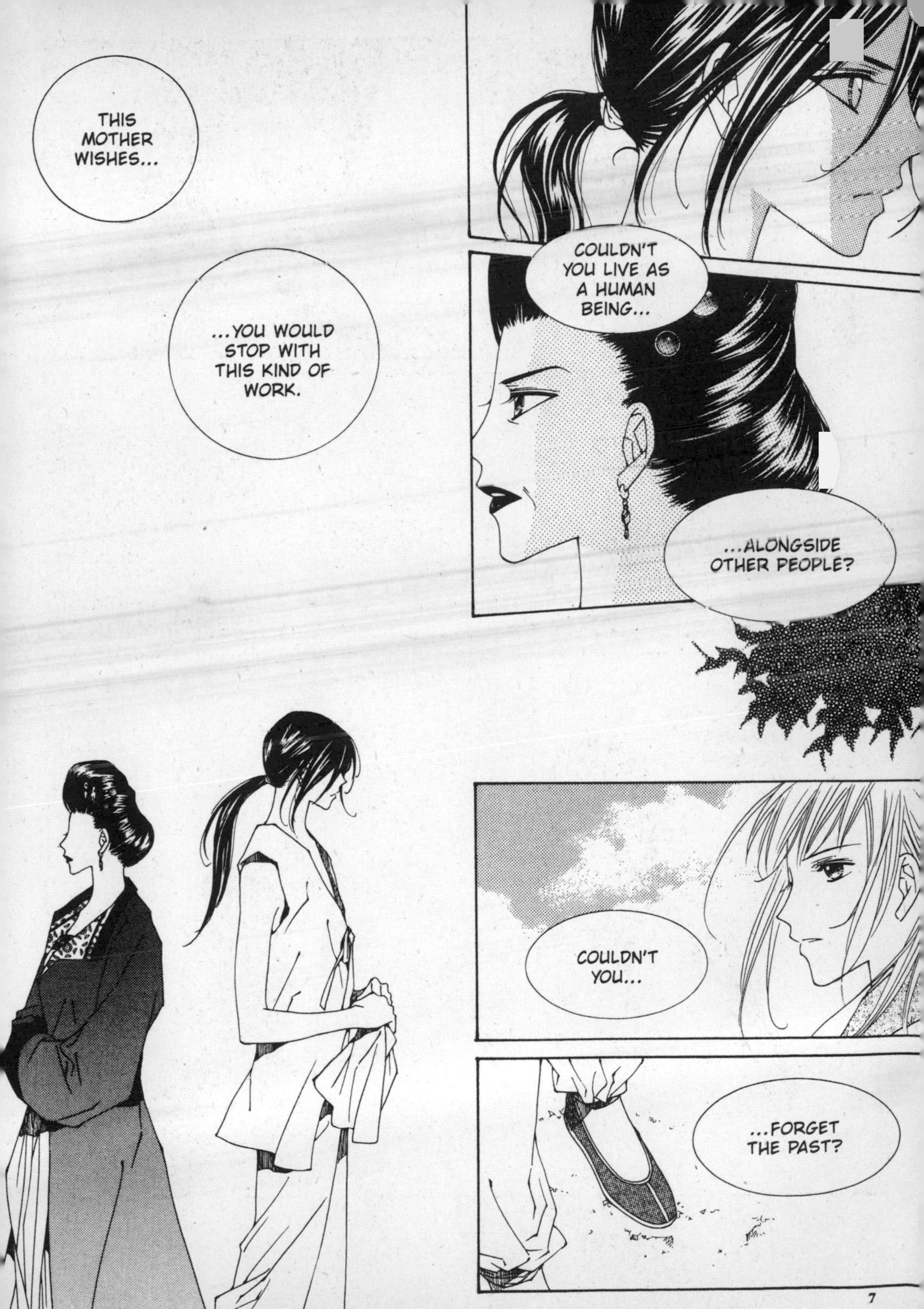
THIS MOTHER WISHES...
...YOU WOULD STOP WITH THIS KIND OF WORK.
COULDN'T YOU LIVE AS A HUMAN BEING...
...ALONGSIDE OTHER PEOPLE?
COULDN'T YOU...
...FORGET THE PAST?

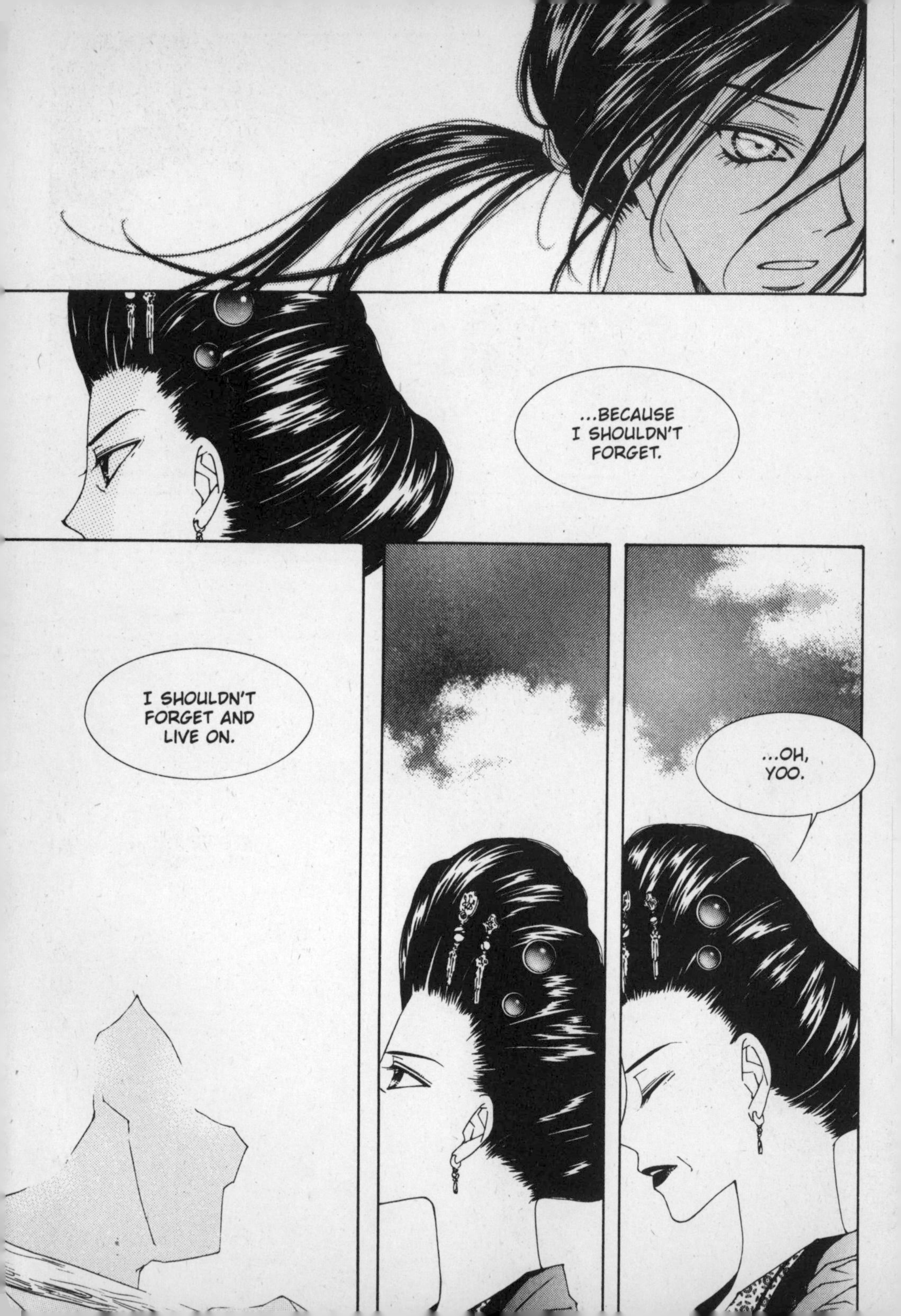
...BECAUSE I SHOULDN'T FORGET.
I SHOULDN'T FORGET AND LIVE ON.
...OH, YOO.

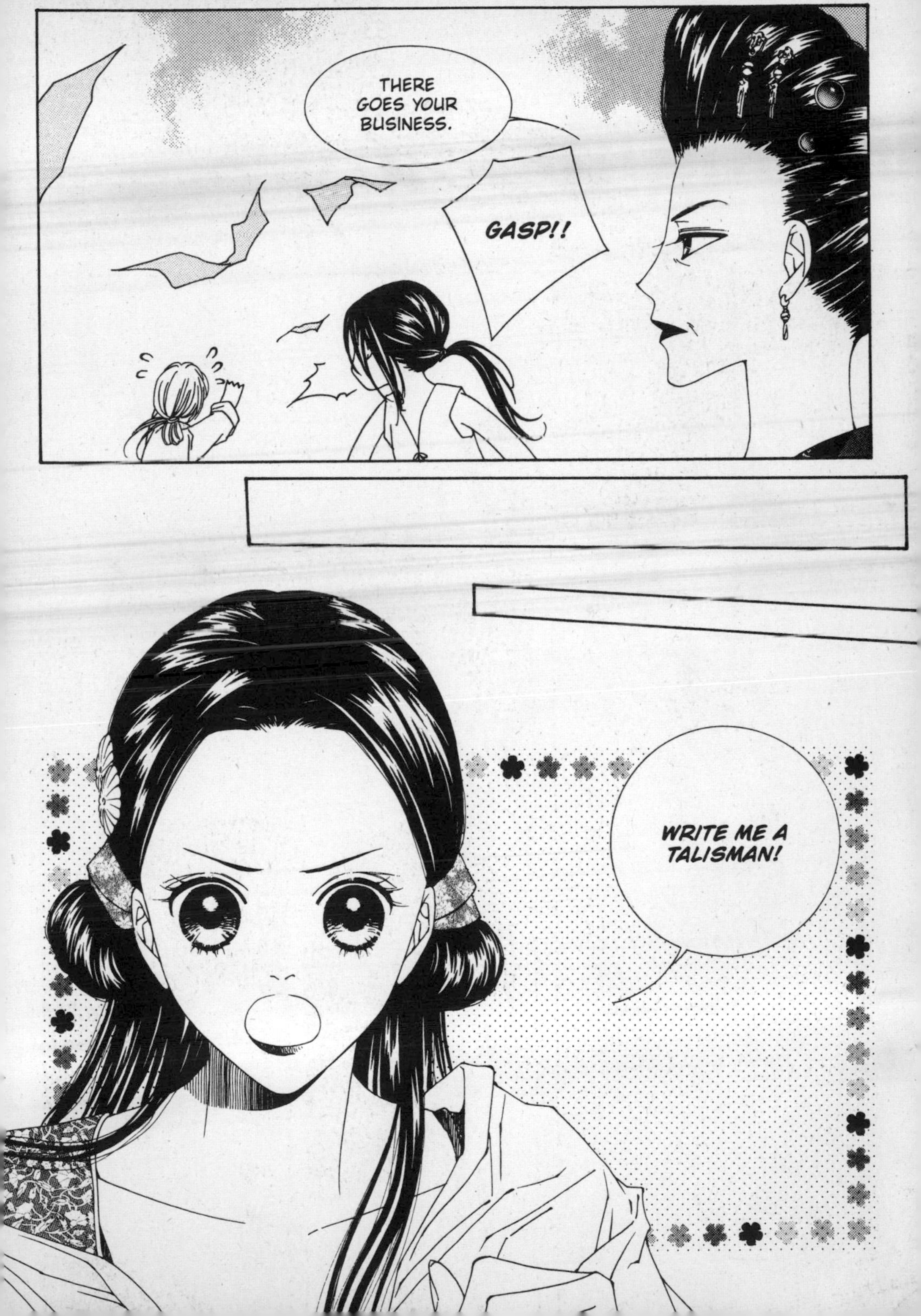
THERE GOES YOUR BUSINESS.
GASP!!
WRITE ME A TALISMAN!

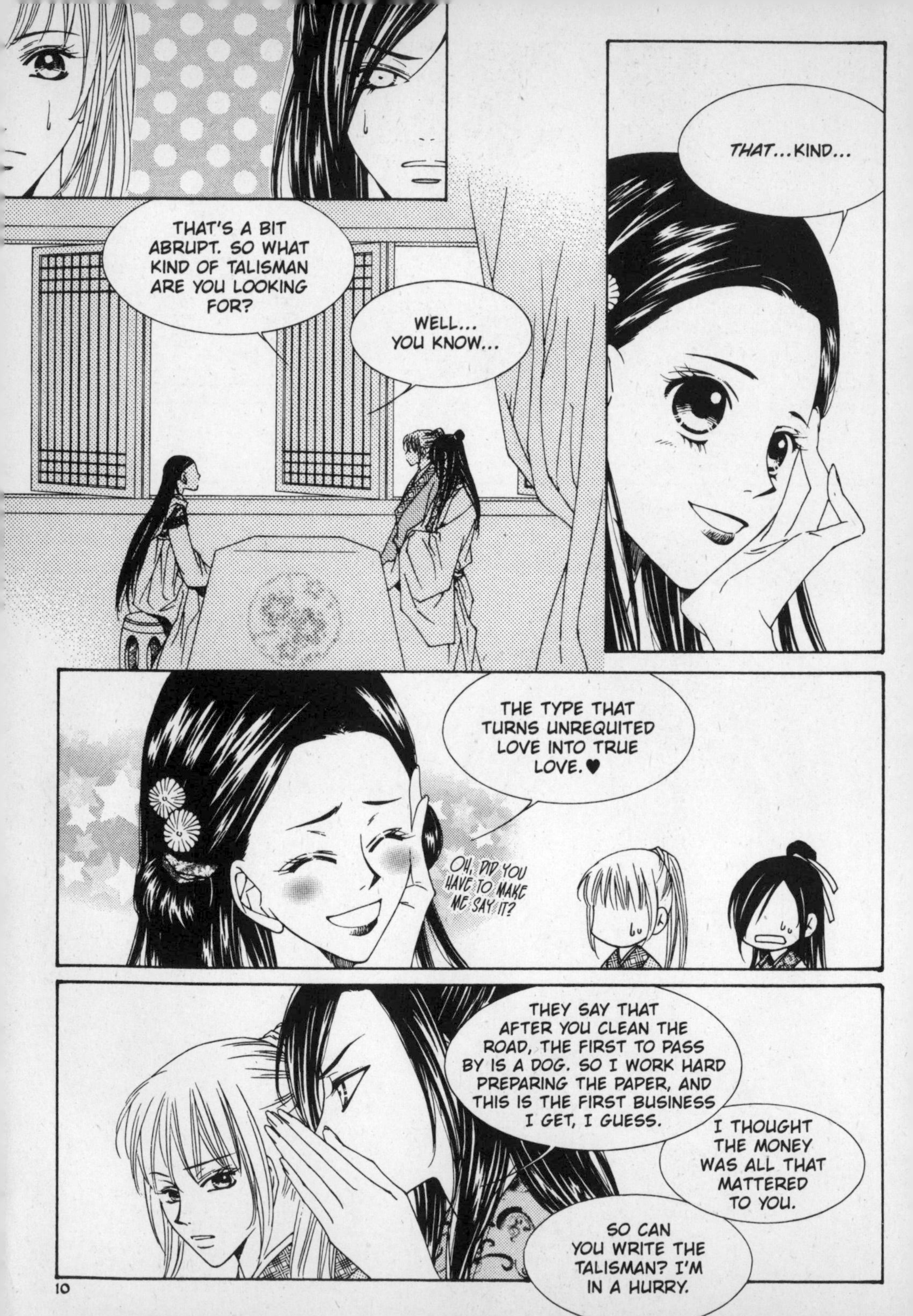
THAT...KIND...
THAT'S A BIT ABRUPT. SO WHAT KIND OF TALISMAN ARE YOU LOOKING FOR?
WELL... YOU KNOW...
THE TYPE THAT TURNS UNREQUITED LOVE INTO TRUE LOVE.♥
OH, DID YOU HAVE TO MAKE ME SAY IT?
THEY SAY THAT AFTER YOU CLEAN THE ROAD, THE FIRST TO PASS BY IS A DOG. SO I WORK HARD PREPARING THE PAPER, AND THIS IS THE FIRST BUSINESS I GET, I GUESS.
I THOUGHT THE MONEY WAS ALL THAT MATTERED TO YOU.
SO CAN YOU WRITE THE TALISMAN? I'M IN A HURRY.

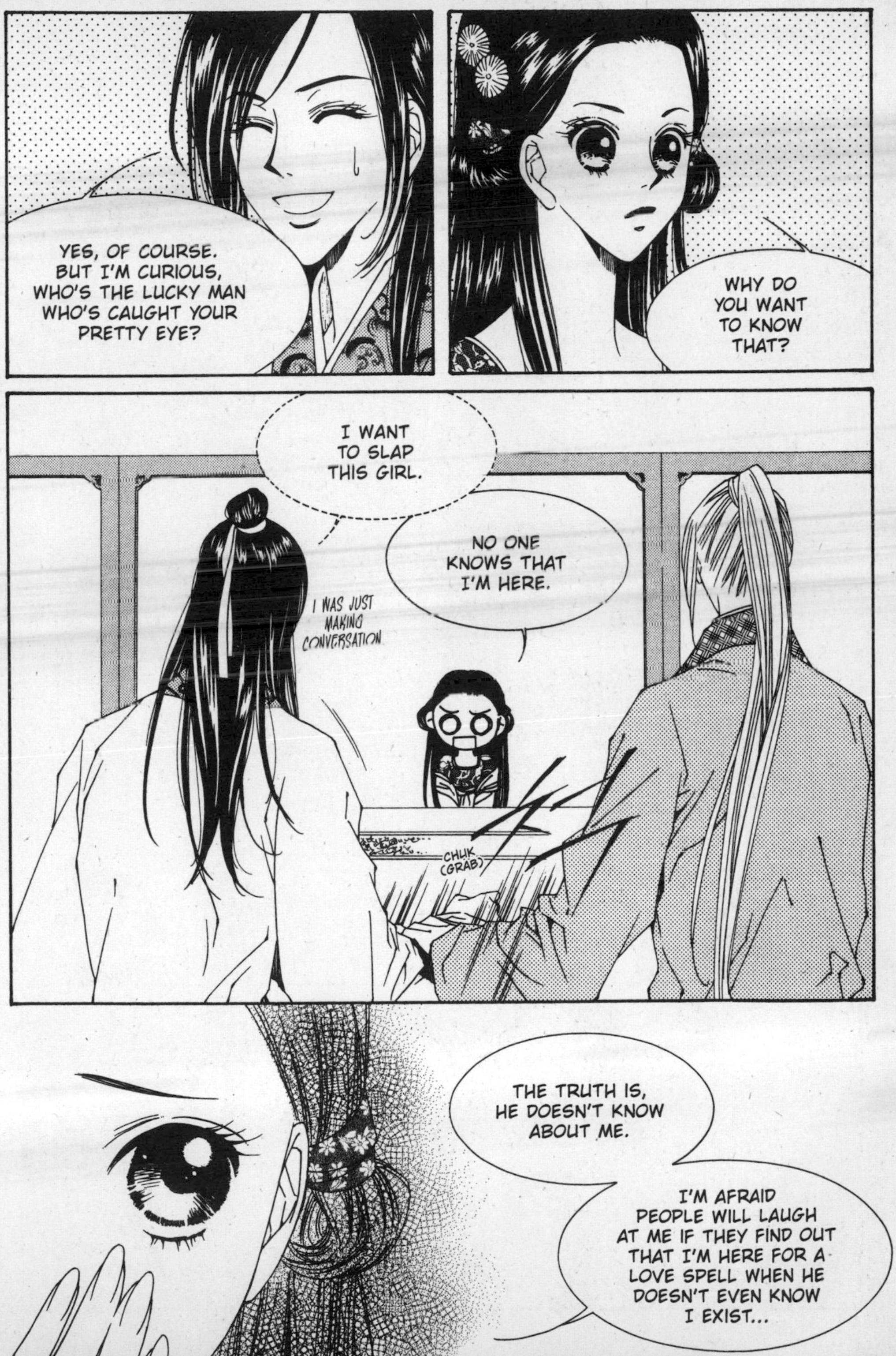
WHY DO YOU WANT TO KNOW THAT?
YES, OF COURSE. BUT I'M CURIOUS, WHO'S THE LUCKY MAN WHO'S CAUGHT YOUR PRETTY EYE?
I WANT TO SLAP THIS GIRL.
NO ONE KNOWS THAT I'M HERE.
I WAS JUST MAKING CONVERSATION.
CHUK (GRAB)
THE TRUTH IS, HE DOESN'T KNOW ABOUT ME.
I'M AFRAID PEOPLE WILL LAUGH AT ME IF THEY FIND OUT THAT I'M HERE FOR A LOVE SPELL WHEN HE DOESN'T EVEN KNOW I EXIST...

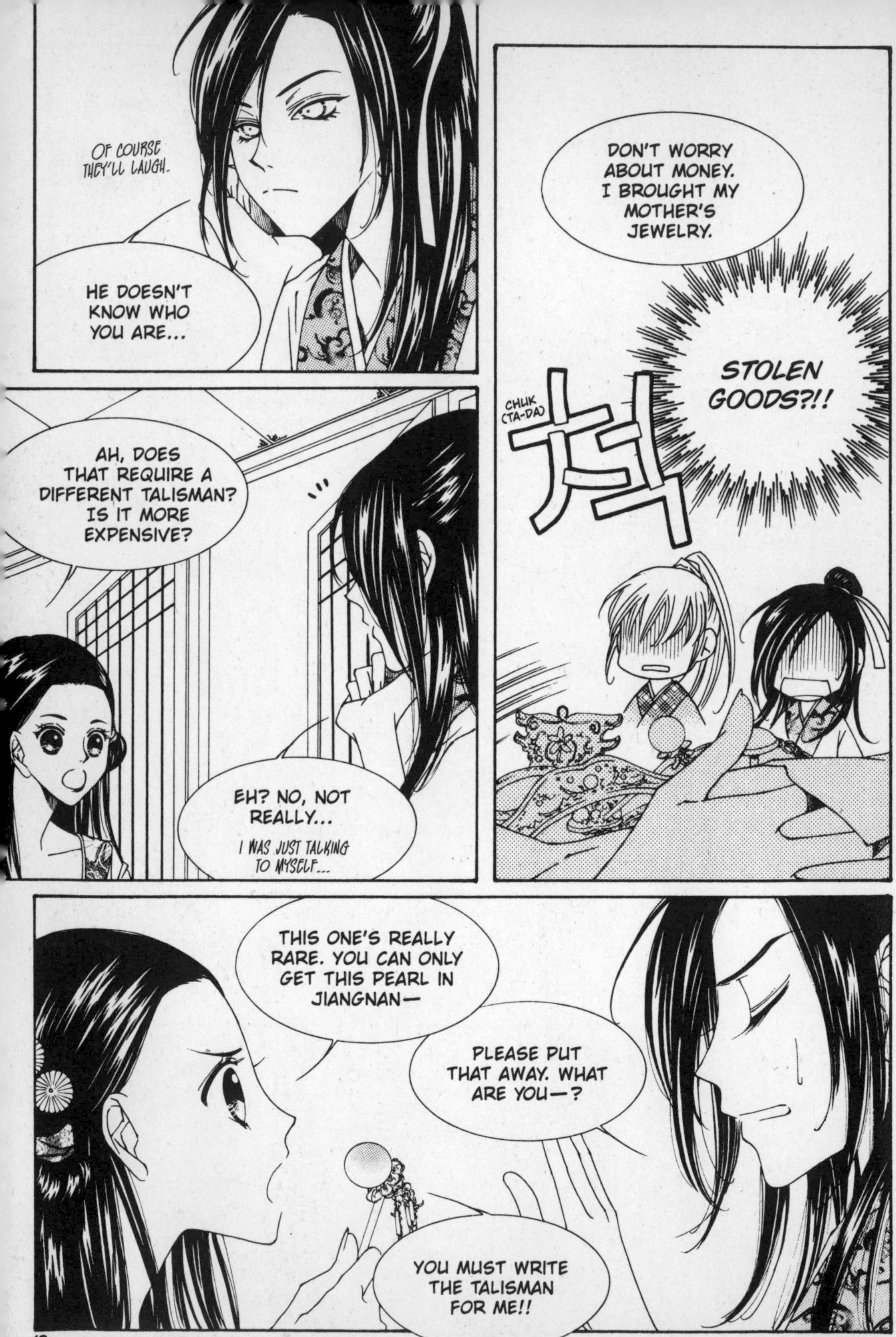
OF COURSE THEY'LL LAUGH.
HE DOESN'T KNOW WHO YOU ARE...
DON'T WORRY ABOUT MONEY. I BROUGHT MY MOTHER'S JEWELRY.
STOLEN GOODS?!!
CHUK (TA-DA)
척
AH, DOES THAT REQUIRE A DIFFERENT TALISMAN? IS IT MORE EXPENSIVE?
EH? NO, NOT REALLY...
I WAS JUST TALKING TO MYSELF...
THIS ONE'S REALLY RARE. YOU CAN ONLY GET THIS PEARL IN JIANGNAN—
PLEASE PUT THAT AWAY. WHAT ARE YOU—?
YOU MUST WRITE THE TALISMAN FOR ME!!

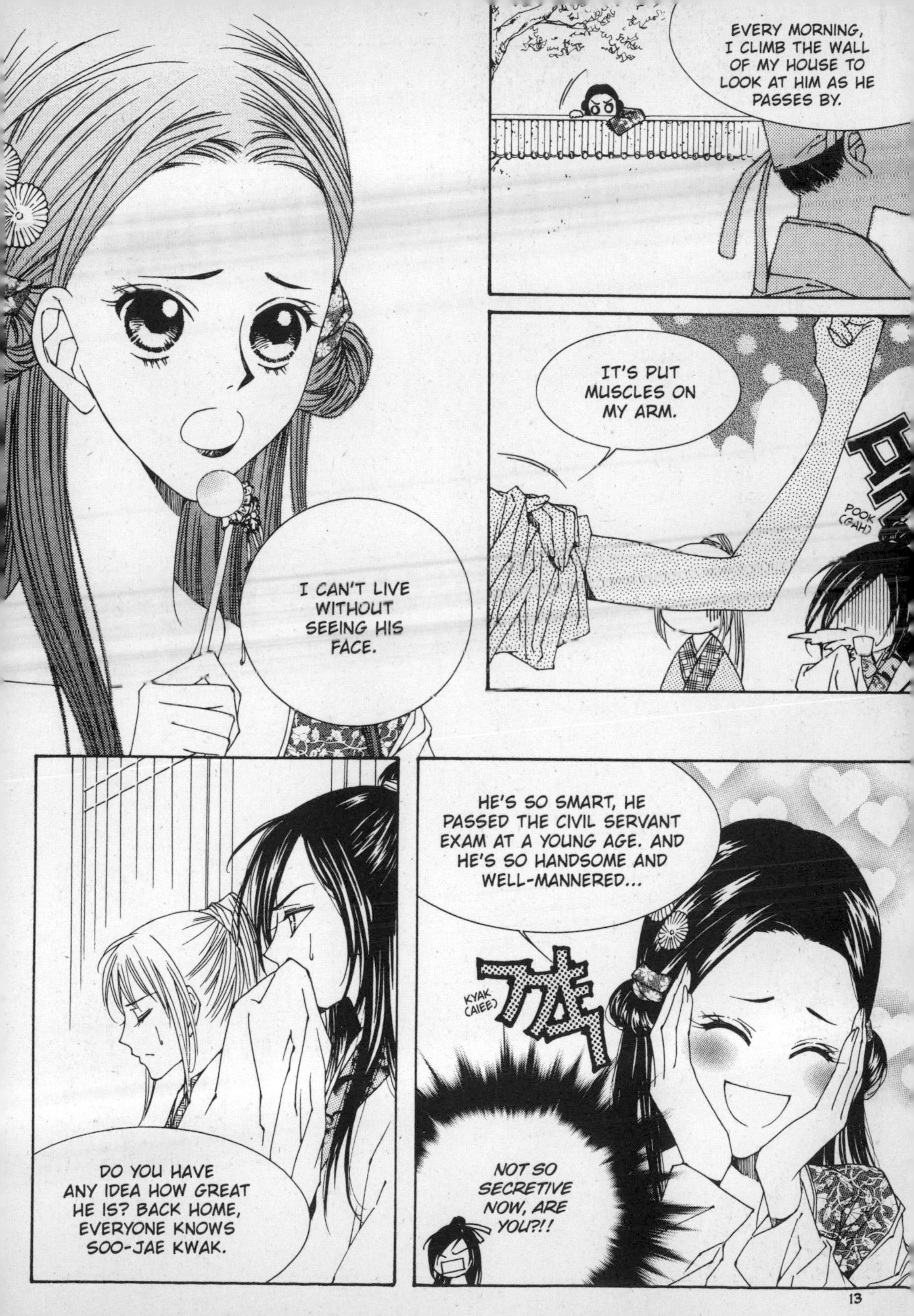
I CAN'T LIVE WITHOUT SEEING HIS FACE.
EVERY MORNING, I CLIMB THE WALL OF MY HOUSE TO LOOK AT HIM AS HE PASSES BY.
IT'S PUT MUSCLES ON MY ARM.
POOK (GAH)
DO YOU HAVE ANY IDEA HOW GREAT HE IS? BACK HOME, EVERYONE KNOWS SOO-JAE KWAK.
HE'S SO SMART, HE PASSED THE CIVIL SERVANT EXAM AT A YOUNG AGE. AND HE'S SO HANDSOME AND WELL-MANNERED...
KYAK (AIEE)
NOT SO SECRETIVE NOW, ARE YOU?!!

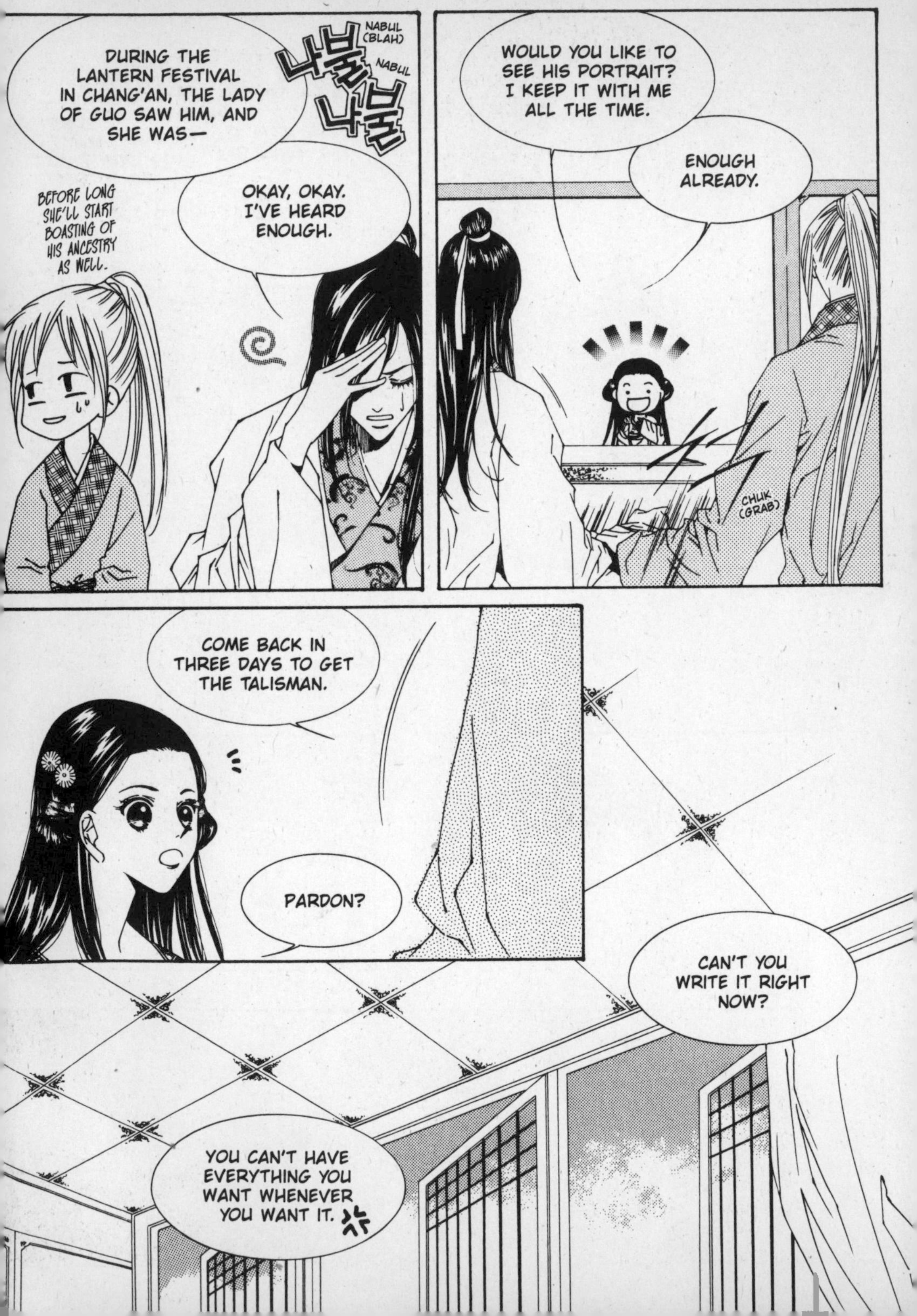

DURING THE LANTERN FESTIVAL IN CHANG'AN, THE LADY OF GUO SAW HIM, AND SHE WAS—
나불 나불
NABUL (BLAH)
NABUL
BEFORE LONG SHE'LL START BOASTING OF HIS ANCESTRY AS WELL.
OKAY, OKAY. I'VE HEARD ENOUGH.
WOULD YOU LIKE TO SEE HIS PORTRAIT? I KEEP IT WITH ME ALL THE TIME.
ENOUGH ALREADY.
CHUK (GRAB)
COME BACK IN THREE DAYS TO GET THE TALISMAN.
PARDON?
CAN'T YOU WRITE IT RIGHT NOW?
YOU CAN'T HAVE EVERYTHING YOU WANT WHENEVER YOU WANT IT.

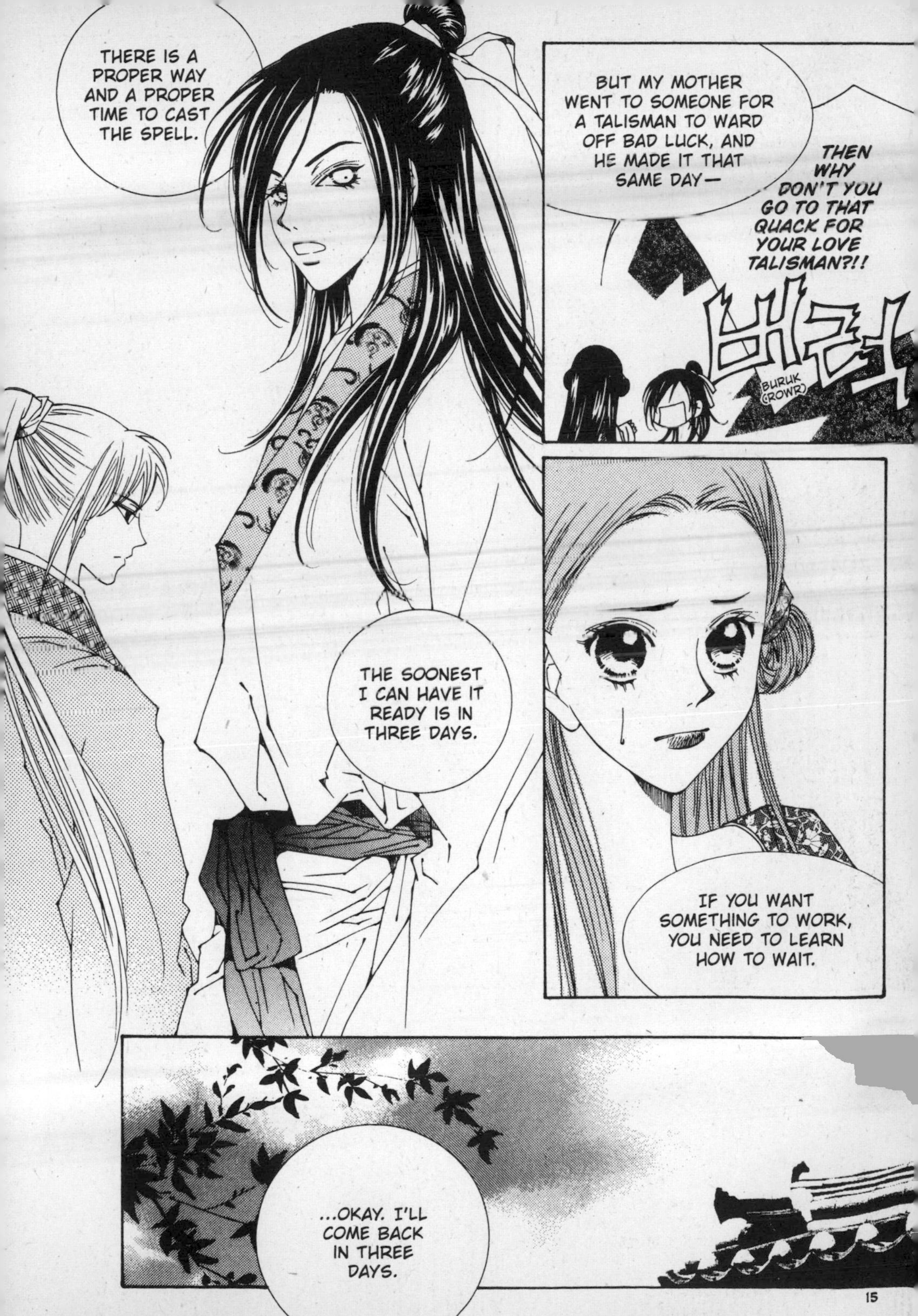

THERE IS A PROPER WAY AND A PROPER TIME TO CAST THE SPELL.
BUT MY MOTHER WENT TO SOMEONE FOR A TALISMAN TO WARD OFF BAD LUCK, AND HE MADE IT THAT SAME DAY—
THEN WHY DON'T YOU GO TO THAT QUACK FOR YOUR LOVE TALISMAN?!!
BURUK (ROWR)
THE SOONEST I CAN HAVE IT READY IS IN THREE DAYS.
IF YOU WANT SOMETHING TO WORK, YOU NEED TO LEARN HOW TO WAIT.
...OKAY. I'LL COME BACK IN THREE DAYS.

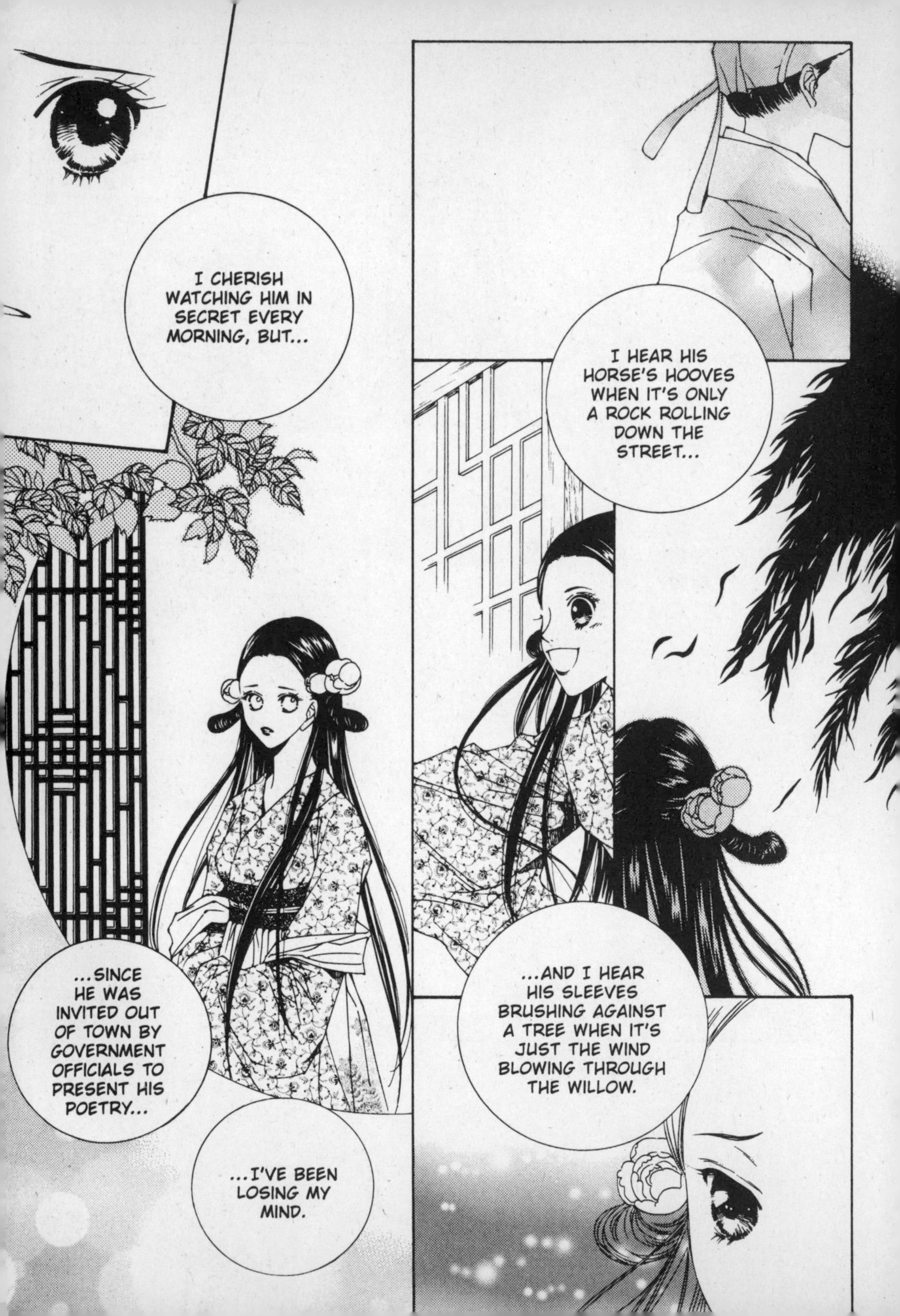
I CHERISH WATCHING HIM IN SECRET EVERY MORNING, BUT...
...SINCE HE WAS INVITED OUT OF TOWN BY GOVERNMENT OFFICIALS TO PRESENT HIS POETRY...
...I'VE BEEN LOSING MY MIND.
I HEAR HIS HORSE'S HOOVES WHEN IT'S ONLY A ROCK ROLLING DOWN THE STREET...
...AND I HEAR HIS SLEEVES BRUSHING AGAINST A TREE WHEN IT'S JUST THE WIND BLOWING THROUGH THE WILLOW.

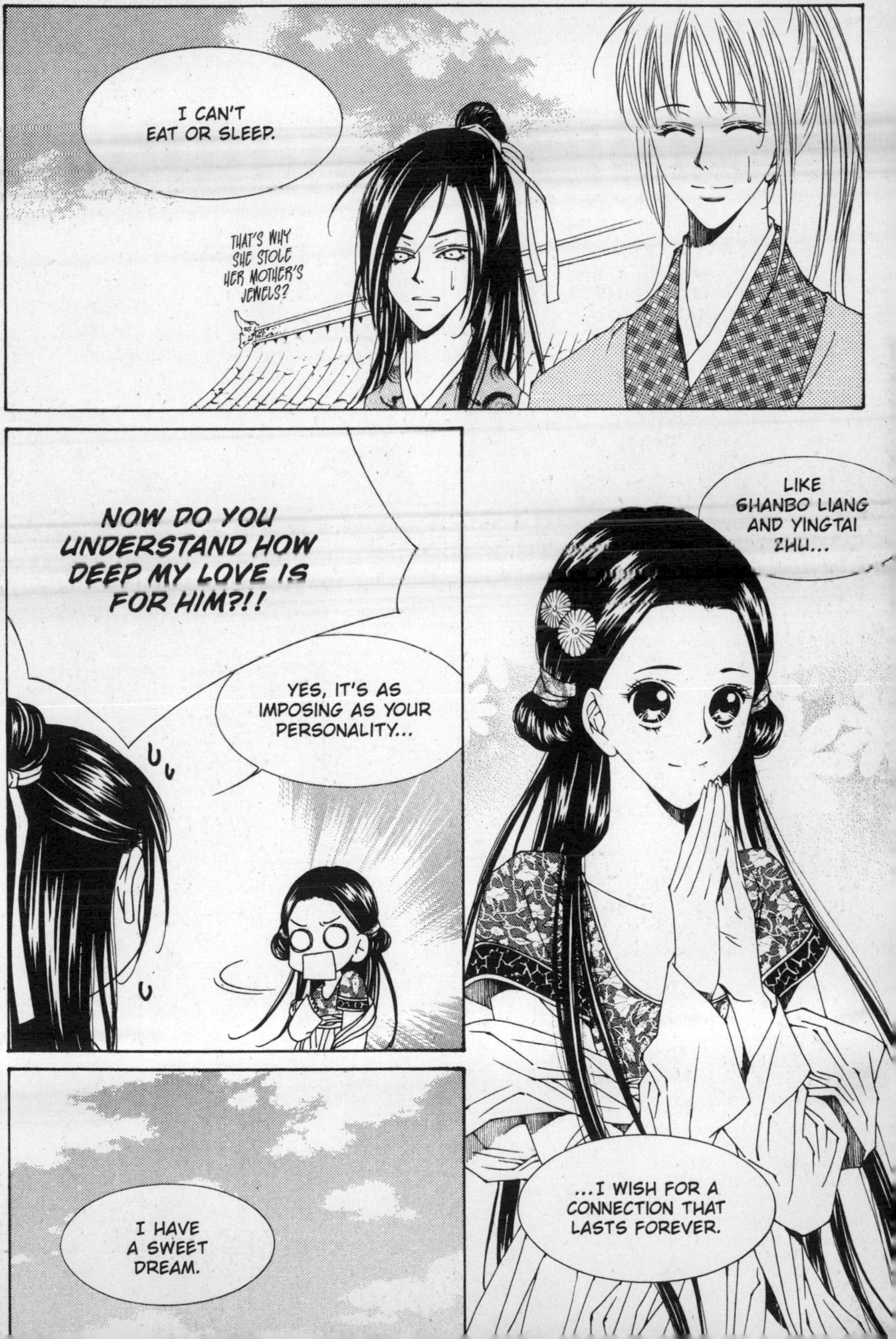
I CAN'T EAT OR SLEEP.
THAT'S WHY SHE STOLE HER MOTHER'S JEWELS?
LIKE SHANBO LIANG AND YINGTAI ZHU...
NOW DO YOU UNDERSTAND HOW DEEP MY LOVE IS FOR HIM?!!
YES, IT'S AS IMPOSING AS YOUR PERSONALITY...
...I WISH FOR A CONNECTION THAT LASTS FOREVER.
I HAVE A SWEET DREAM.

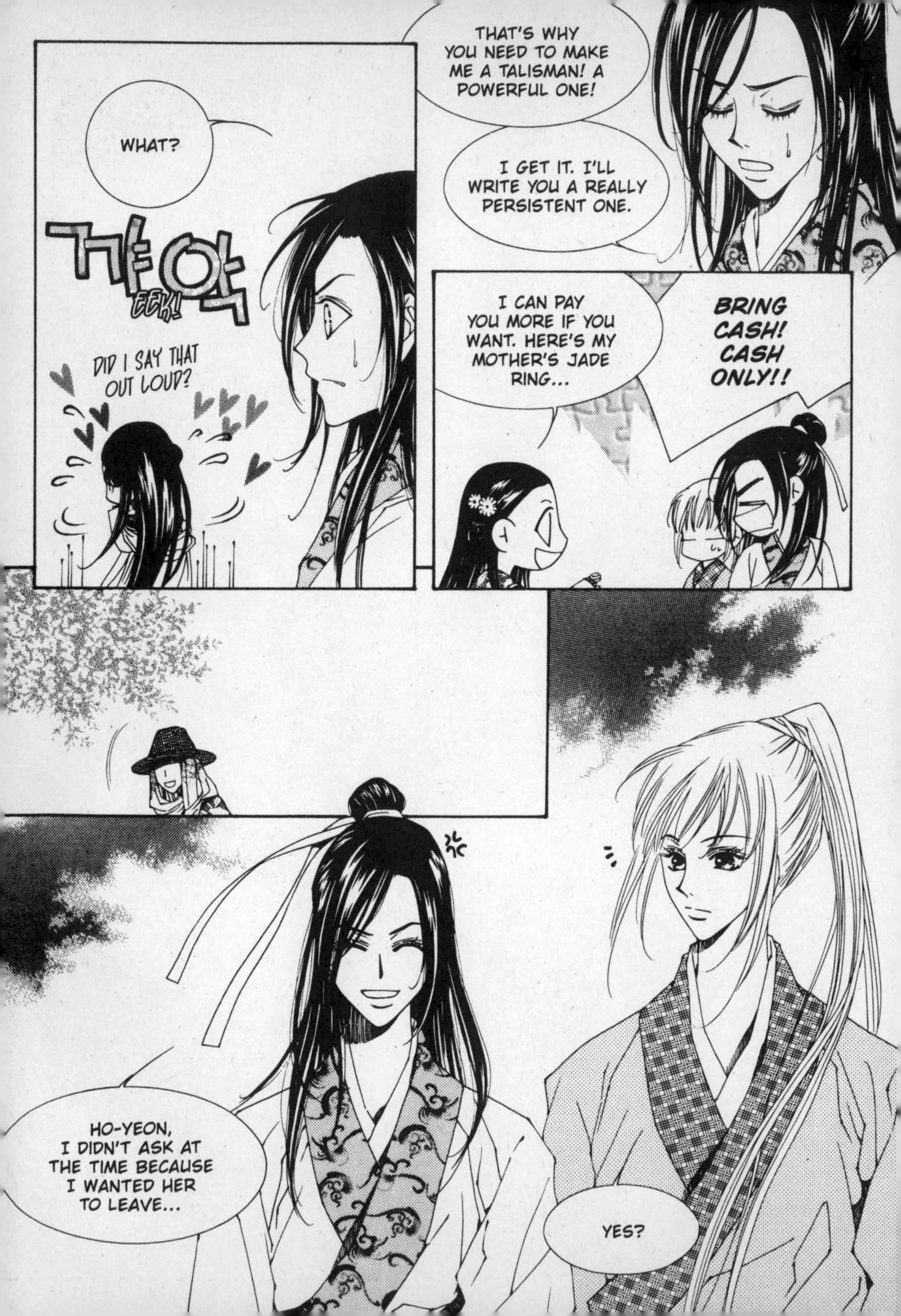
THAT'S WHY YOU NEED TO MAKE ME A TALISMAN! A POWERFUL ONE!
WHAT?
꺄악
EEK!
DID I SAY THAT OUT LOUD?
I GET IT. I'LL WRITE YOU A REALLY PERSISTENT ONE.
I CAN PAY YOU MORE IF YOU WANT. HERE'S MY MOTHER'S JADE RING...
BRING CASH! CASH ONLY!!
HO-YEON, I DIDN'T ASK AT THE TIME BECAUSE I WANTED HER TO LEAVE...
YES?

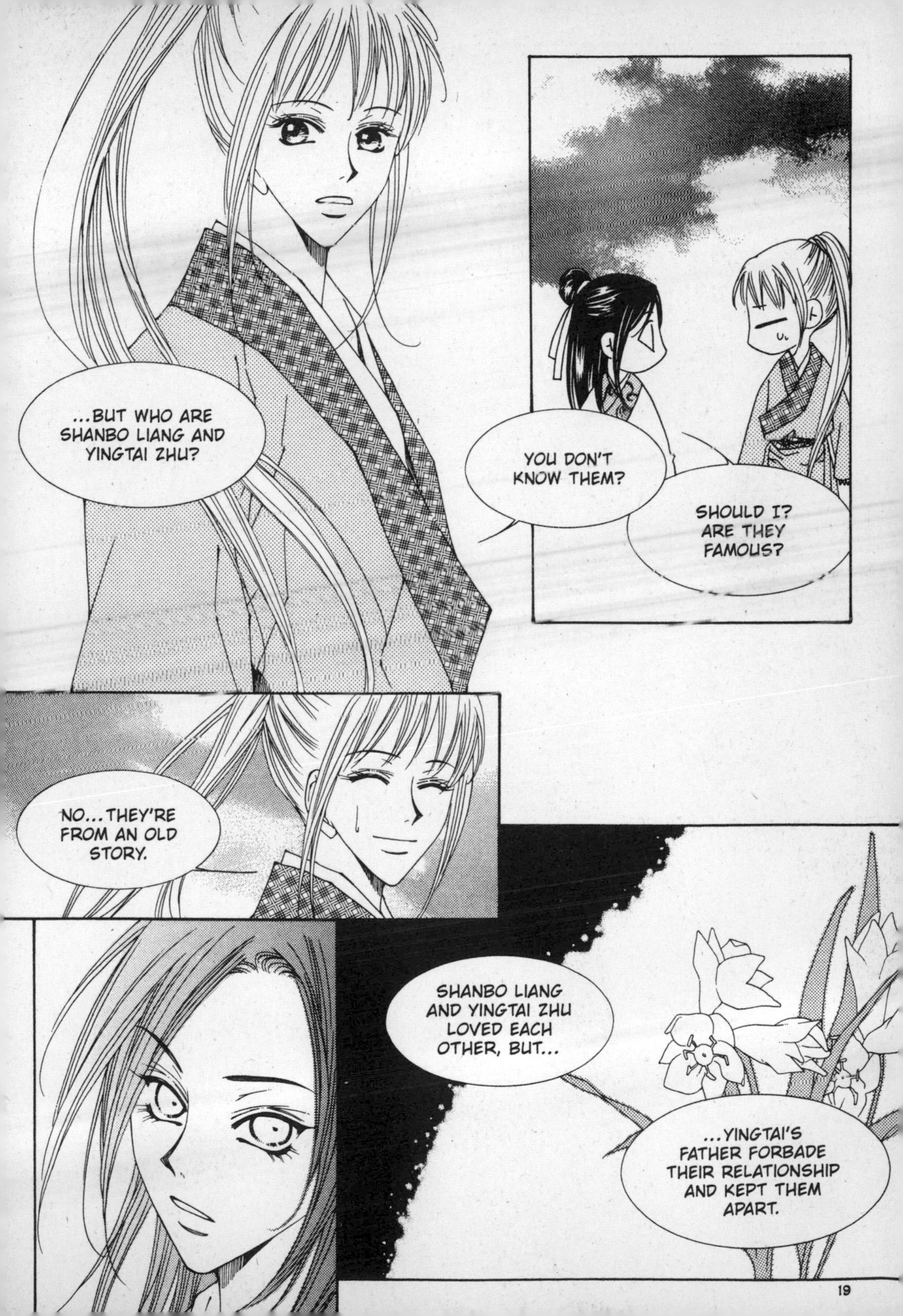
...BUT WHO ARE SHANBO LIANG AND YINGTAI ZHU?
YOU DON'T KNOW THEM?
SHOULD I? ARE THEY FAMOUS?
NO...THEY'RE FROM AN OLD STORY.
SHANBO LIANG AND YINGTAI ZHU LOVED EACH OTHER, BUT...
...YINGTAI'S FATHER FORBADE THEIR RELATIONSHIP AND KEPT THEM APART.

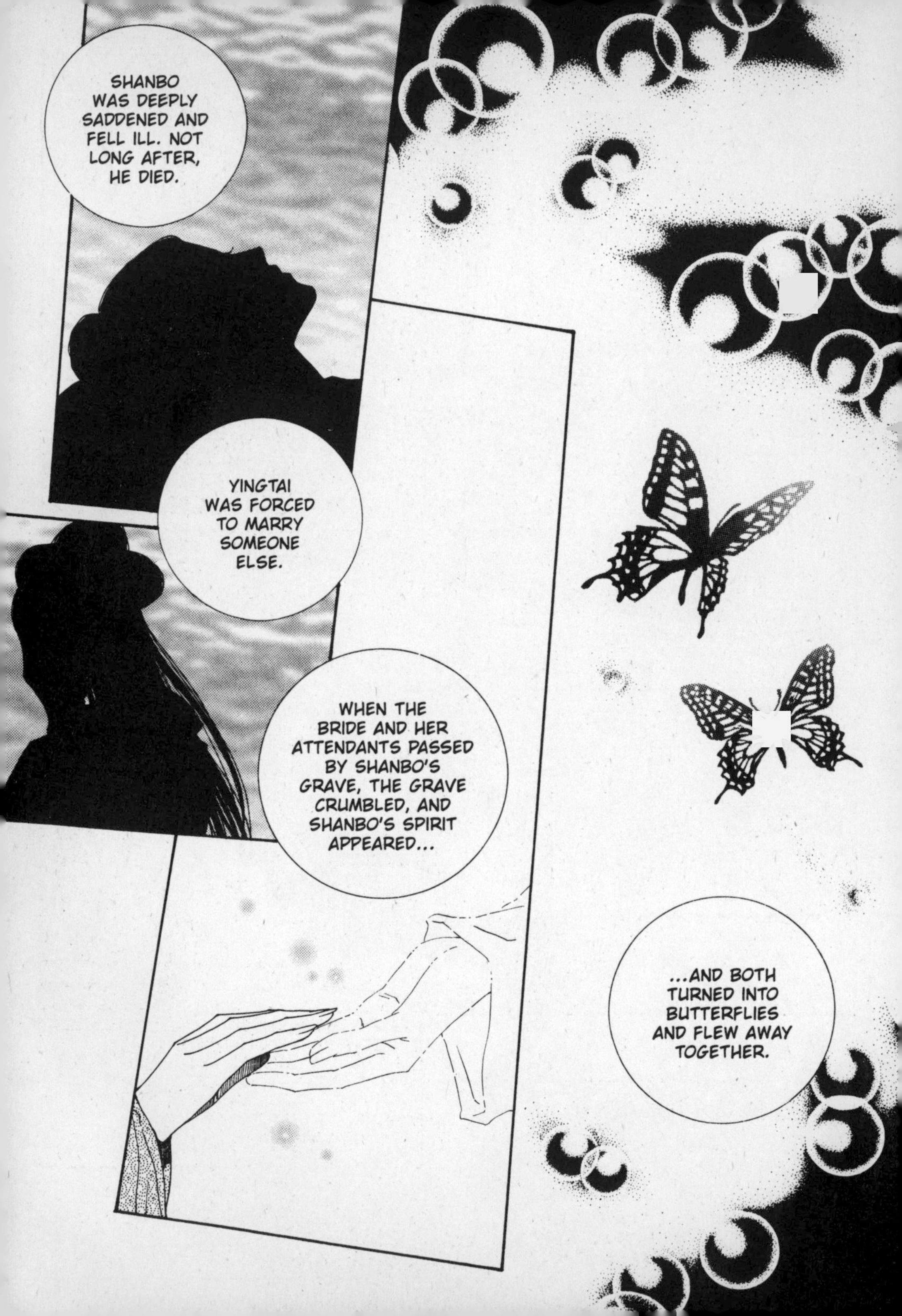
SHANBO WAS DEEPLY SADDENED AND FELL ILL. NOT LONG AFTER, HE DIED.
YINGTAI WAS FORCED TO MARRY SOMEONE ELSE.
WHEN THE BRIDE AND HER ATTENDANTS PASSED BY SHANBO'S GRAVE, THE GRAVE CRUMBLED, AND SHANBO'S SPIRIT APPEARED...
...AND BOTH TURNED INTO BUTTERFLIES AND FLEW AWAY TOGETHER.

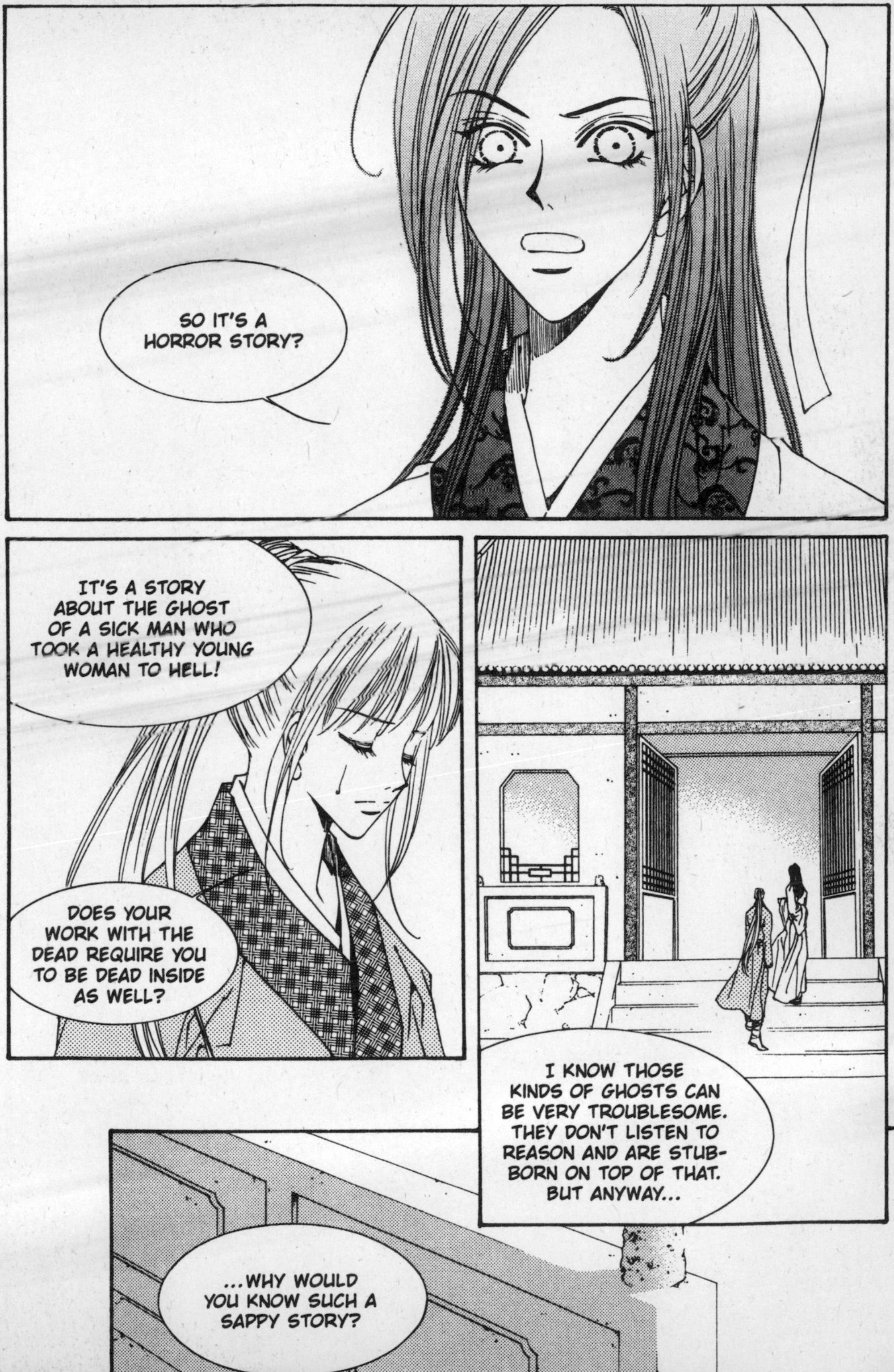
SO IT'S A HORROR STORY?
IT'S A STORY ABOUT THE GHOST OF A SICK MAN WHO TOOK A HEALTHY YOUNG WOMAN TO HELL!
DOES YOUR WORK WITH THE DEAD REQUIRE YOU TO BE DEAD INSIDE AS WELL?
I KNOW THOSE KINDS OF GHOSTS CAN BE VERY TROUBLESOME. THEY DON'T LISTEN TO REASON AND ARE STUBBORN ON TOP OF THAT. BUT ANYWAY...
...WHY WOULD YOU KNOW SUCH A SAPPY STORY?

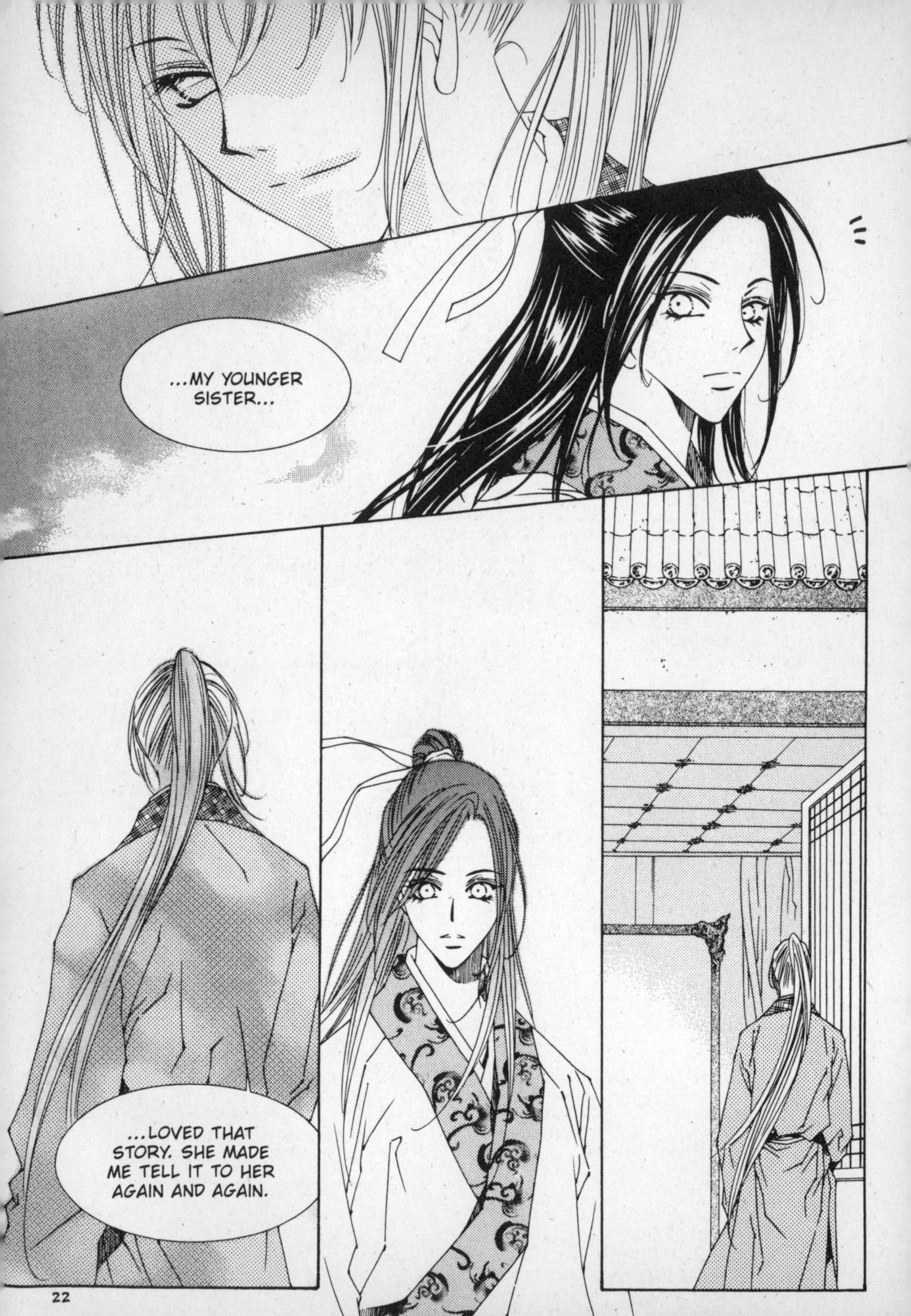
...MY YOUNGER SISTER...
...LOVED THAT STORY. SHE MADE ME TELL IT TO HER AGAIN AND AGAIN.

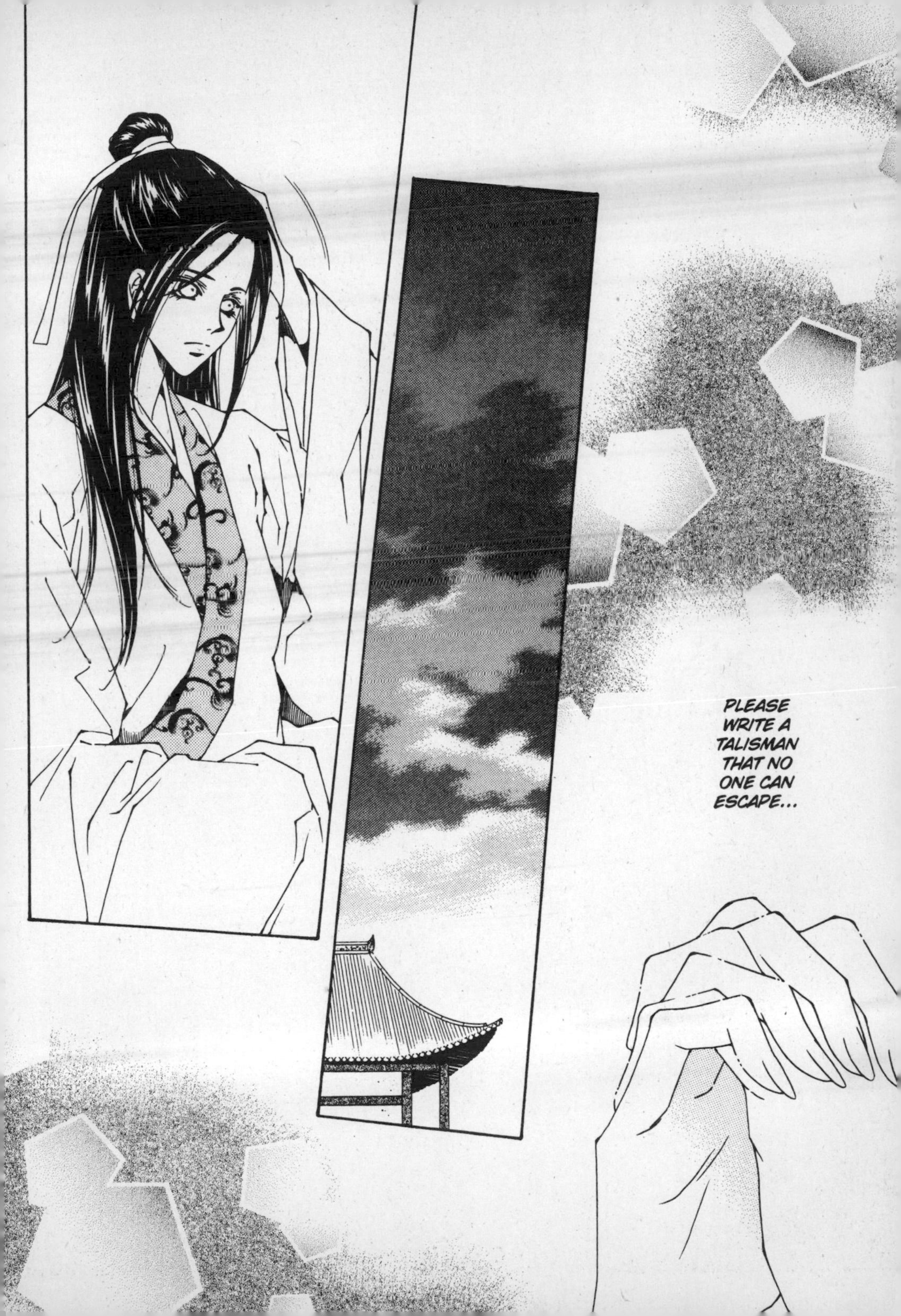
PLEASE WRITE A TALISMAN THAT NO ONE CAN ESCAPE...

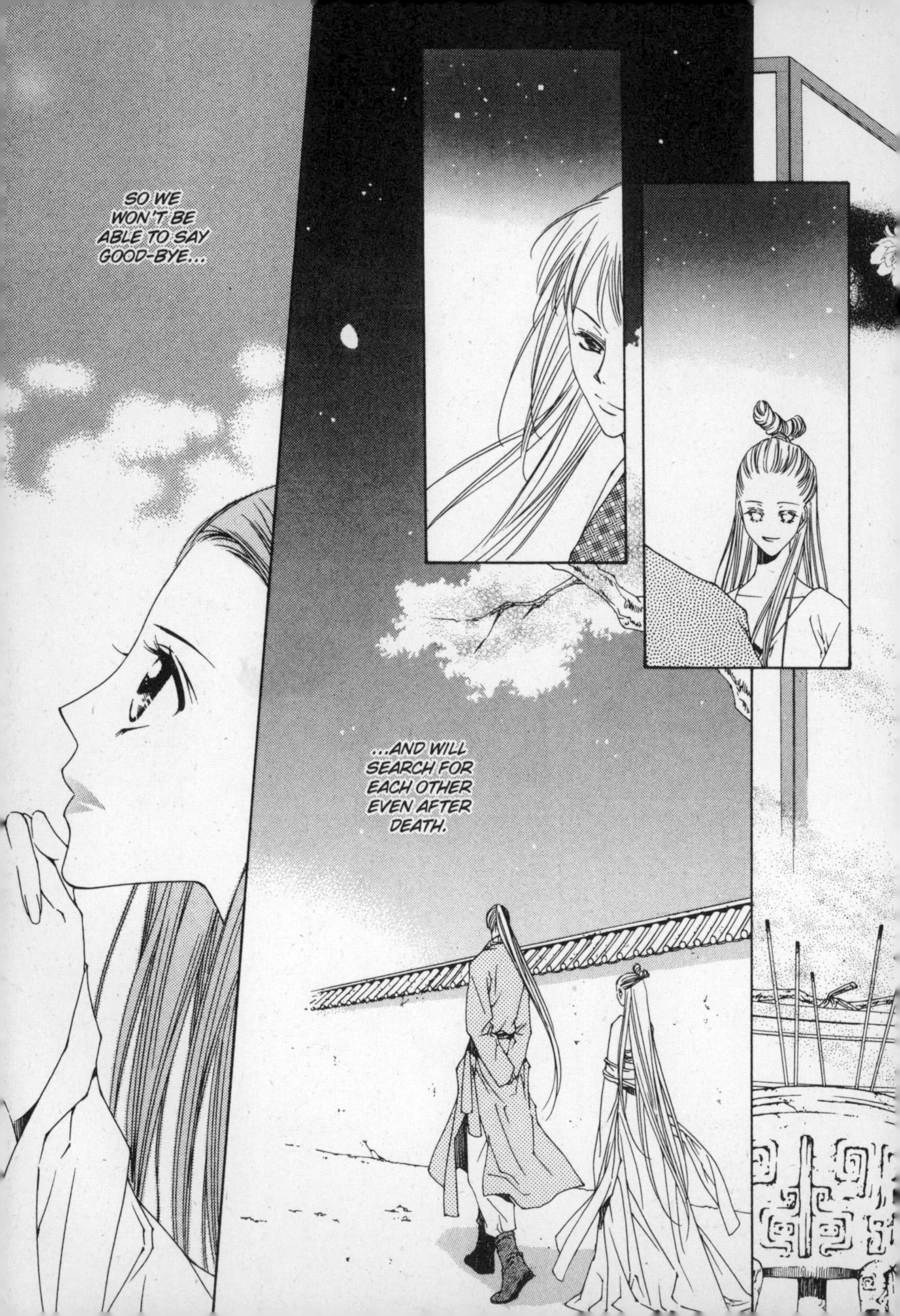
SO WE WON'T BE ABLE TO SAY GOOD-BYE...
...AND WILL SEARCH FOR EACH OTHER EVEN AFTER DEATH.

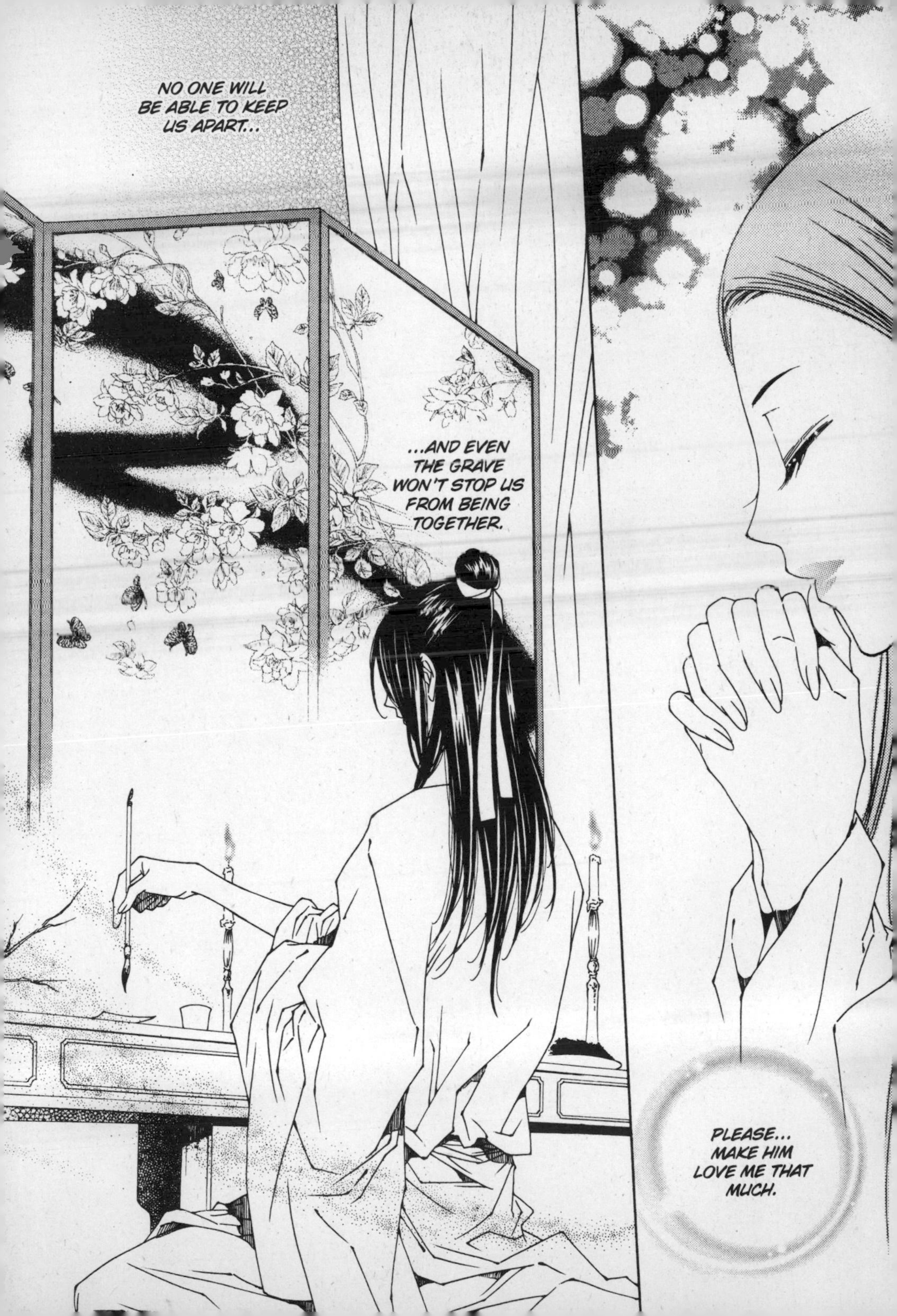
NO ONE WILL BE ABLE TO KEEP US APART...
...AND EVEN THE GRAVE WON'T STOP US FROM BEING TOGETHER.
PLEASE... MAKE HIM LOVE ME THAT MUCH.

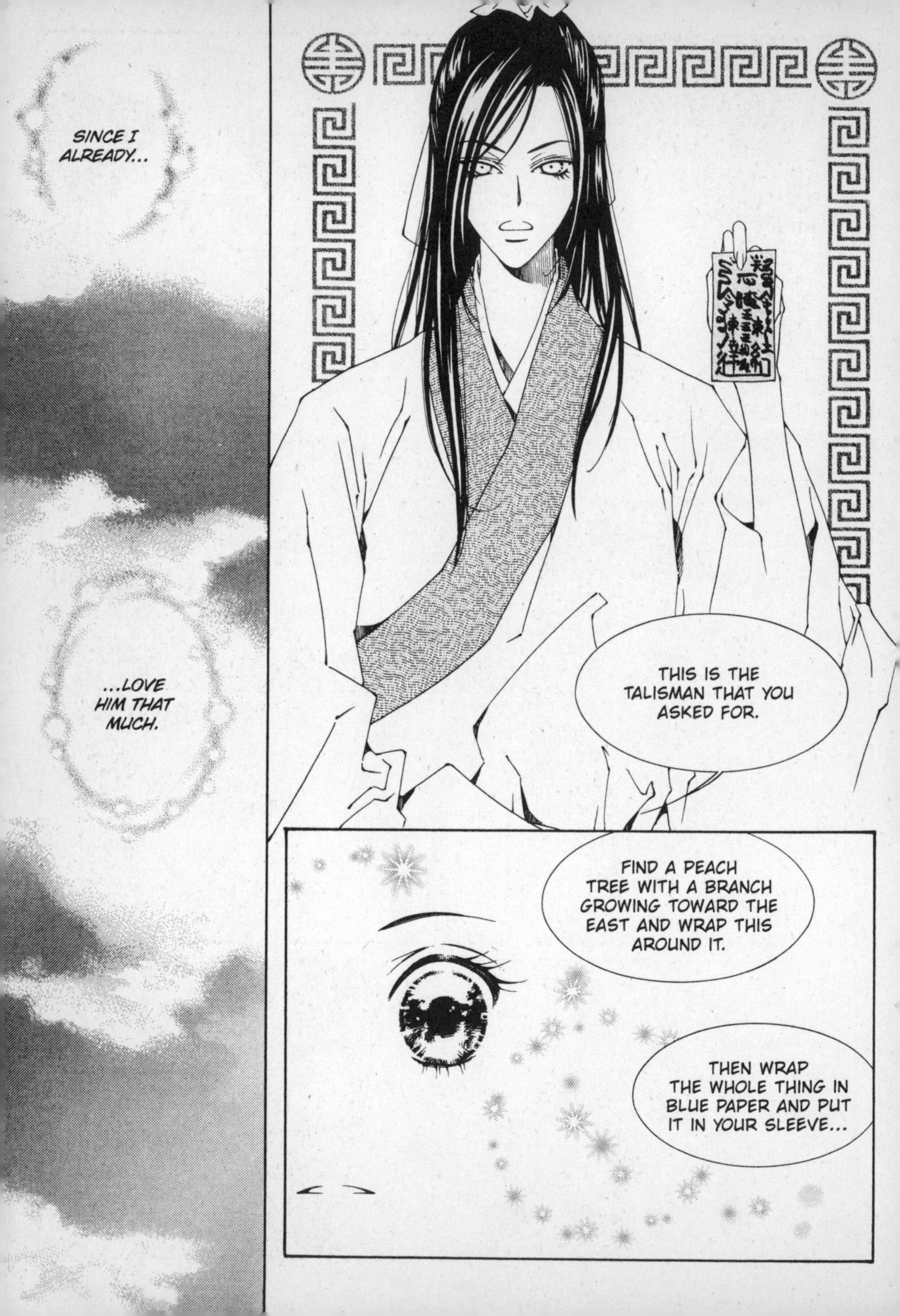

SINCE I ALREADY...
...LOVE HIM THAT MUCH.
THIS IS THE TALISMAN THAT YOU ASKED FOR.
FIND A PEACH TREE WITH A BRANCH GROWING TOWARD THE EAST AND WRAP THIS AROUND IT.
THEN WRAP THE WHOLE THING IN BLUE PAPER AND PUT IT IN YOUR SLEEVE...

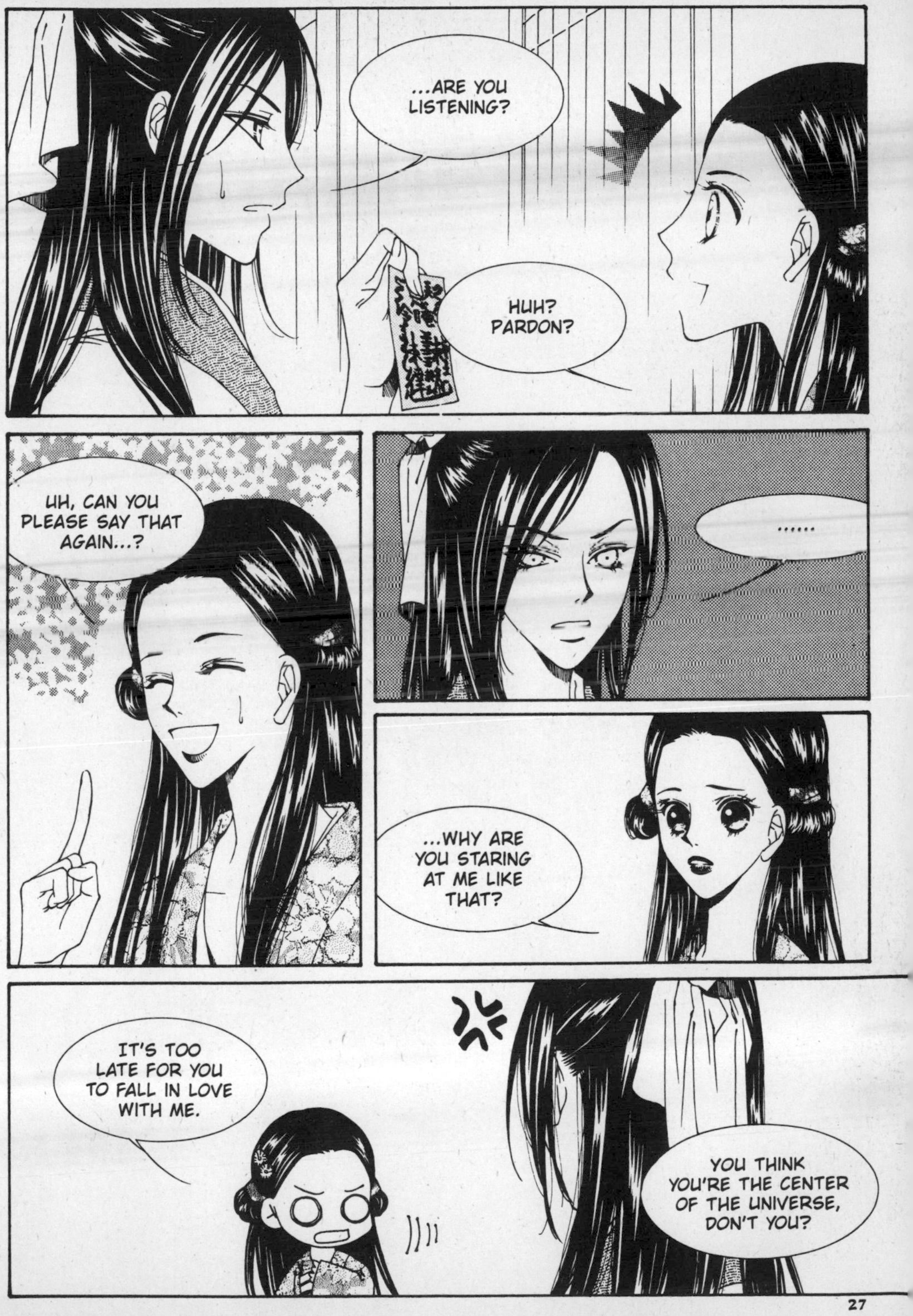
...ARE YOU LISTENING?
HUH? PARDON?
UH, CAN YOU PLEASE SAY THAT AGAIN...?
......
...WHY ARE YOU STARING AT ME LIKE THAT?
IT'S TOO LATE FOR YOU TO FALL IN LOVE WITH ME.
YOU THINK YOU'RE THE CENTER OF THE UNIVERSE, DON'T YOU?

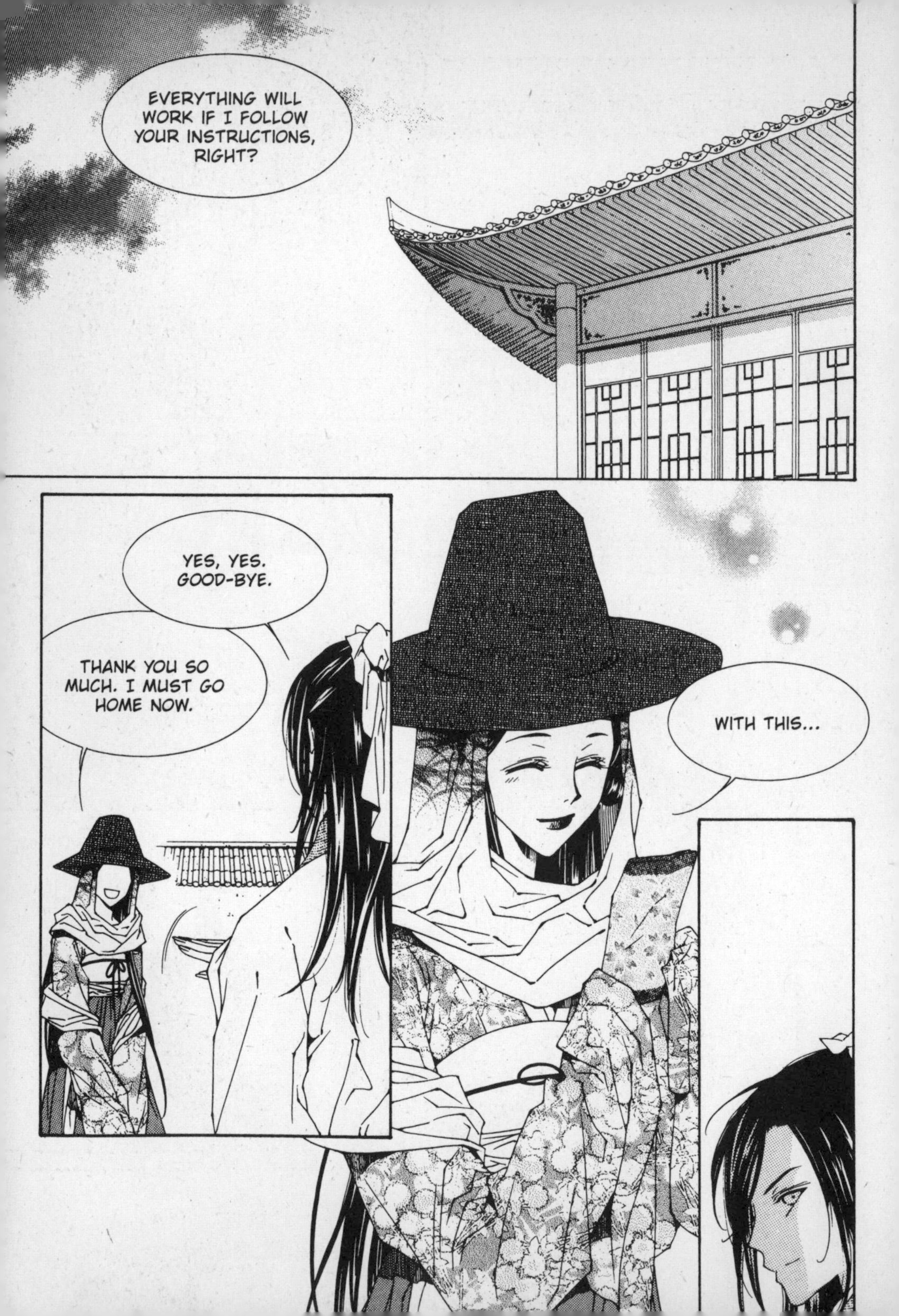
EVERYTHING WILL WORK IF I FOLLOW YOUR INSTRUCTIONS, RIGHT?
YES, YES. GOOD-BYE.
THANK YOU SO MUCH. I MUST GO HOME NOW.
WITH THIS...

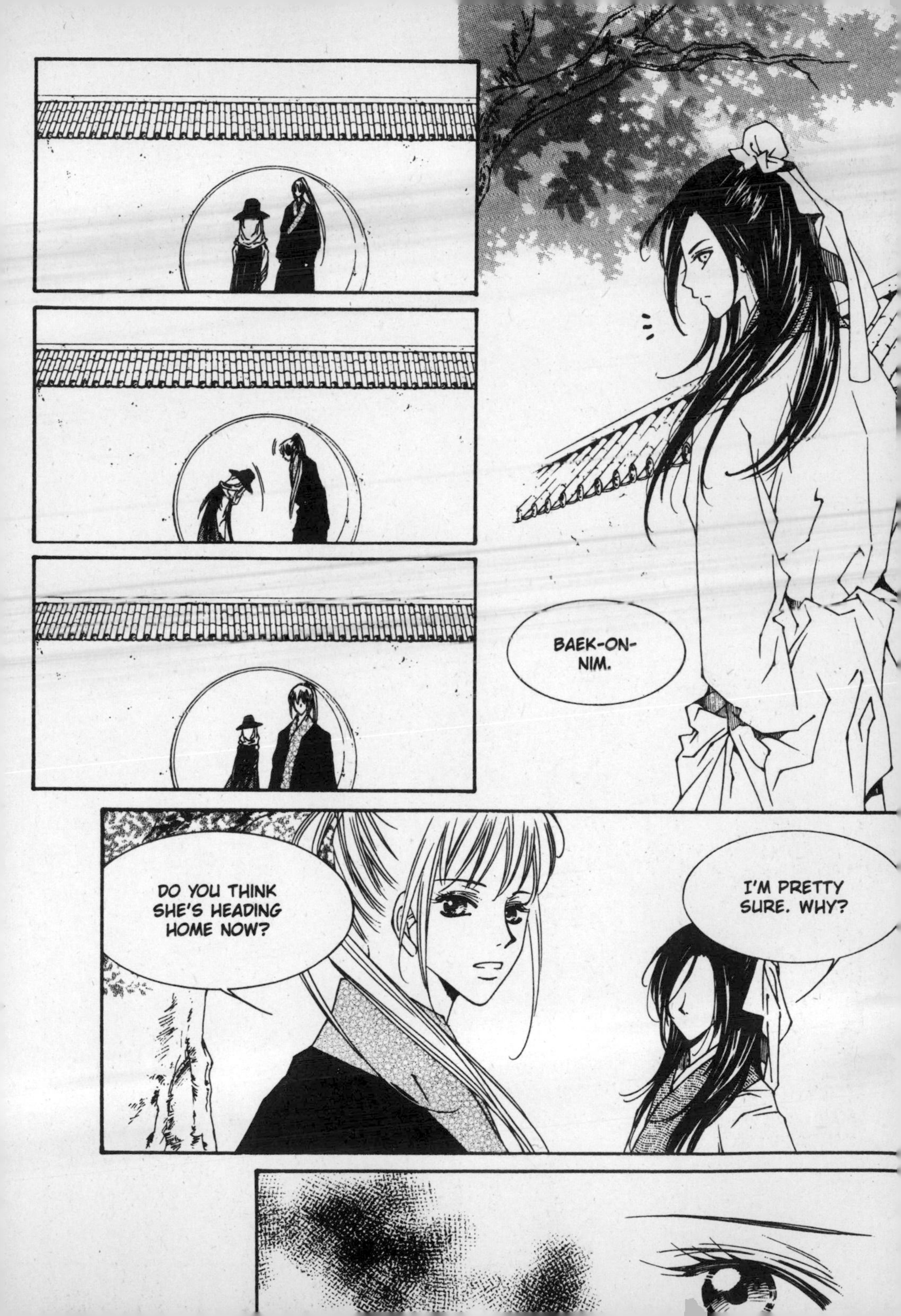
BAEK-ON-NIM.
I'M PRETTY SURE. WHY?
DO YOU THINK SHE'S HEADING HOME NOW?

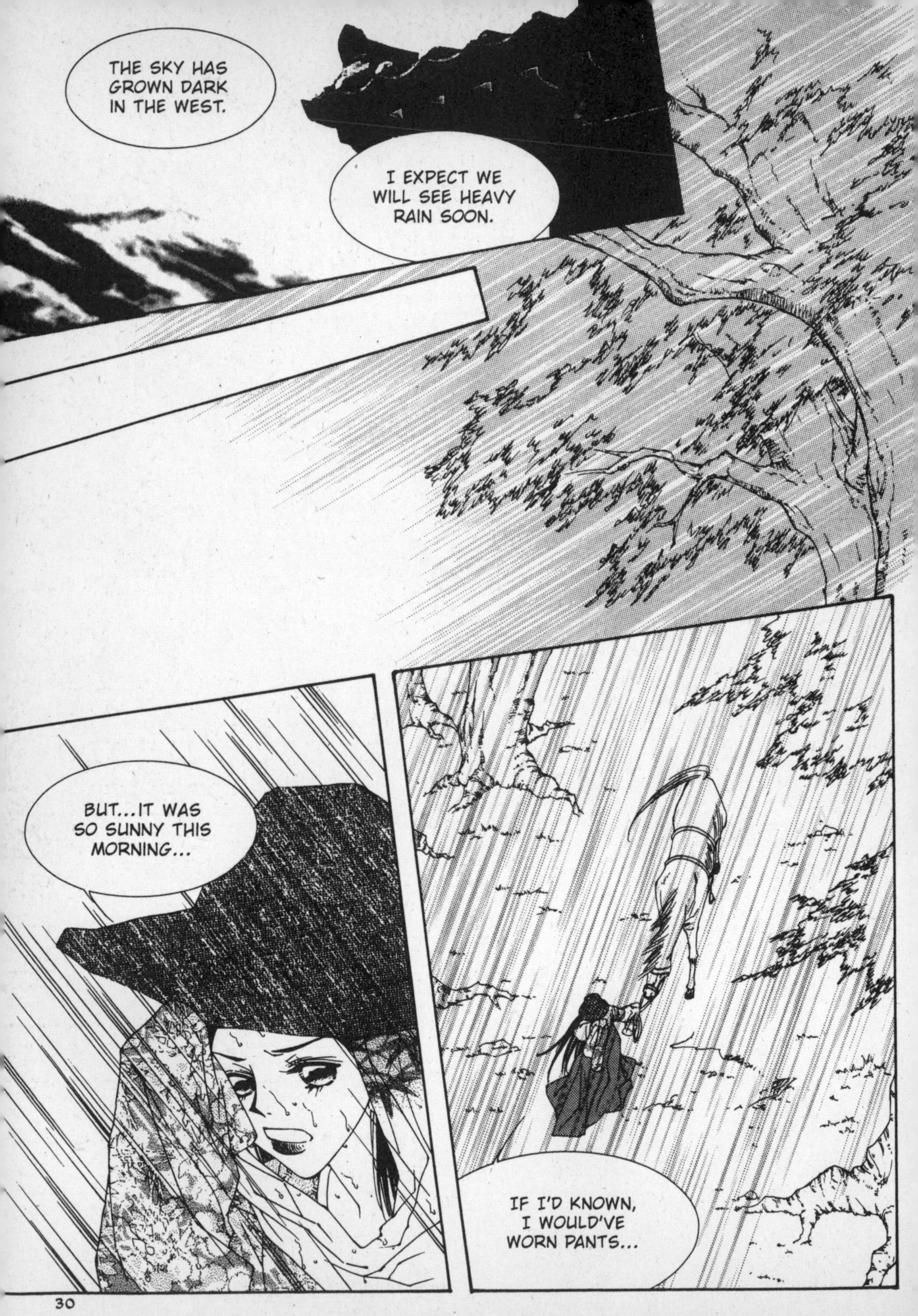
THE SKY HAS GROWN DARK IN THE WEST.
I EXPECT WE WILL SEE HEAVY RAIN SOON.
BUT...IT WAS SO SUNNY THIS MORNING...
IF I'D KNOWN, I WOULD'VE WORN PANTS...

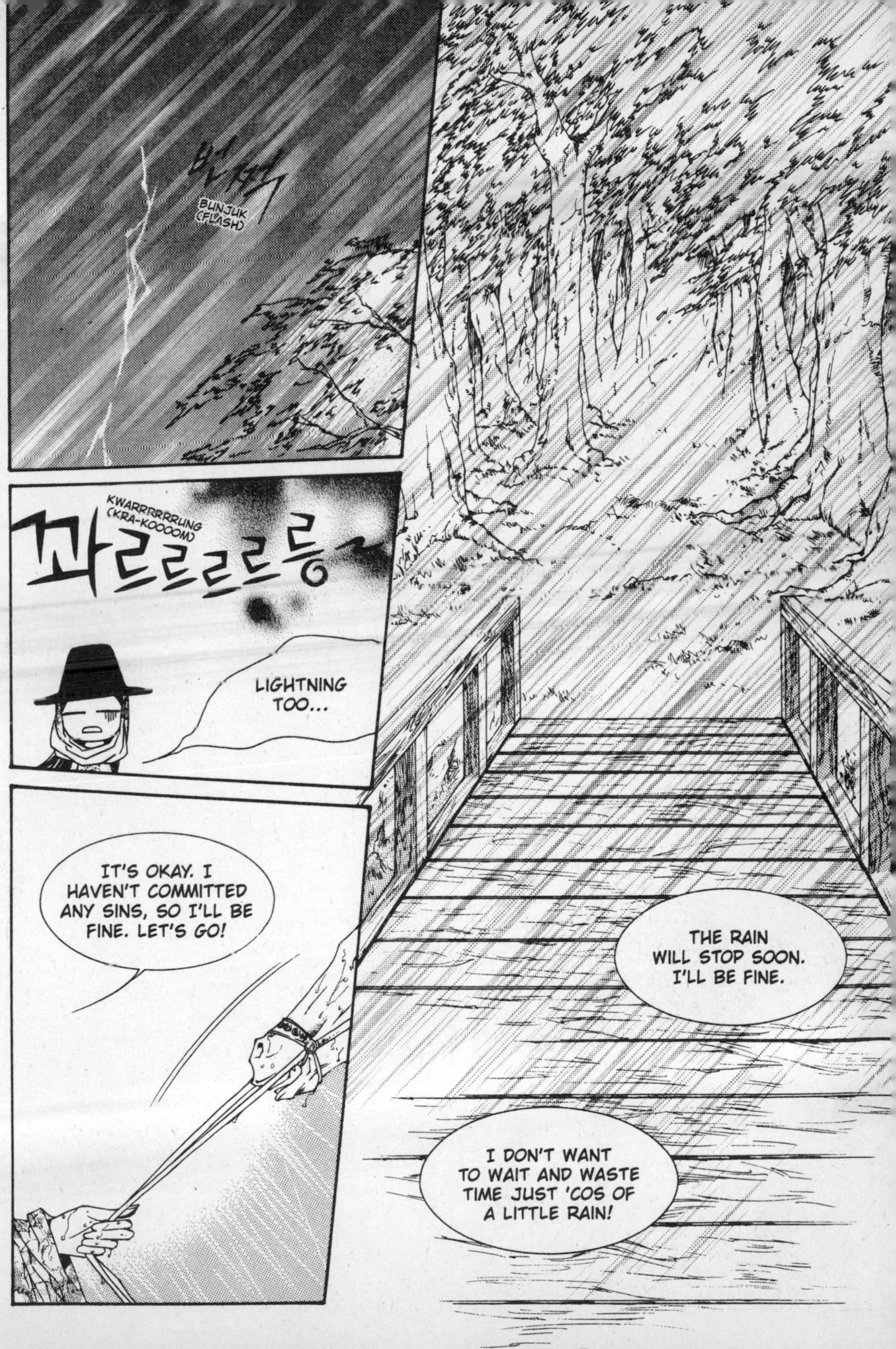

번쩍
BUNJUK (FLASH)
파르르르르릉
KWARRRRRRUNG (KRA-KOOOOM)
LIGHTNING TOO...
IT'S OKAY. I HAVEN'T COMMITTED ANY SINS, SO I'LL BE FINE. LET'S GO!
THE RAIN WILL STOP SOON. I'LL BE FINE.
I DON'T WANT TO WAIT AND WASTE TIME JUST 'COS OF A LITTLE RAIN!

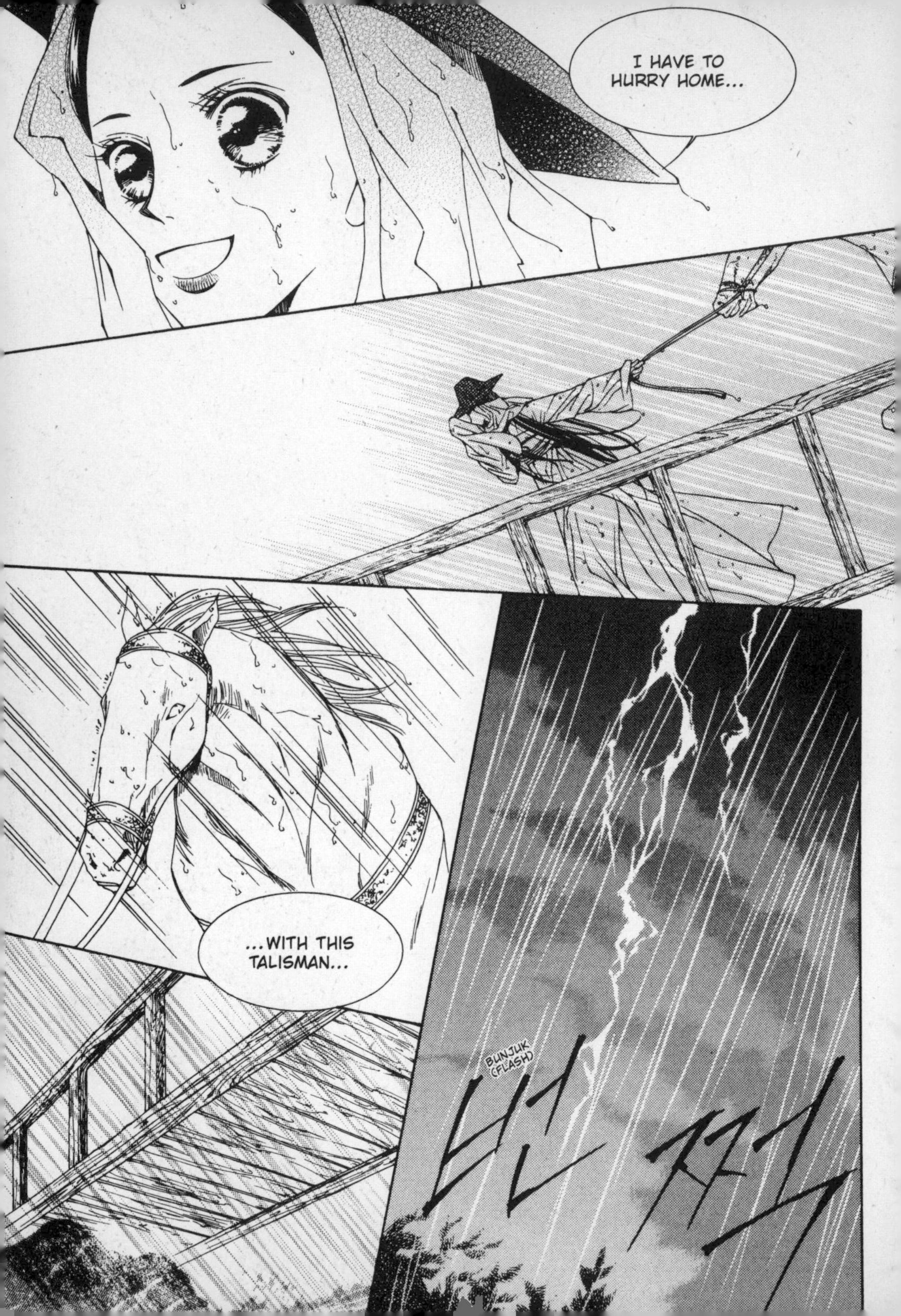
I HAVE TO HURRY HOME...
...WITH THIS TALISMAN...
BUNJUK (FLASH)

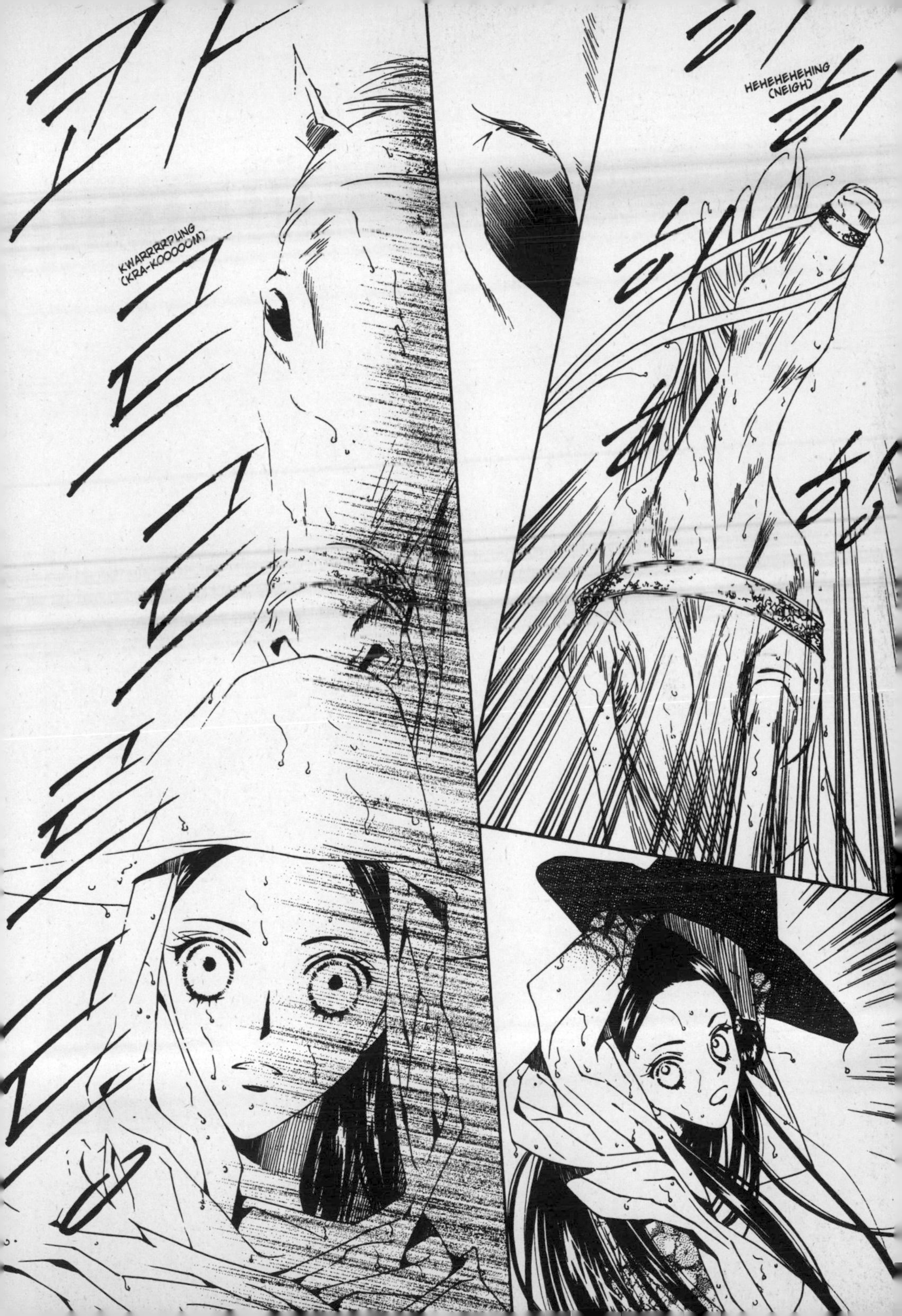
HEHEHEHEHING
(NEIGH)
KWARRRRPUNG
(KRA-KOOOOOM)

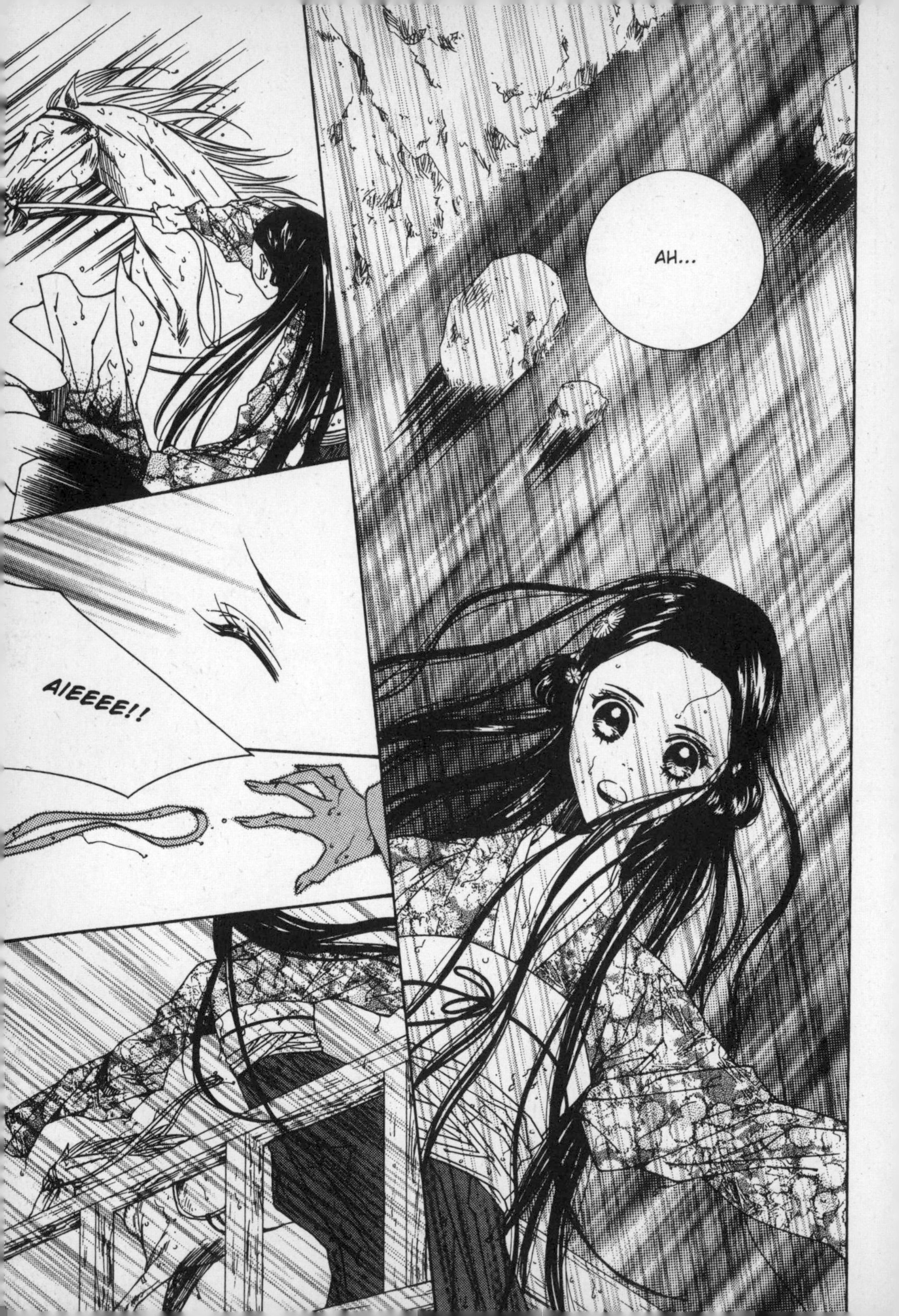
AH...
AIEEEE!!

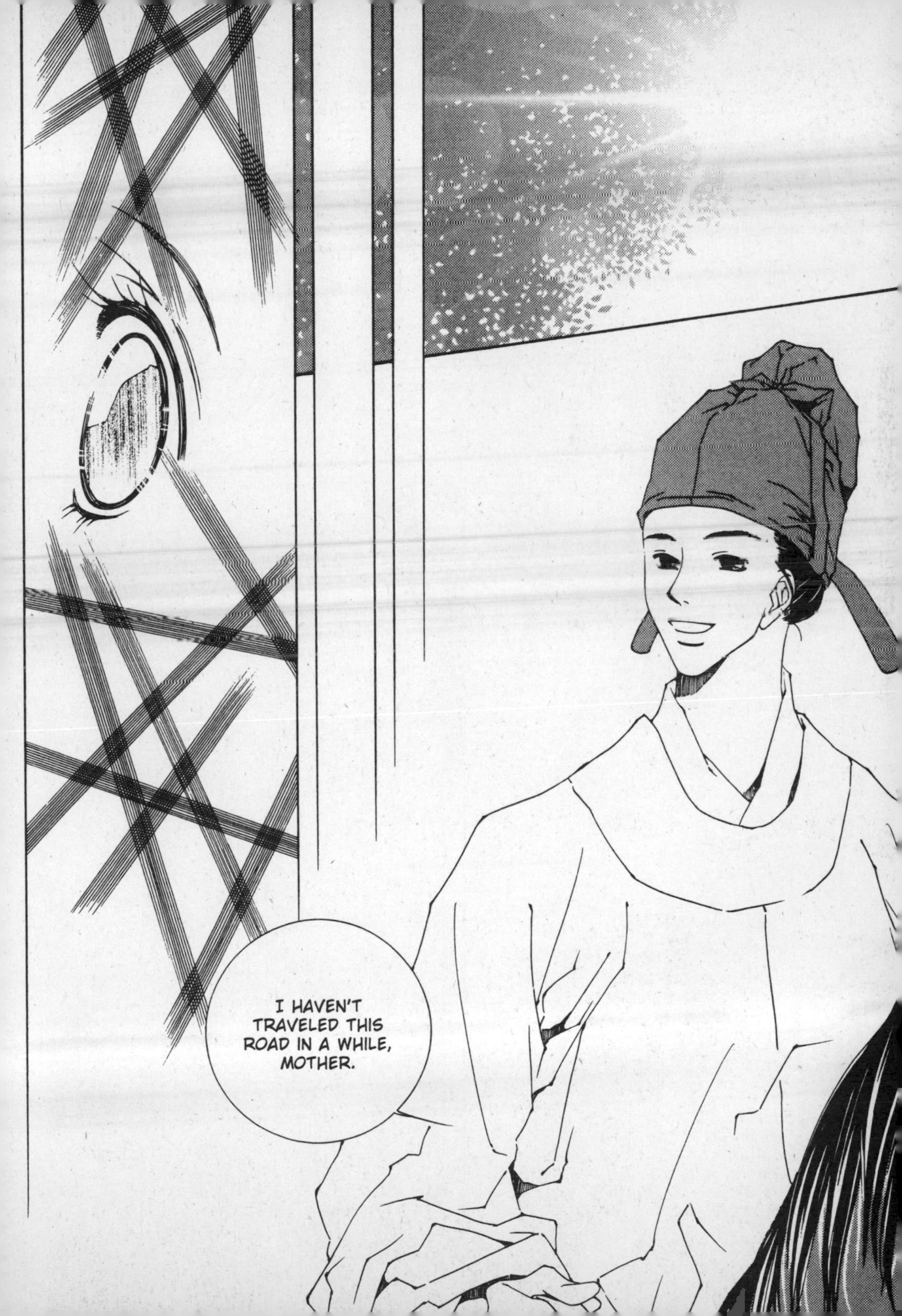
I HAVEN'T TRAVELED THIS ROAD IN A WHILE, MOTHER.

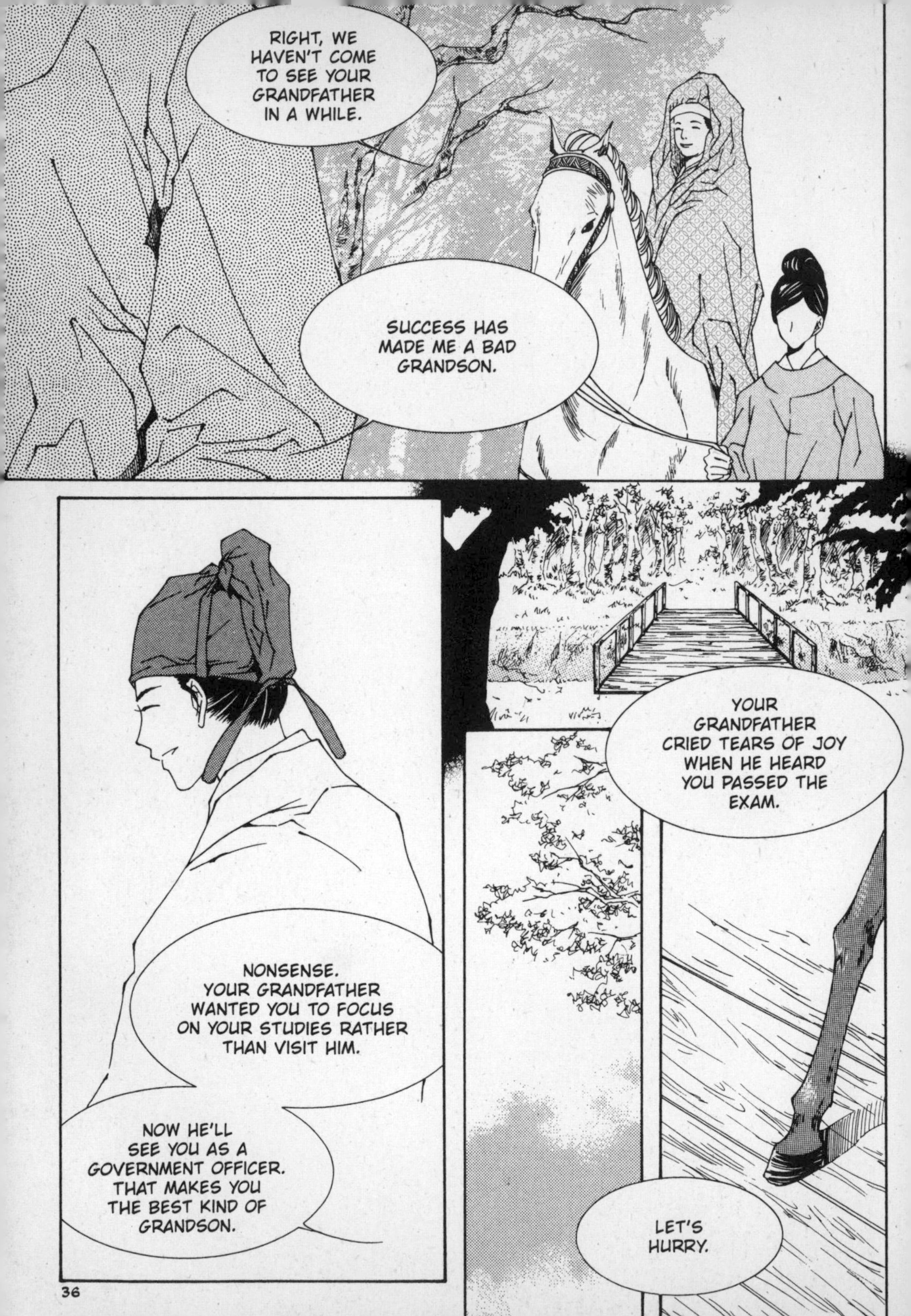
RIGHT, WE HAVEN'T COME TO SEE YOUR GRANDFATHER IN A WHILE.
SUCCESS HAS MADE ME A BAD GRANDSON.
NONSENSE. YOUR GRANDFATHER WANTED YOU TO FOCUS ON YOUR STUDIES RATHER THAN VISIT HIM.
NOW HE'LL SEE YOU AS A GOVERNMENT OFFICER. THAT MAKES YOU THE BEST KIND OF GRANDSON.
YOUR GRANDFATHER CRIED TEARS OF JOY WHEN HE HEARD YOU PASSED THE EXAM.
LET'S HURRY.

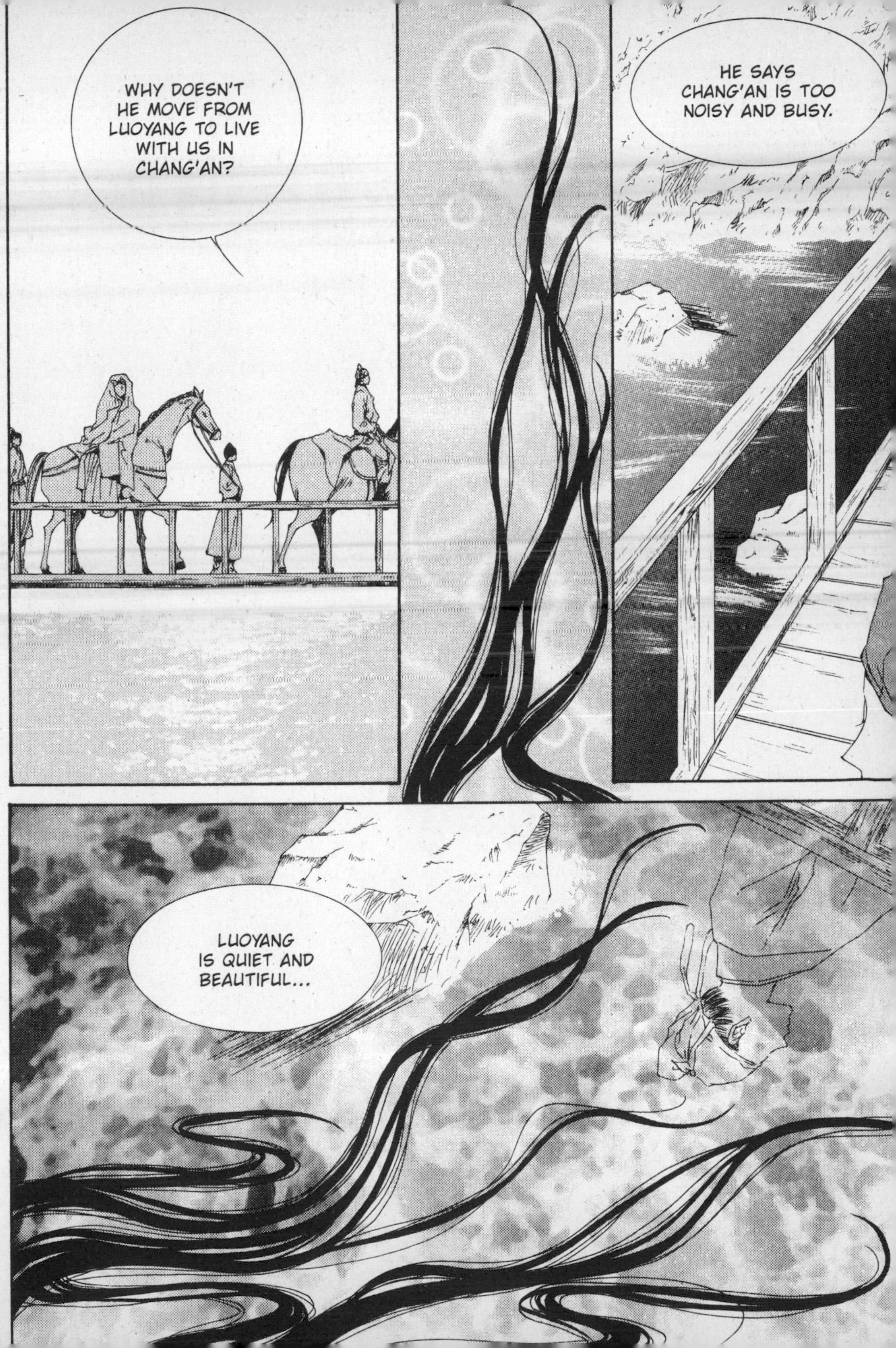
HE SAYS CHANG'AN IS TOO NOISY AND BUSY.
WHY DOESN'T HE MOVE FROM LUOYANG TO LIVE WITH US IN CHANG'AN?
LUOYANG IS QUIET AND BEAUTIFUL...

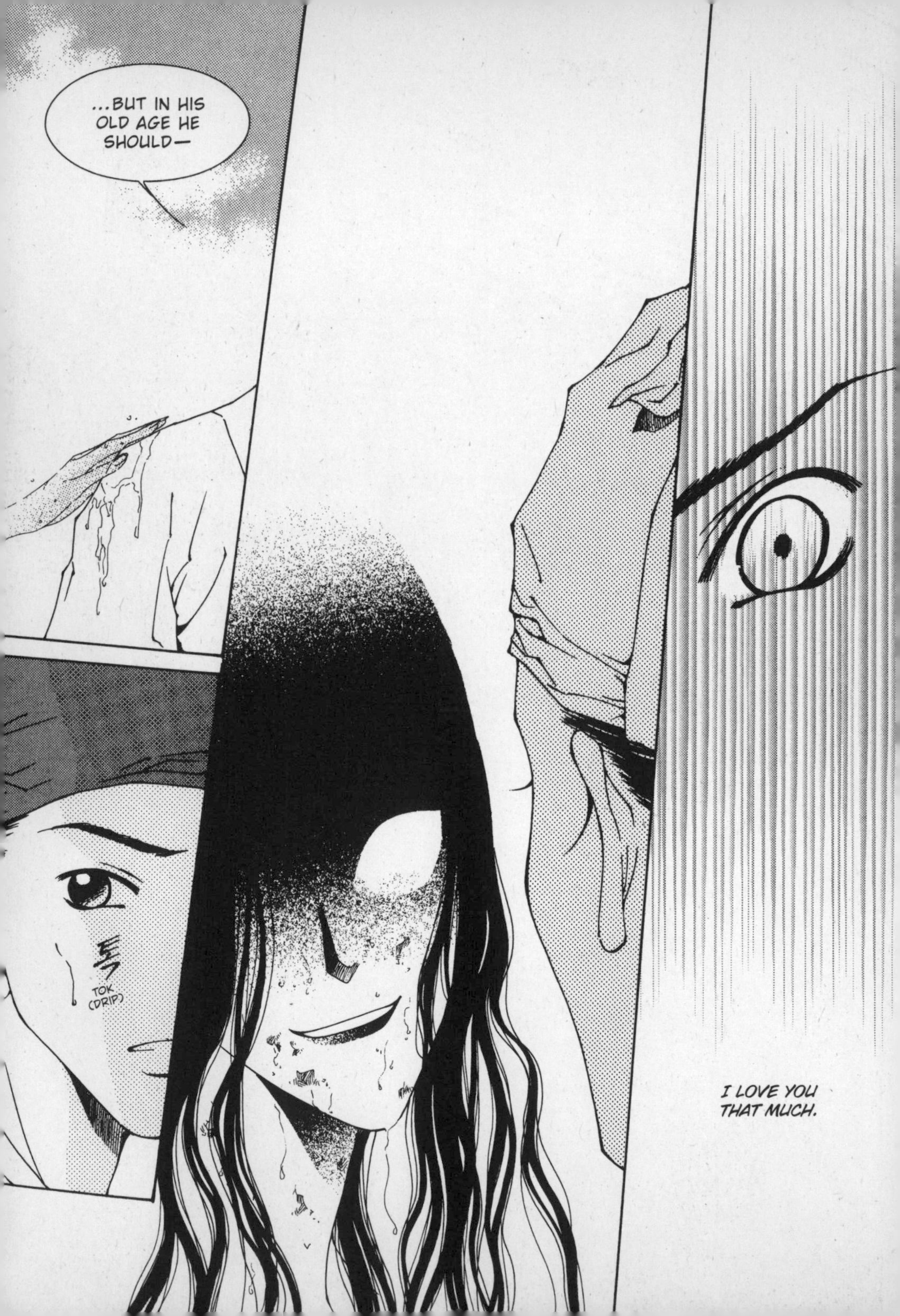
...BUT IN HIS OLD AGE HE SHOULD—
TOK (DRIP)
I LOVE YOU THAT MUCH.

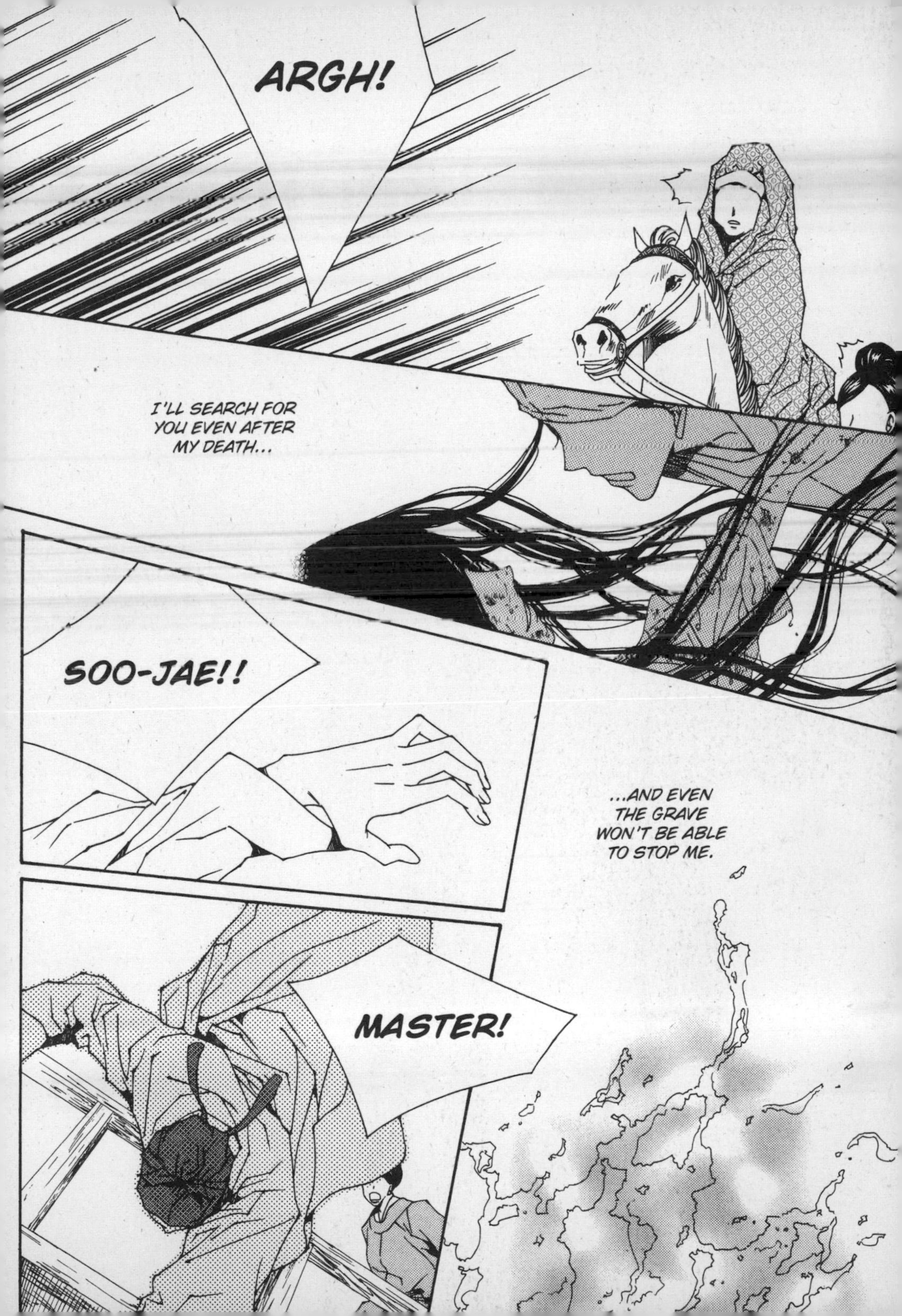
ARGH!
I'LL SEARCH FOR YOU EVEN AFTER MY DEATH...
SOO-JAE!!
...AND EVEN THE GRAVE WON'T BE ABLE TO STOP ME.
MASTER!

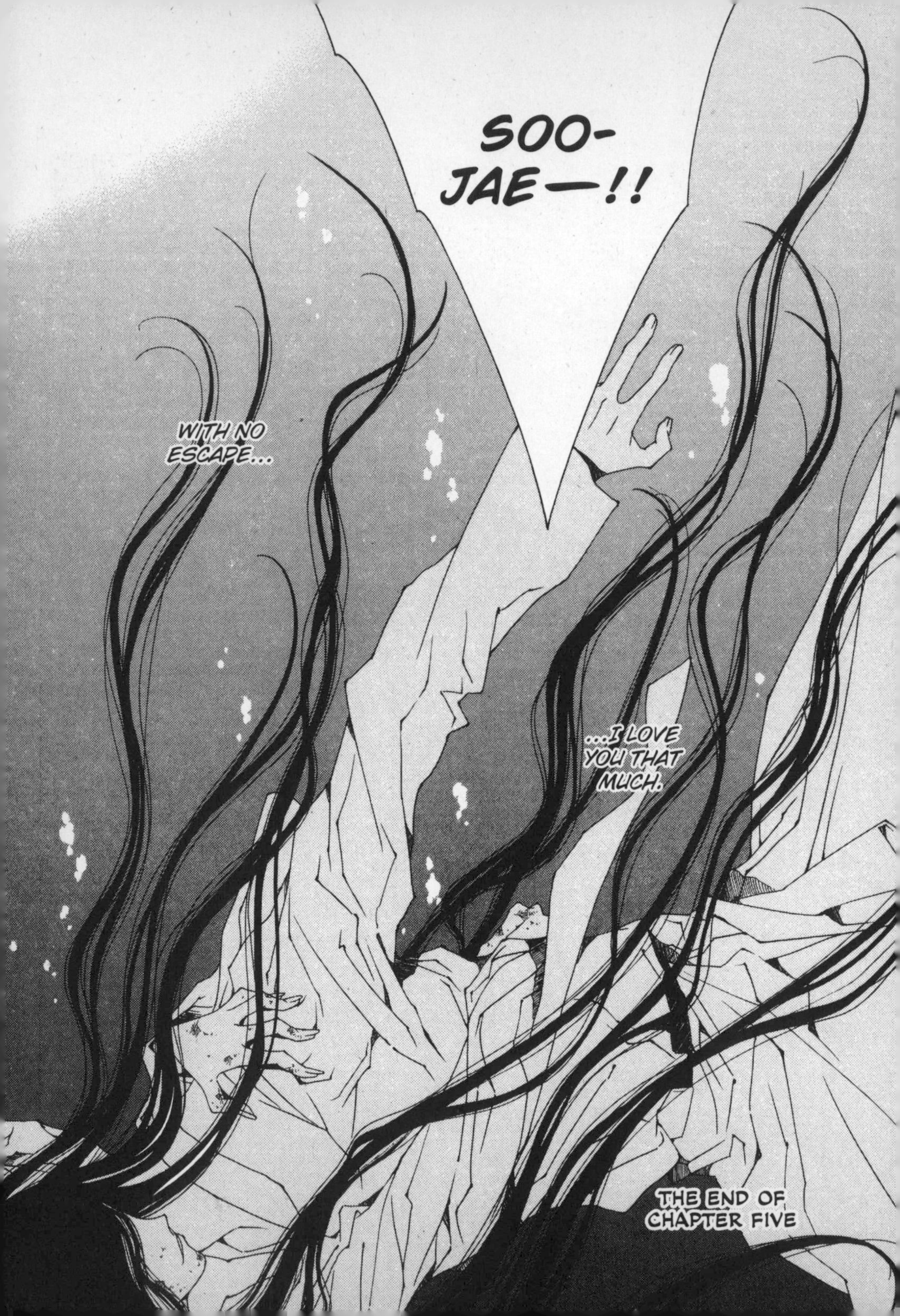
SOO-
JAE—!!
WITH NO ESCAPE...
...I LOVE YOU THAT MUCH.
THE END OF CHAPTER FIVE

CHAPTER SIX
LOVE

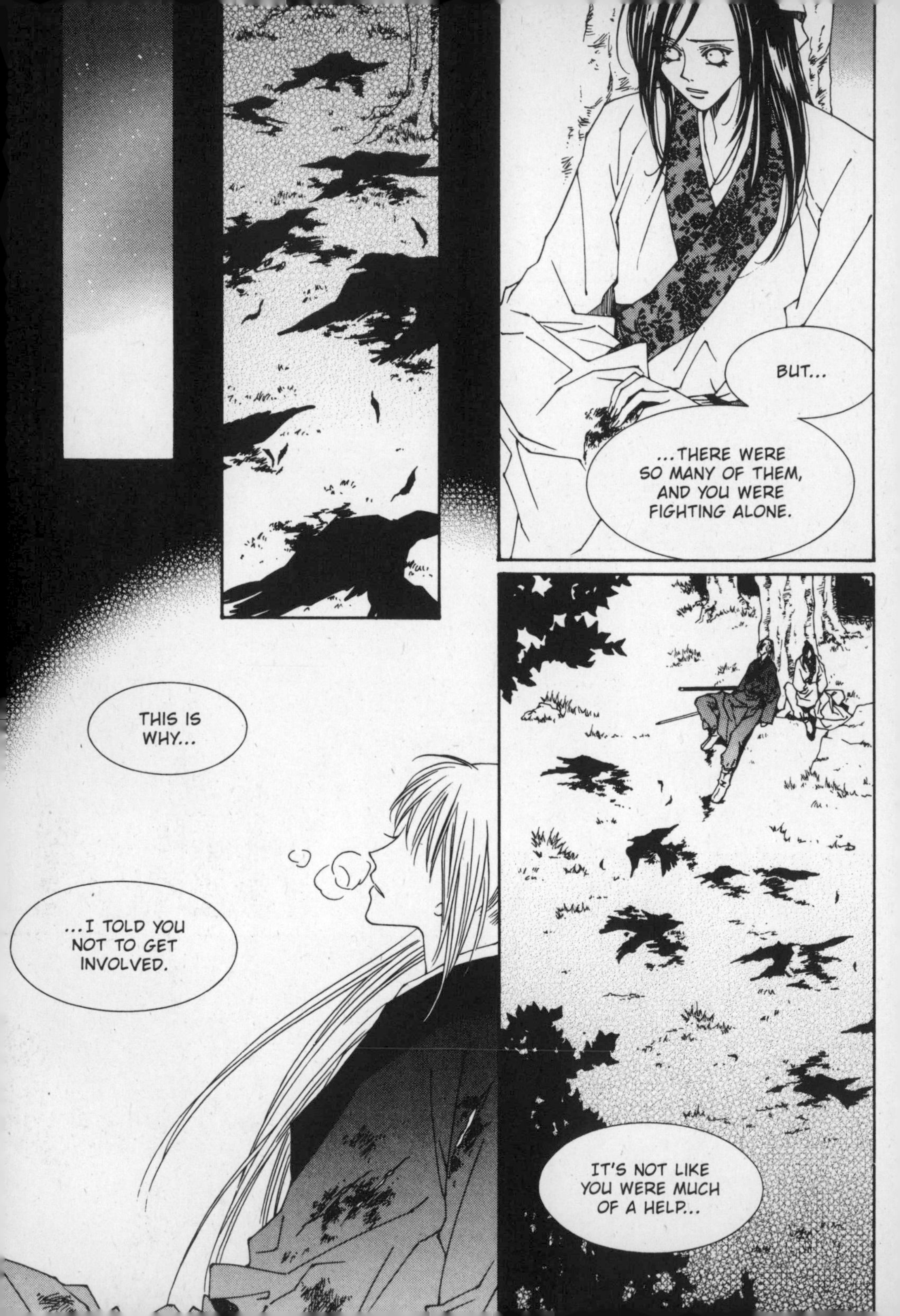
BUT...
...THERE WERE SO MANY OF THEM, AND YOU WERE FIGHTING ALONE.
IT'S NOT LIKE YOU WERE MUCH OF A HELP...
THIS IS WHY...
...I TOLD YOU NOT TO GET INVOLVED.

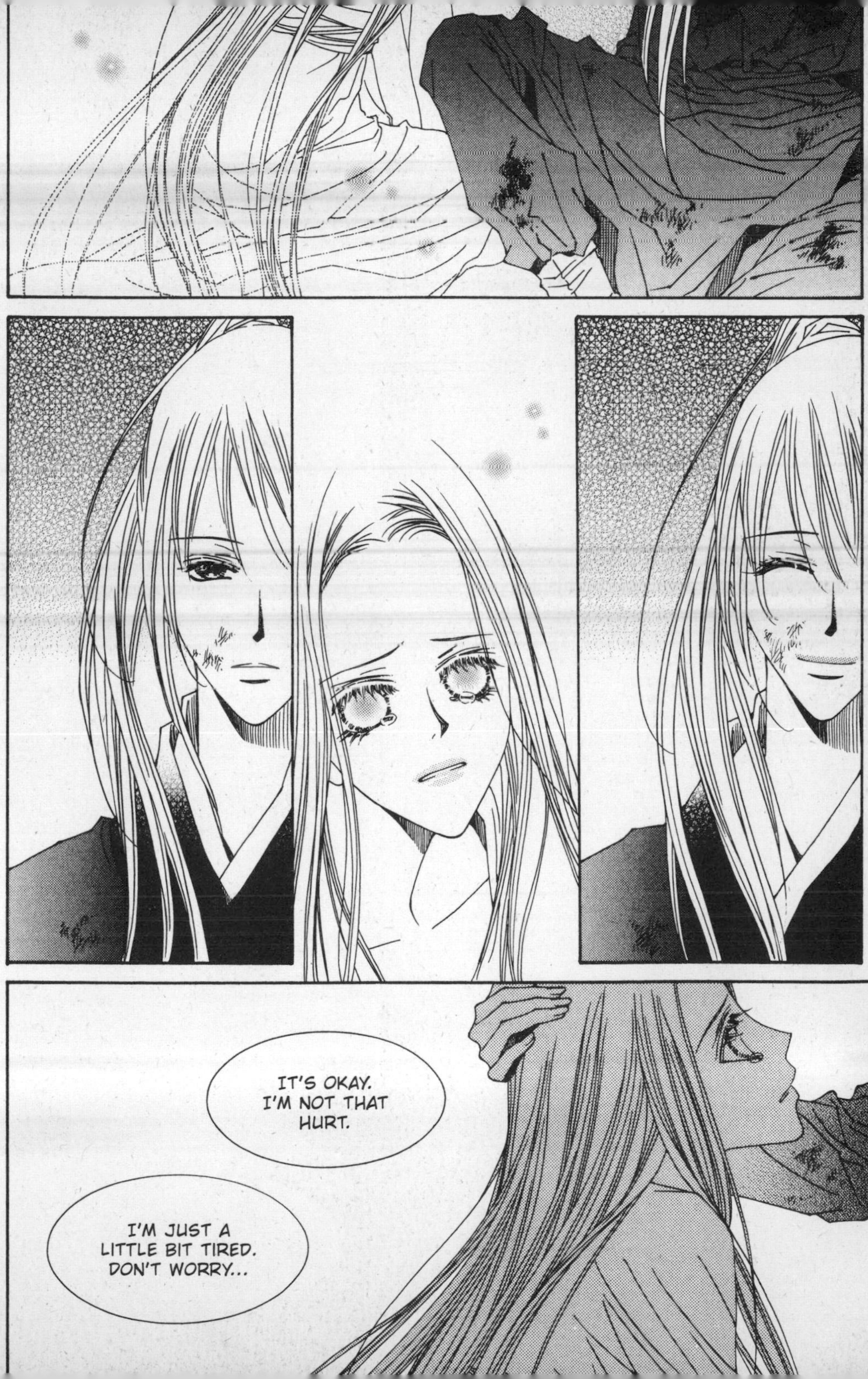
IT'S OKAY. I'M NOT THAT HURT.
I'M JUST A LITTLE BIT TIRED. DON'T WORRY...

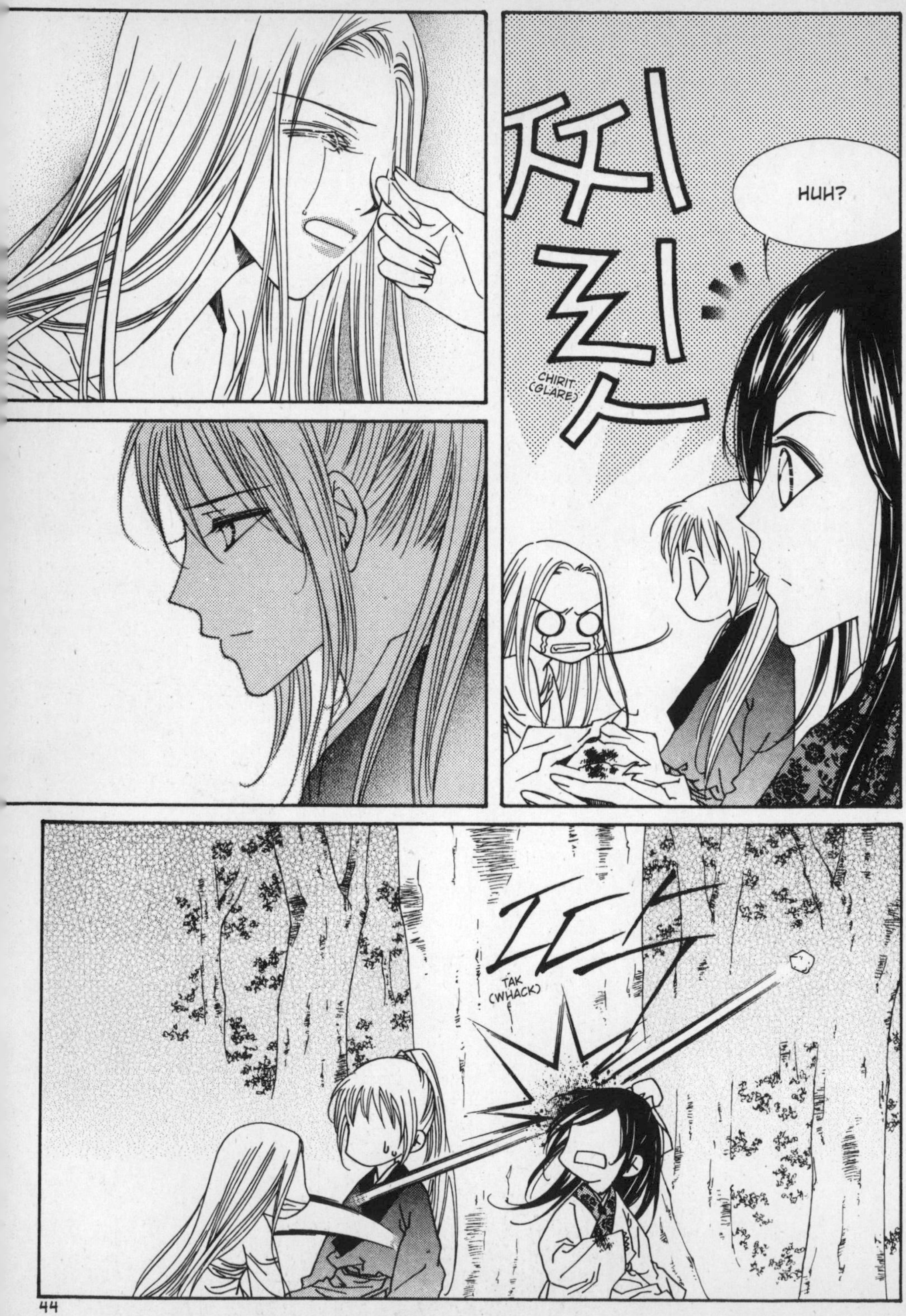
HUH?
CHIRIT (GLARE)
TAK (WHACK)

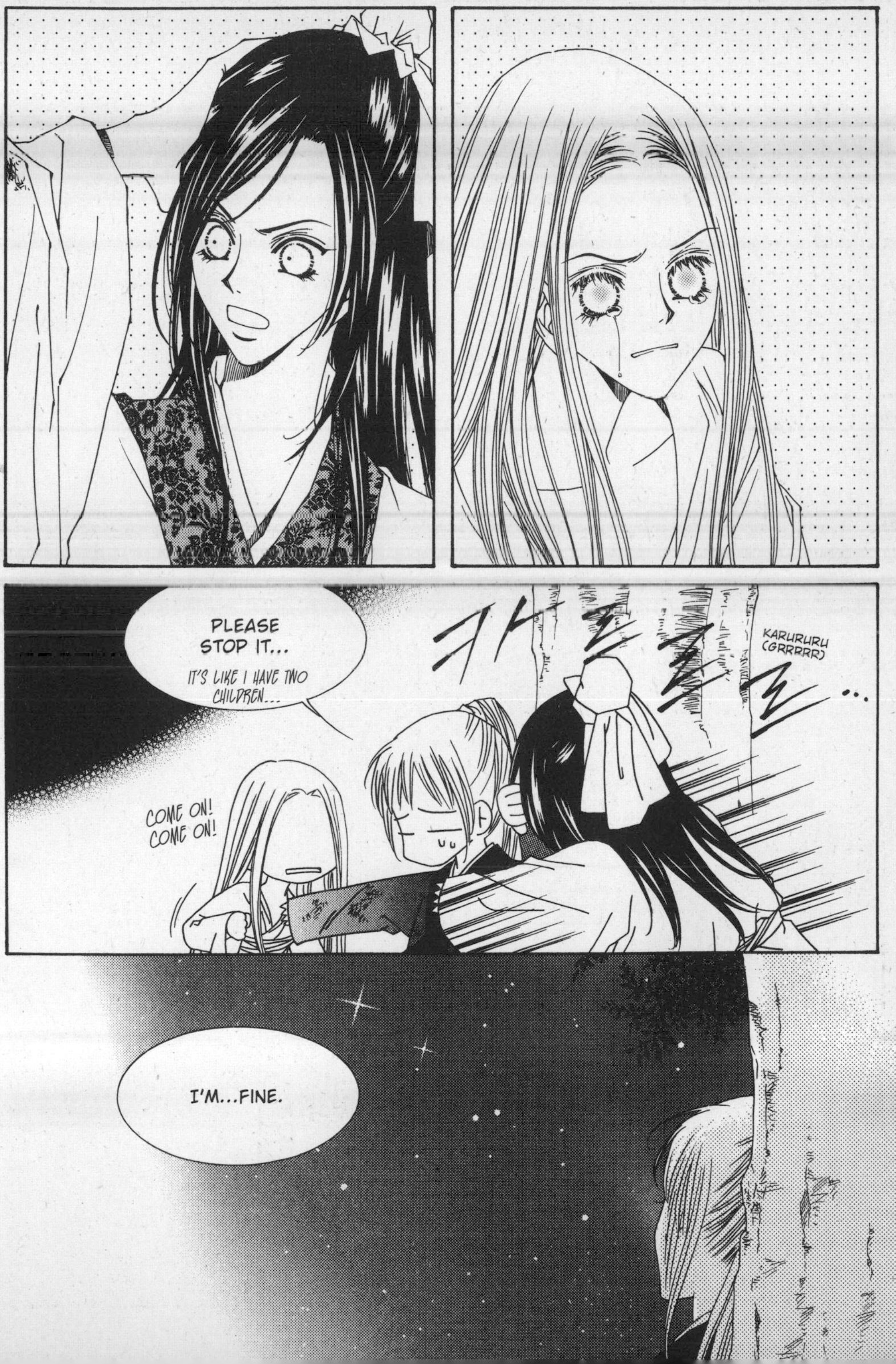
KARURURU (GRRRRR)
PLEASE STOP IT...
IT'S LIKE I HAVE TWO CHILDREN...
COME ON! COME ON!
I'M...FINE.

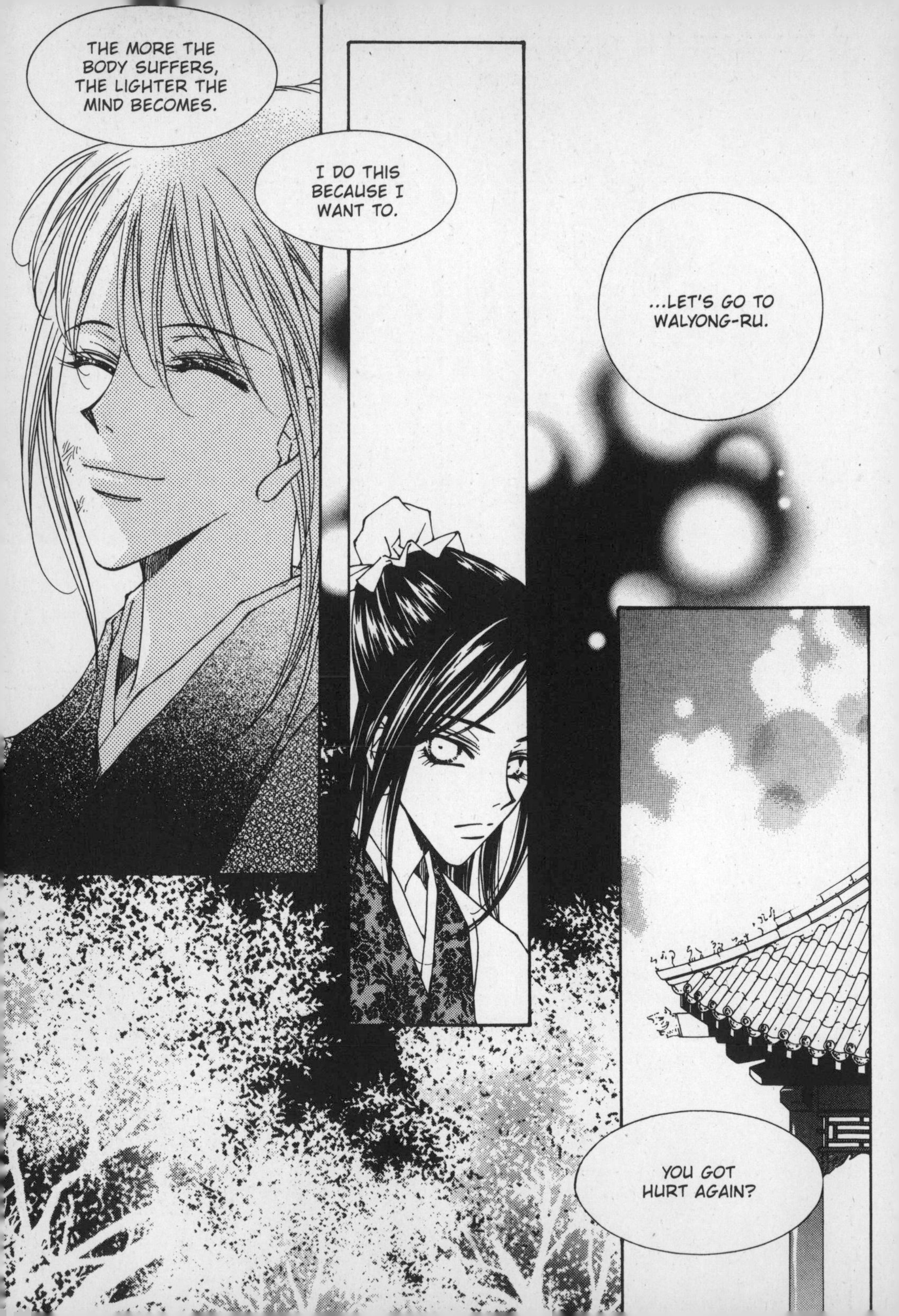
THE MORE THE BODY SUFFERS, THE LIGHTER THE MIND BECOMES.
I DO THIS BECAUSE I WANT TO.
...LET'S GO TO WALYONG-RU.
YOU GOT HURT AGAIN?

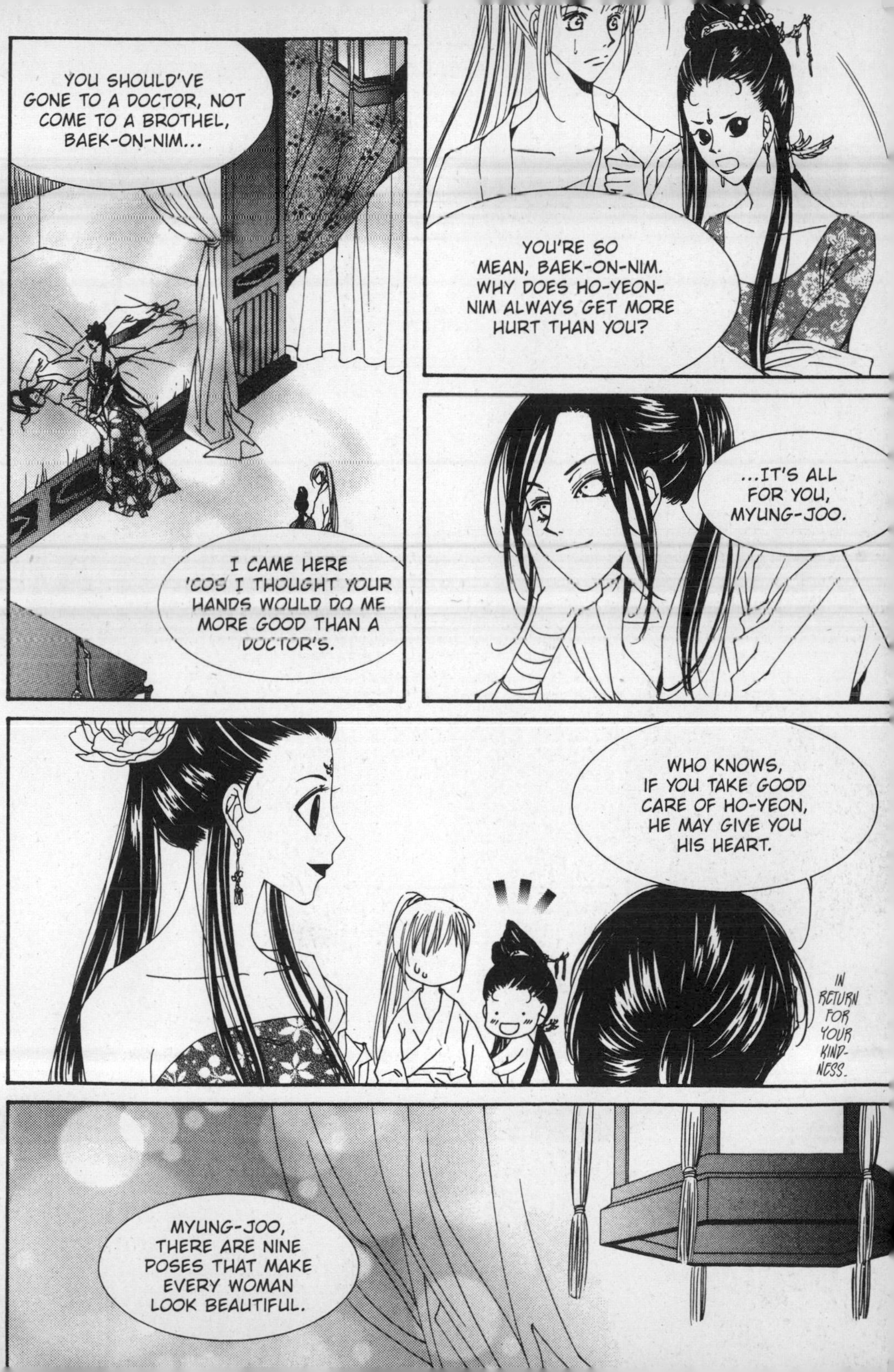
YOU SHOULD'VE GONE TO A DOCTOR, NOT COME TO A BROTHEL, BAEK-ON-NIM...
YOU'RE SO MEAN, BAEK-ON-NIM. WHY DOES HO-YEON-NIM ALWAYS GET MORE HURT THAN YOU?
I CAME HERE 'COS I THOUGHT YOUR HANDS WOULD DO ME MORE GOOD THAN A DOCTOR'S.
...IT'S ALL FOR YOU, MYUNG-JOO.
WHO KNOWS, IF YOU TAKE GOOD CARE OF HO-YEON, HE MAY GIVE YOU HIS HEART.
IN RETURN FOR YOUR KINDNESS.
MYUNG-JOO, THERE ARE NINE POSES THAT MAKE EVERY WOMAN LOOK BEAUTIFUL.

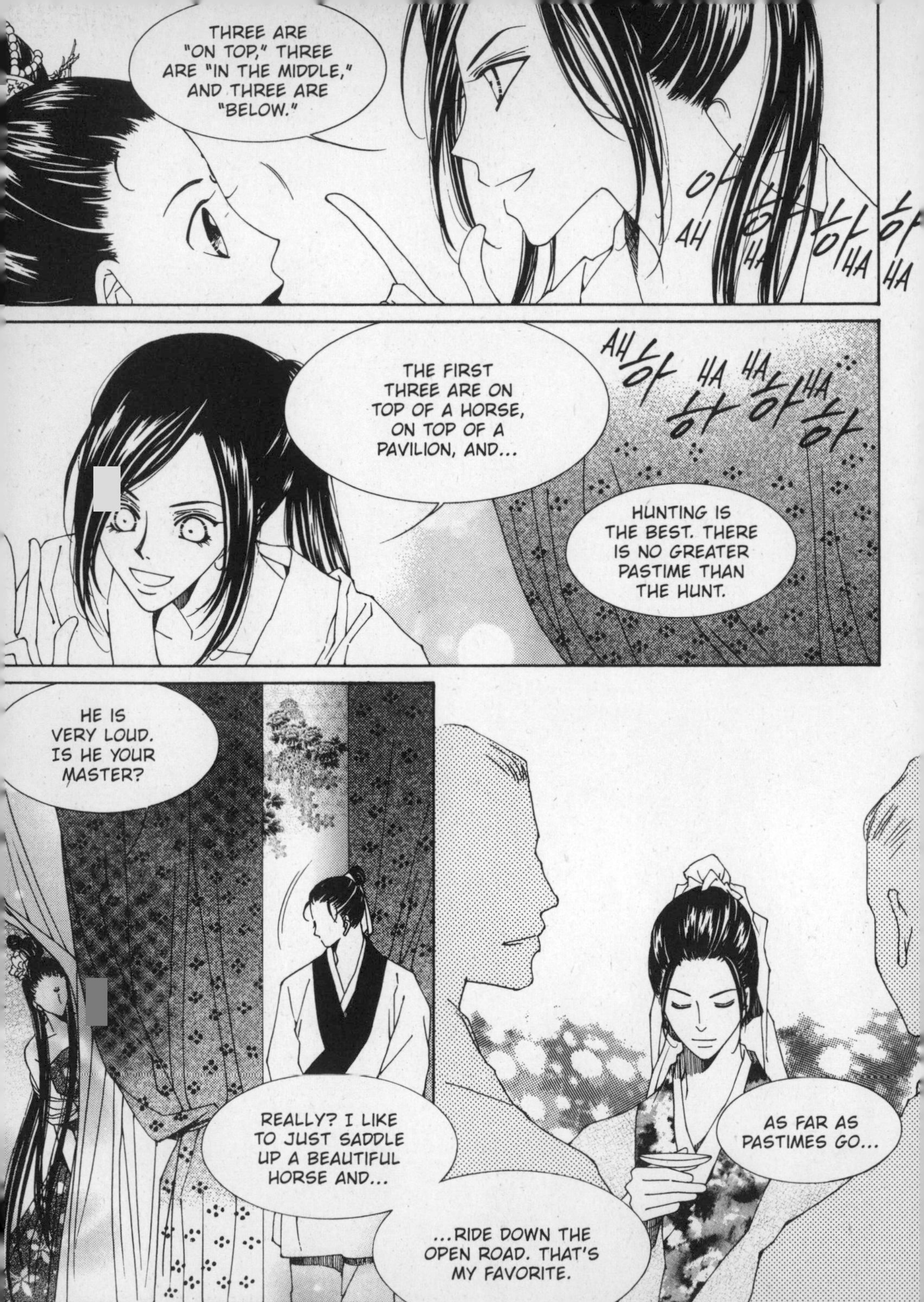
THREE ARE "ON TOP," THREE ARE "IN THE MIDDLE," AND THREE ARE "BELOW."
아 하 하 하
AH HA HA HA
THE FIRST THREE ARE ON TOP OF A HORSE, ON TOP OF A PAVILION, AND...
아 하 하 하 하
AH HA HA HA
HUNTING IS THE BEST. THERE IS NO GREATER PASTIME THAN THE HUNT.
HE IS VERY LOUD. IS HE YOUR MASTER?
REALLY? I LIKE TO JUST SADDLE UP A BEAUTIFUL HORSE AND...
...RIDE DOWN THE OPEN ROAD. THAT'S MY FAVORITE.
AS FAR AS PASTIMES GO...

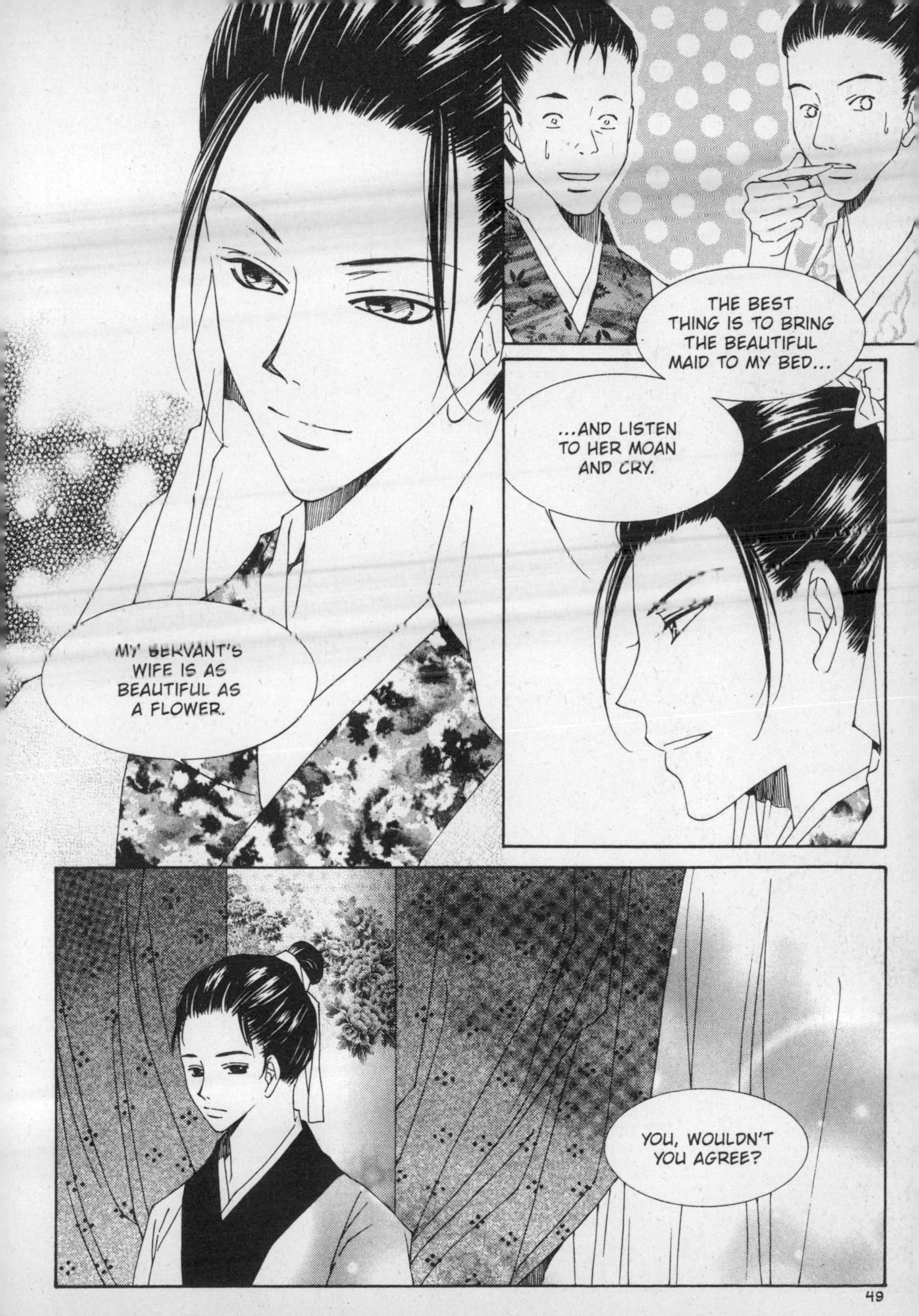
MY SERVANT'S WIFE IS AS BEAUTIFUL AS A FLOWER.
THE BEST THING IS TO BRING THE BEAUTIFUL MAID TO MY BED...
...AND LISTEN TO HER MOAN AND CRY.
YOU, WOULDN'T YOU AGREE?

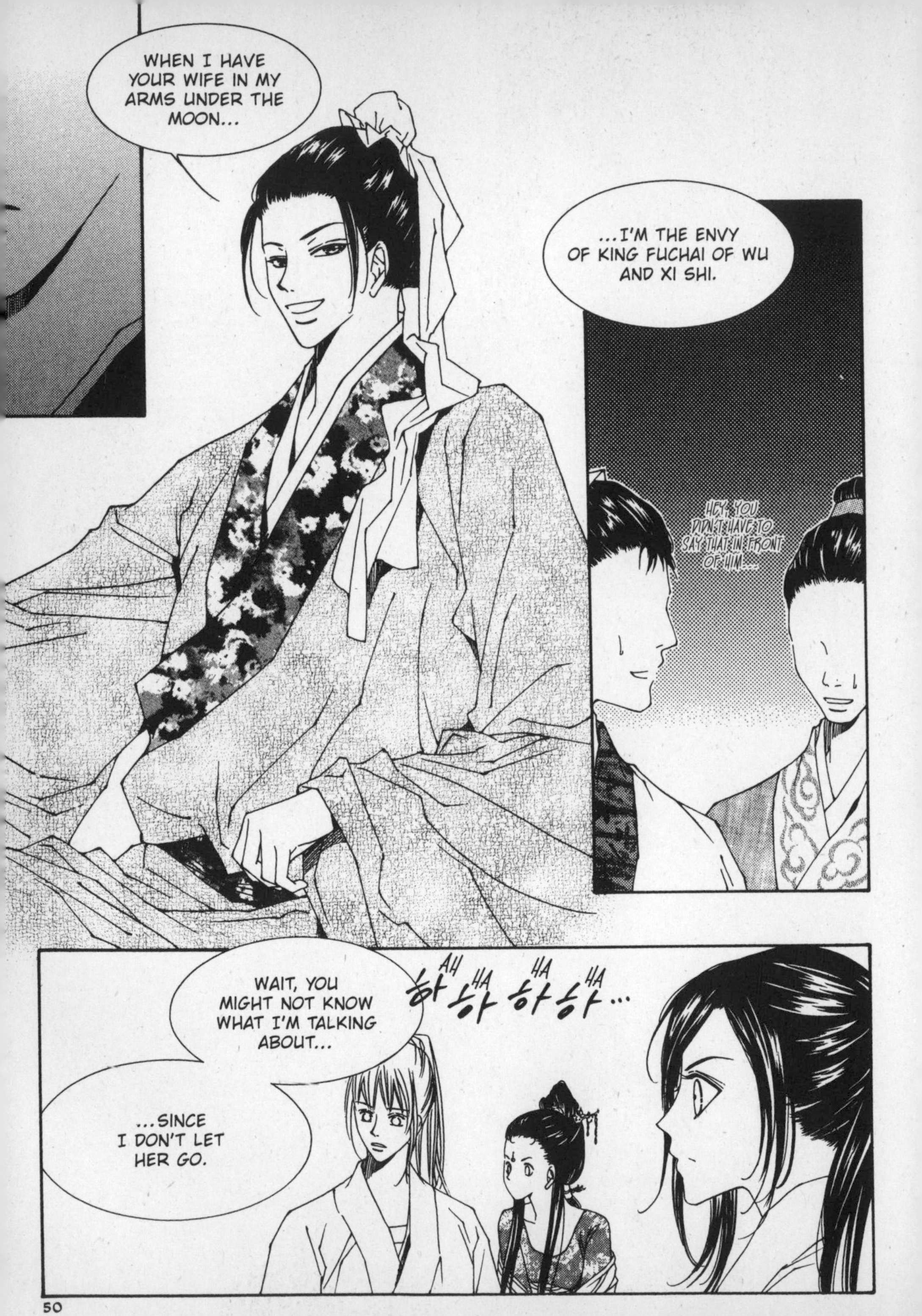
WHEN I HAVE YOUR WIFE IN MY ARMS UNDER THE MOON...
...I'M THE ENVY OF KING FUCHAI OF WU AND XI SHI.
HEY, YOU DIDN'T HAVE TO SAY THAT IN FRONT OF HIM...
WAIT, YOU MIGHT NOT KNOW WHAT I'M TALKING ABOUT...
...SINCE I DON'T LET HER GO.
하하하하...
AH HA HA HA

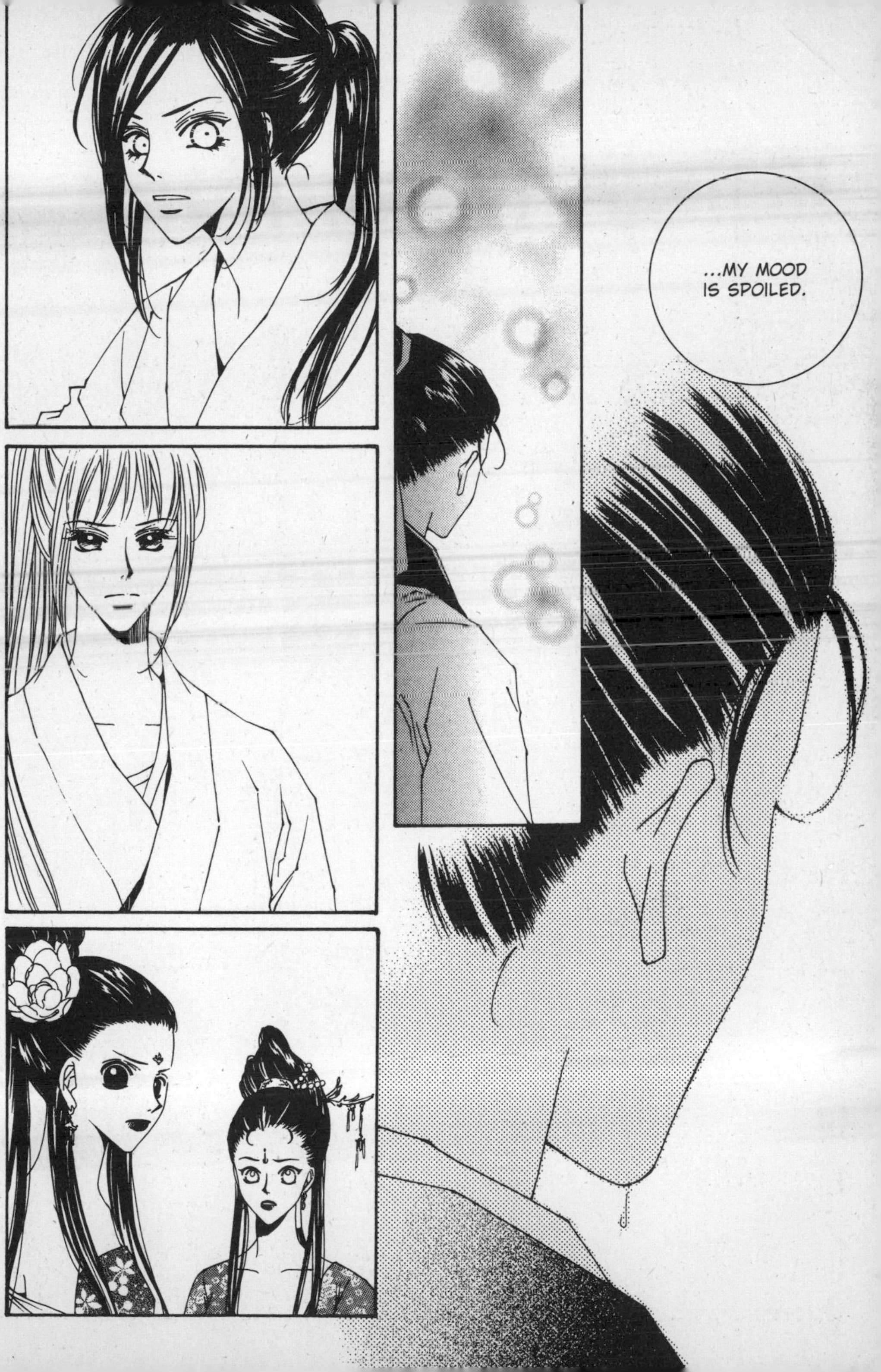
...MY MOOD IS SPOILED.

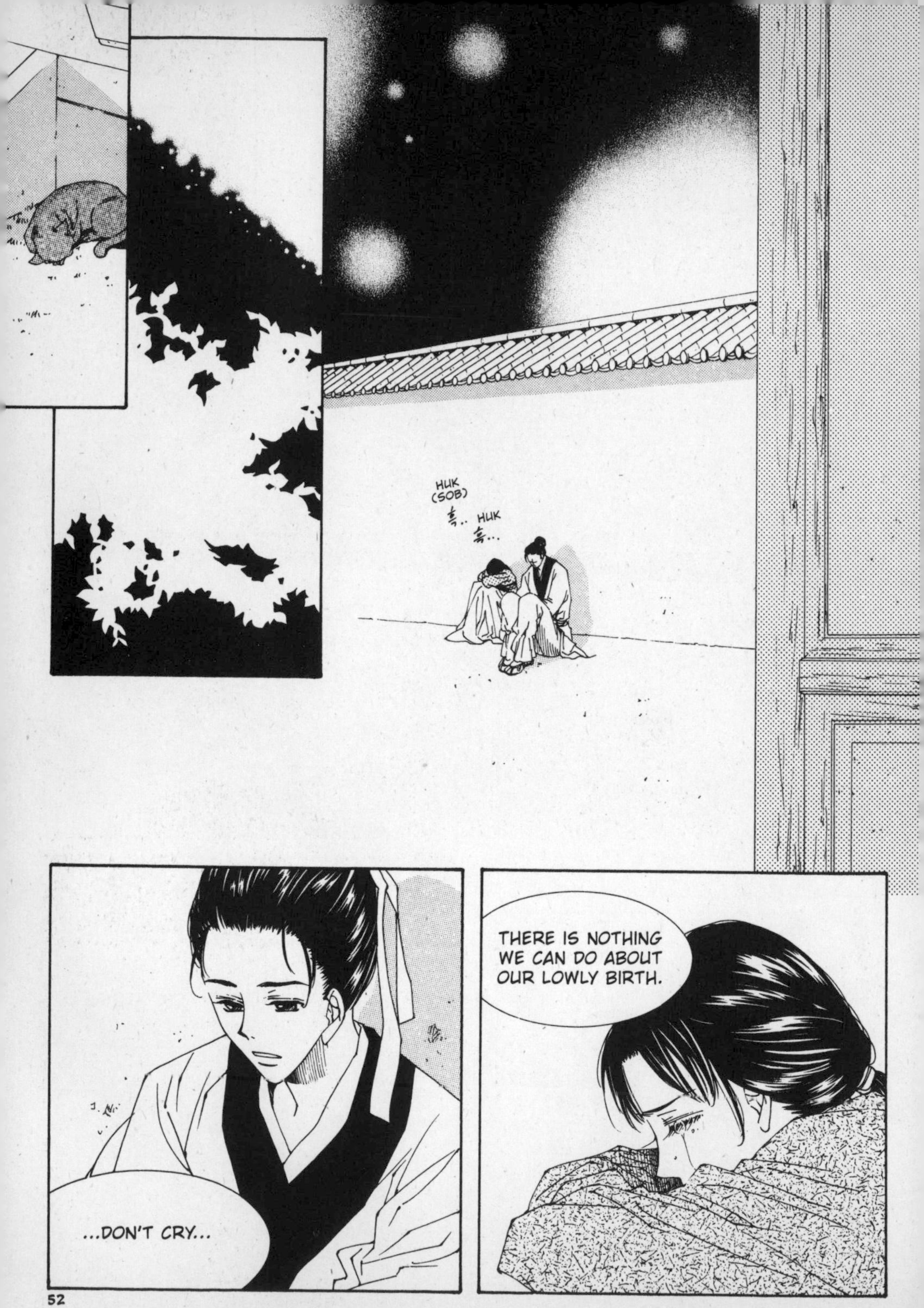
HUK
(SOB)
흑..
HUK
흑...
...DON'T CRY...
THERE IS NOTHING WE CAN DO ABOUT OUR LOWLY BIRTH.

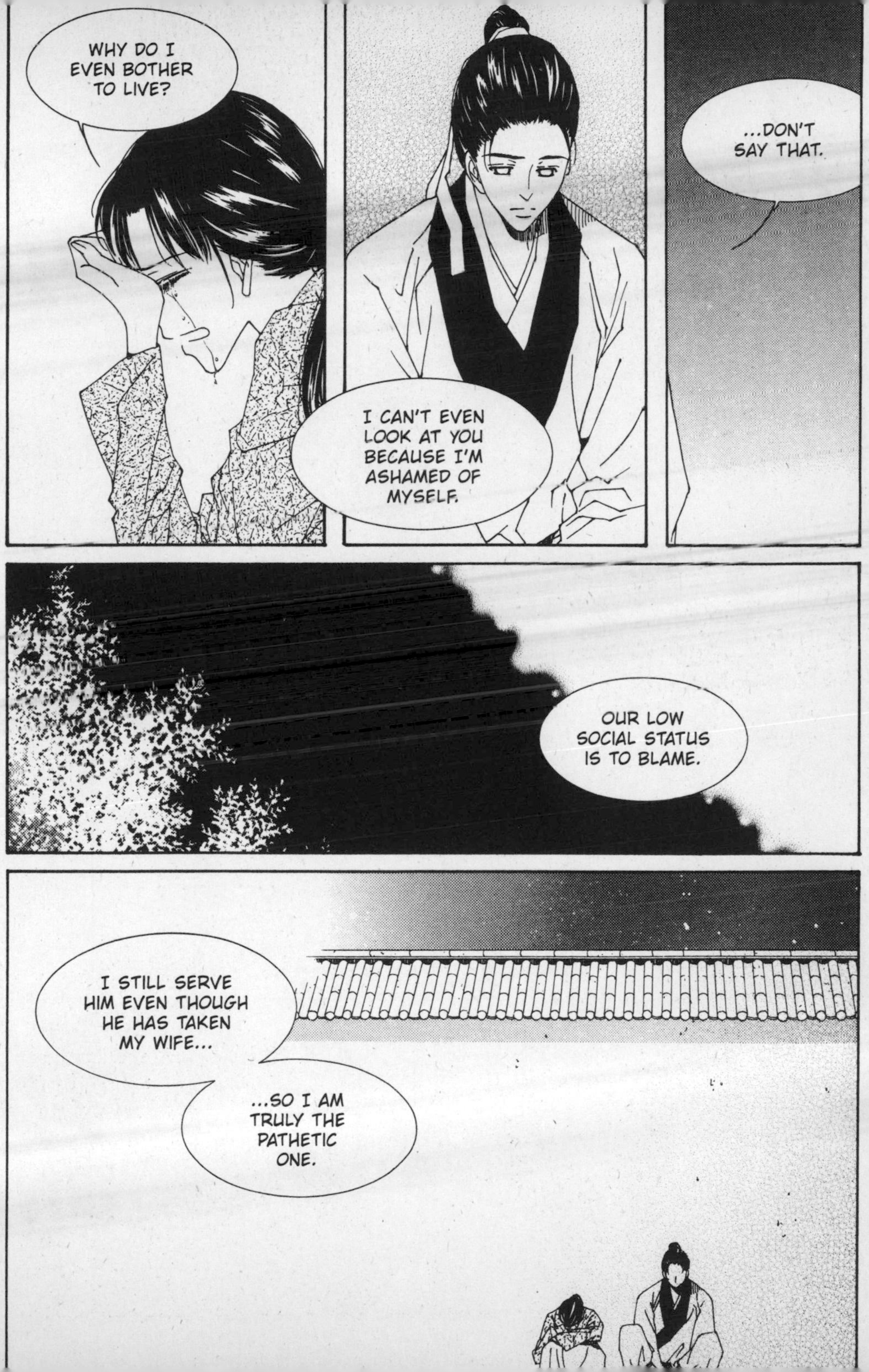

WHY DO I EVEN BOTHER TO LIVE?
I CAN'T EVEN LOOK AT YOU BECAUSE I'M ASHAMED OF MYSELF.
...DON'T SAY THAT.
OUR LOW SOCIAL STATUS IS TO BLAME.
I STILL SERVE HIM EVEN THOUGH HE HAS TAKEN MY WIFE...
...SO I AM TRULY THE PATHETIC ONE.

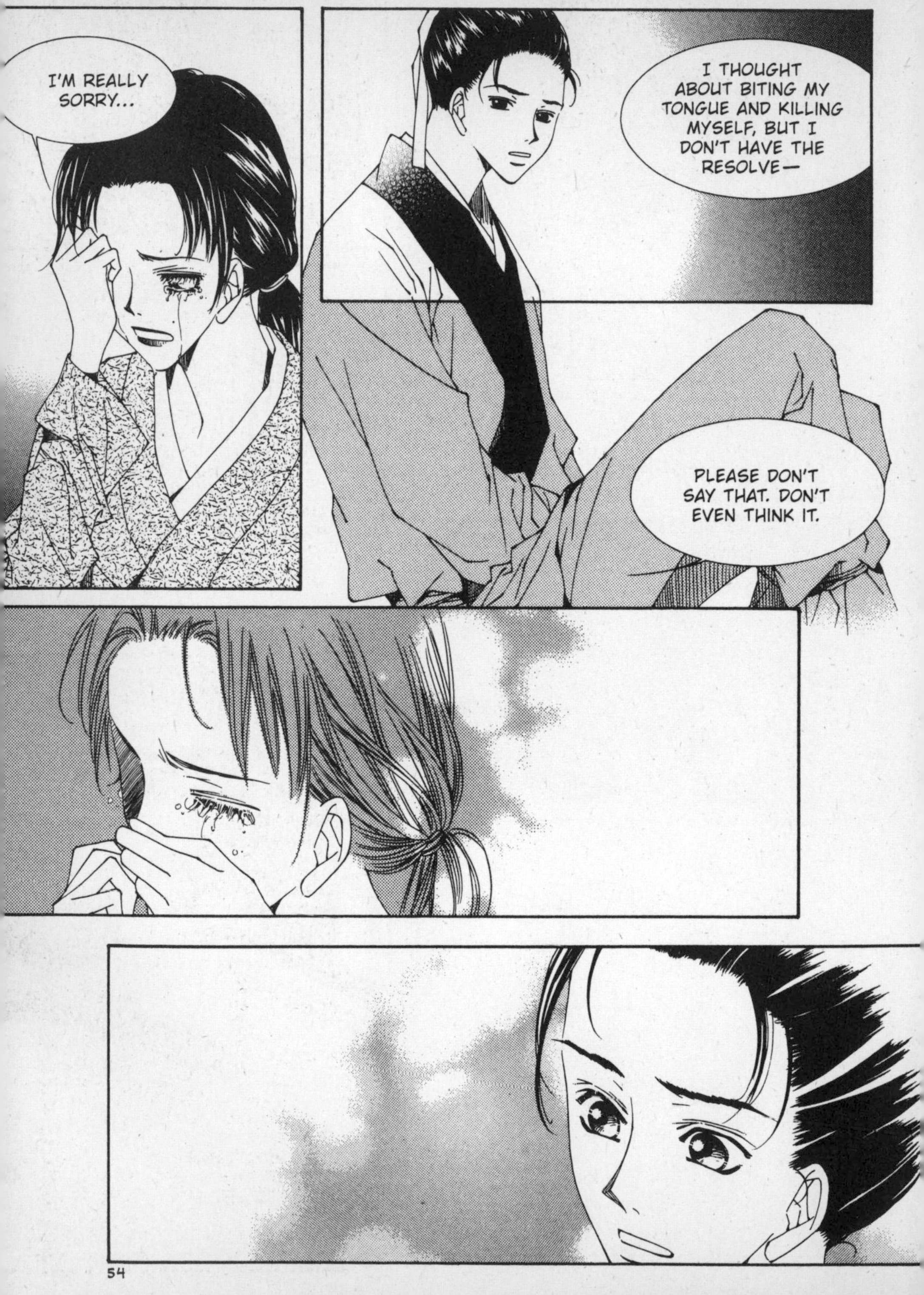
I THOUGHT ABOUT BITING MY TONGUE AND KILLING MYSELF, BUT I DON'T HAVE THE RESOLVE—
I'M REALLY SORRY...
PLEASE DON'T SAY THAT. DON'T EVEN THINK IT.

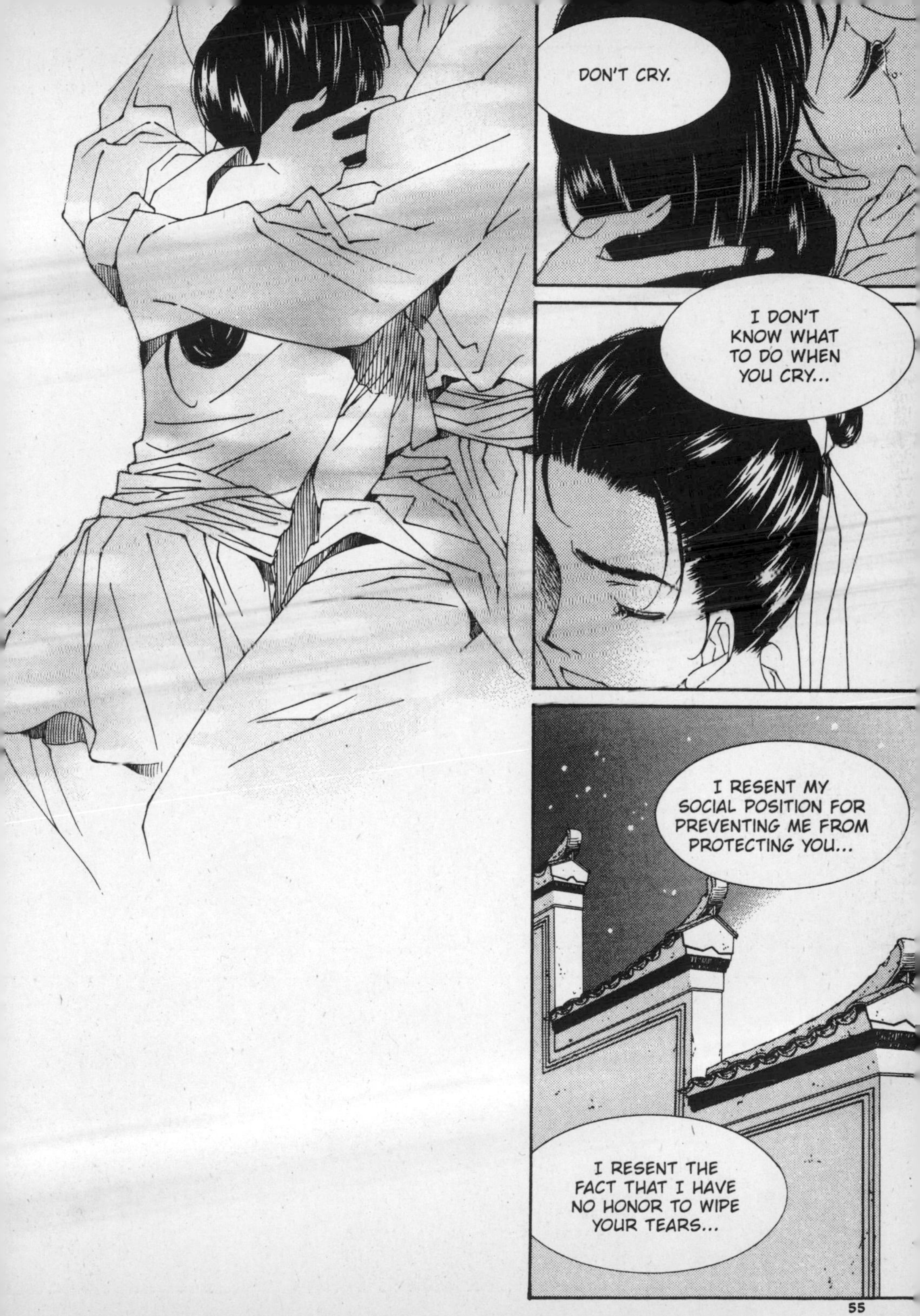
DON'T CRY.
I DON'T KNOW WHAT TO DO WHEN YOU CRY...
I RESENT MY SOCIAL POSITION FOR PREVENTING ME FROM PROTECTING YOU...
I RESENT THE FACT THAT I HAVE NO HONOR TO WIPE YOUR TEARS...

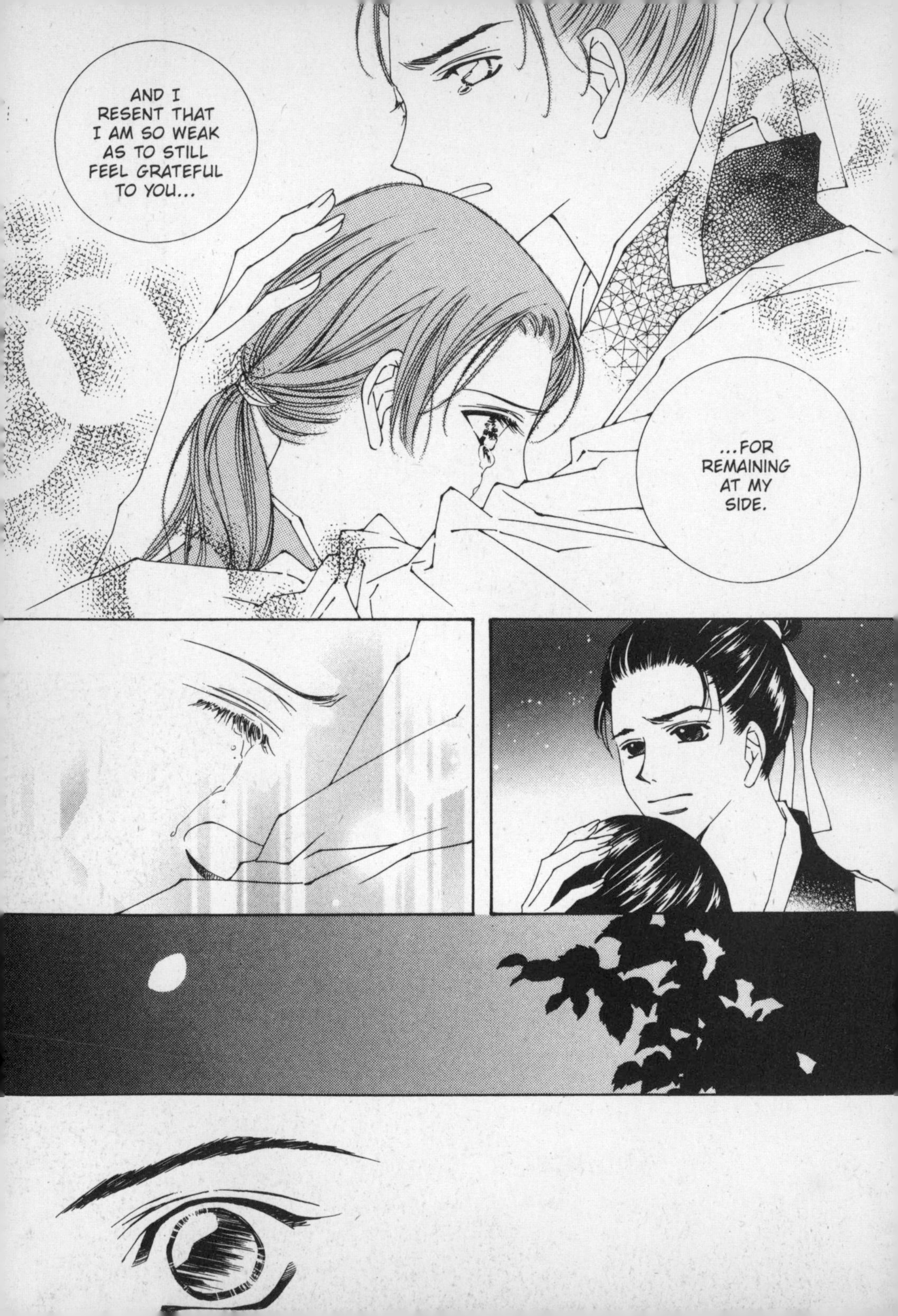
...FOR REMAINING AT MY SIDE.
AND I RESENT THAT I AM SO WEAK AS TO STILL FEEL GRATEFUL TO YOU...

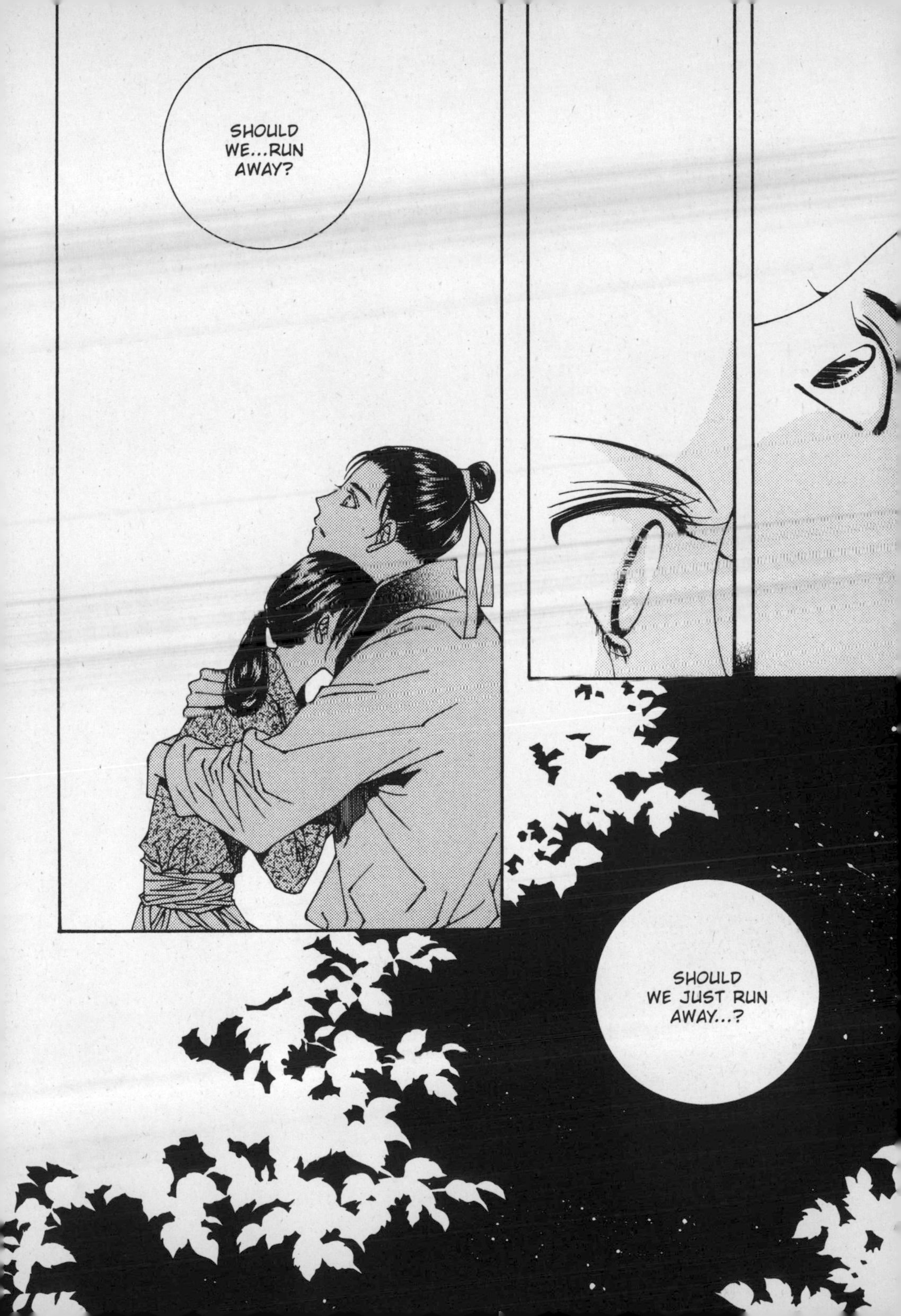
SHOULD WE...RUN AWAY?
SHOULD WE JUST RUN AWAY...?

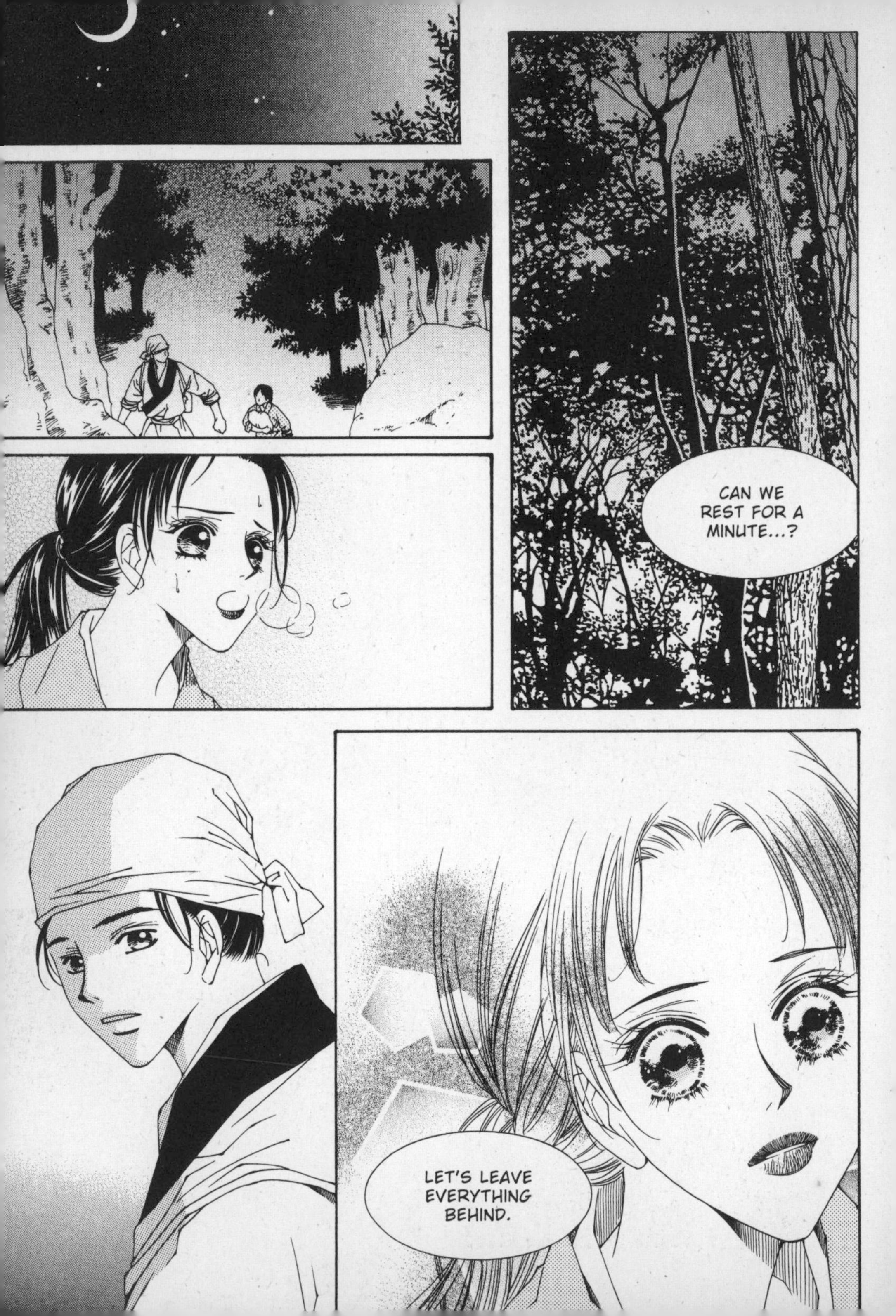
CAN WE REST FOR A MINUTE...?
LET'S LEAVE EVERYTHING BEHIND.

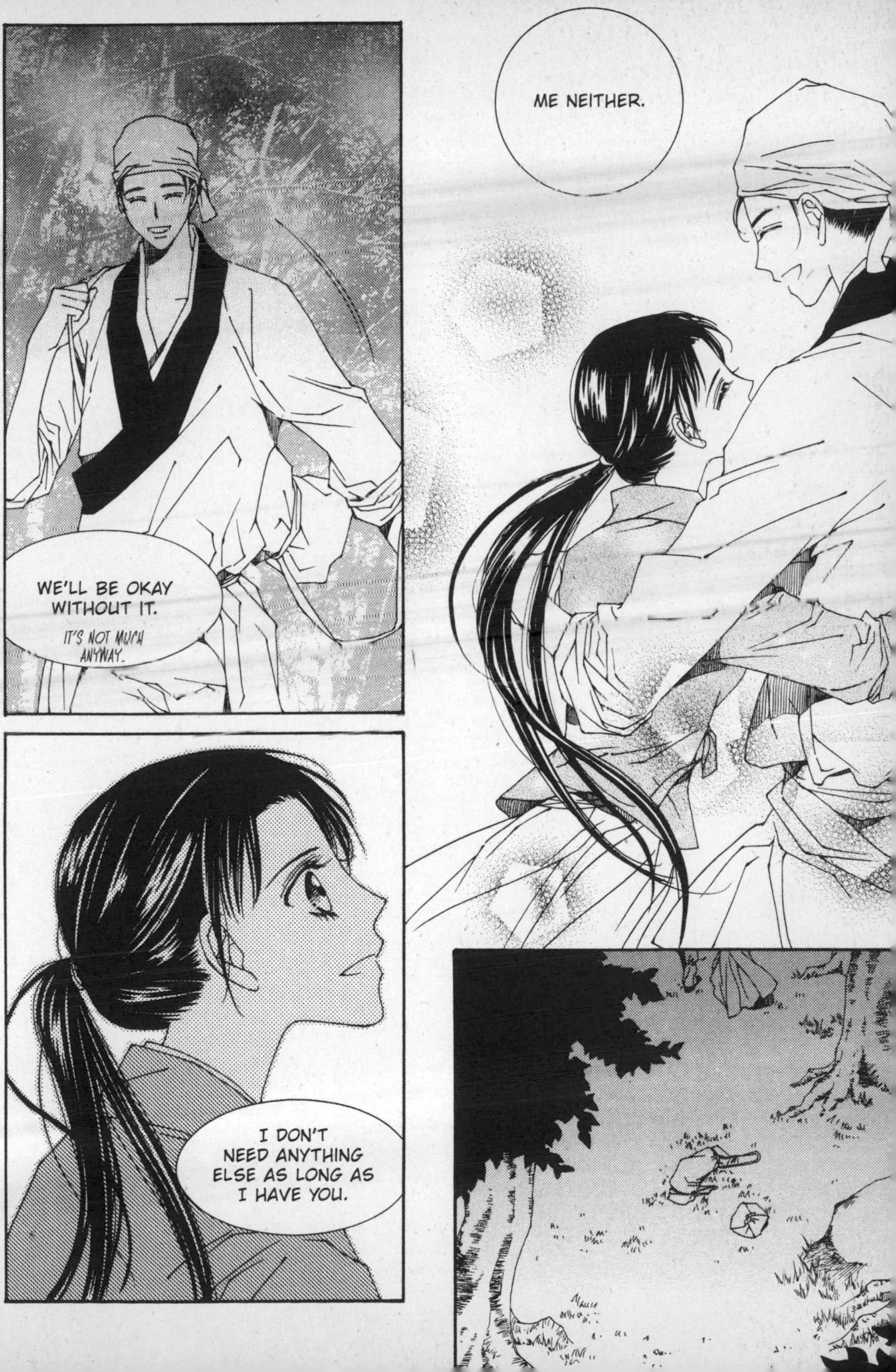
WE'LL BE OKAY WITHOUT IT.
IT'S NOT MUCH ANYWAY.
I DON'T NEED ANYTHING ELSE AS LONG AS I HAVE YOU.
ME NEITHER.

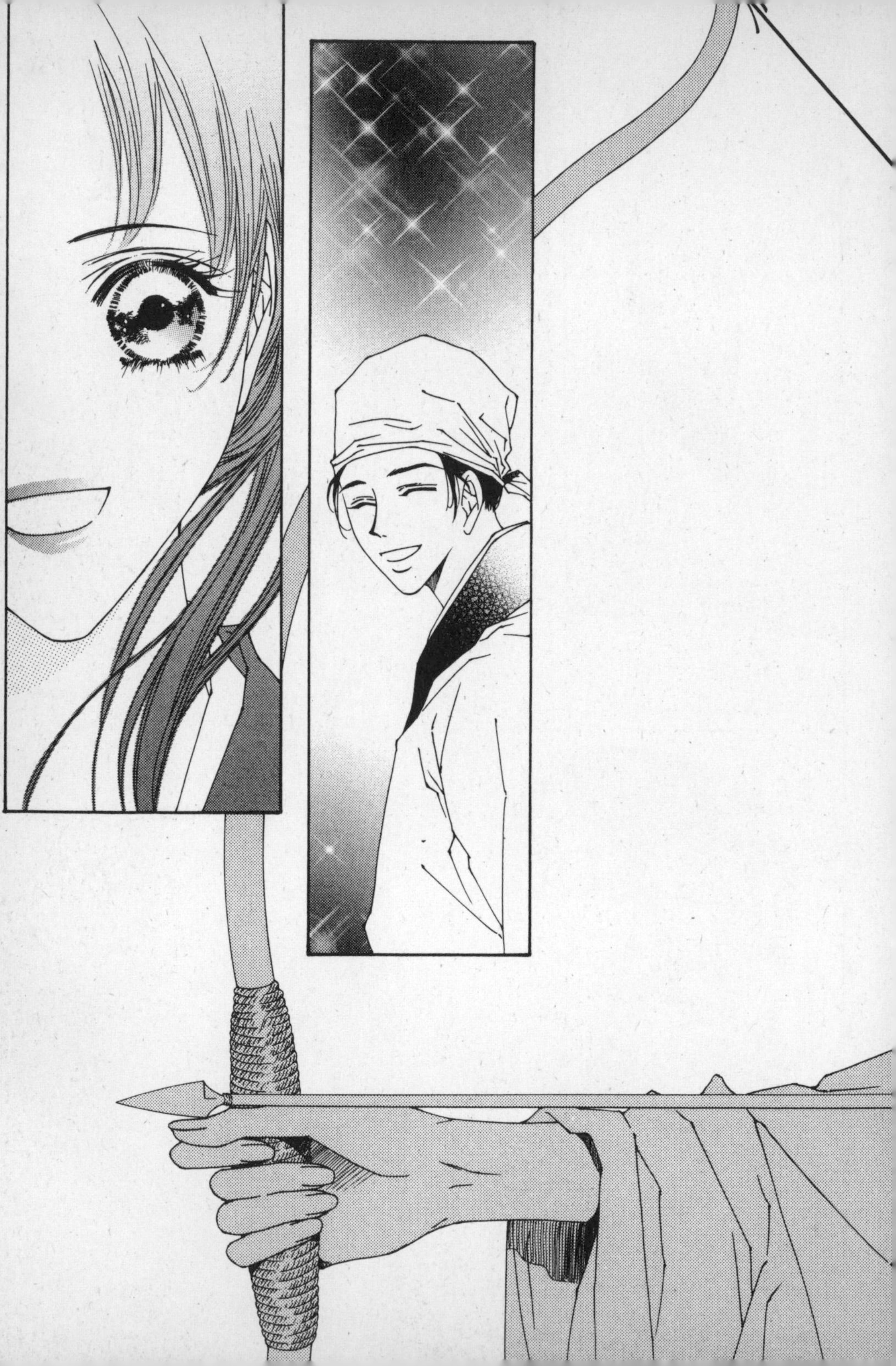

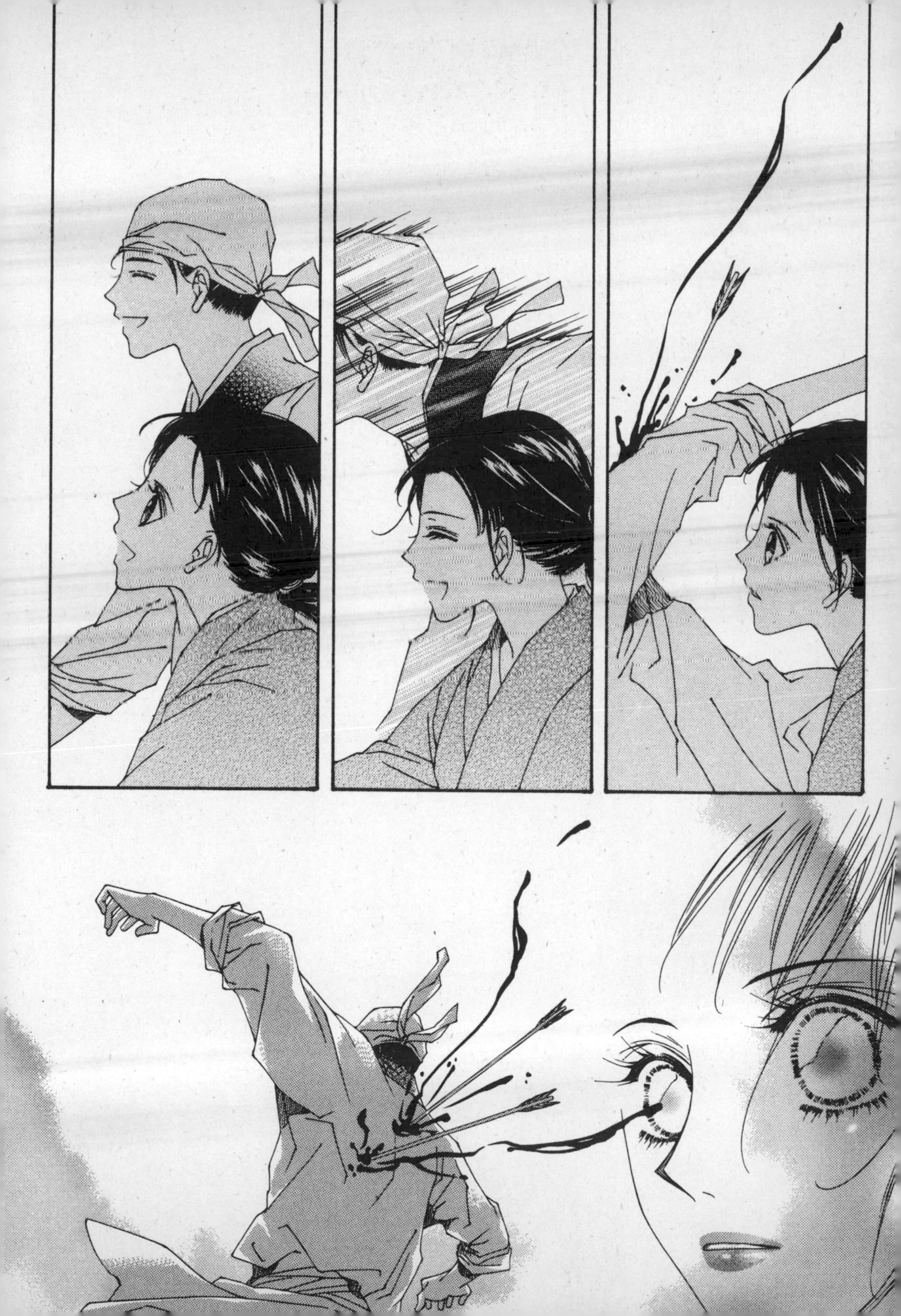

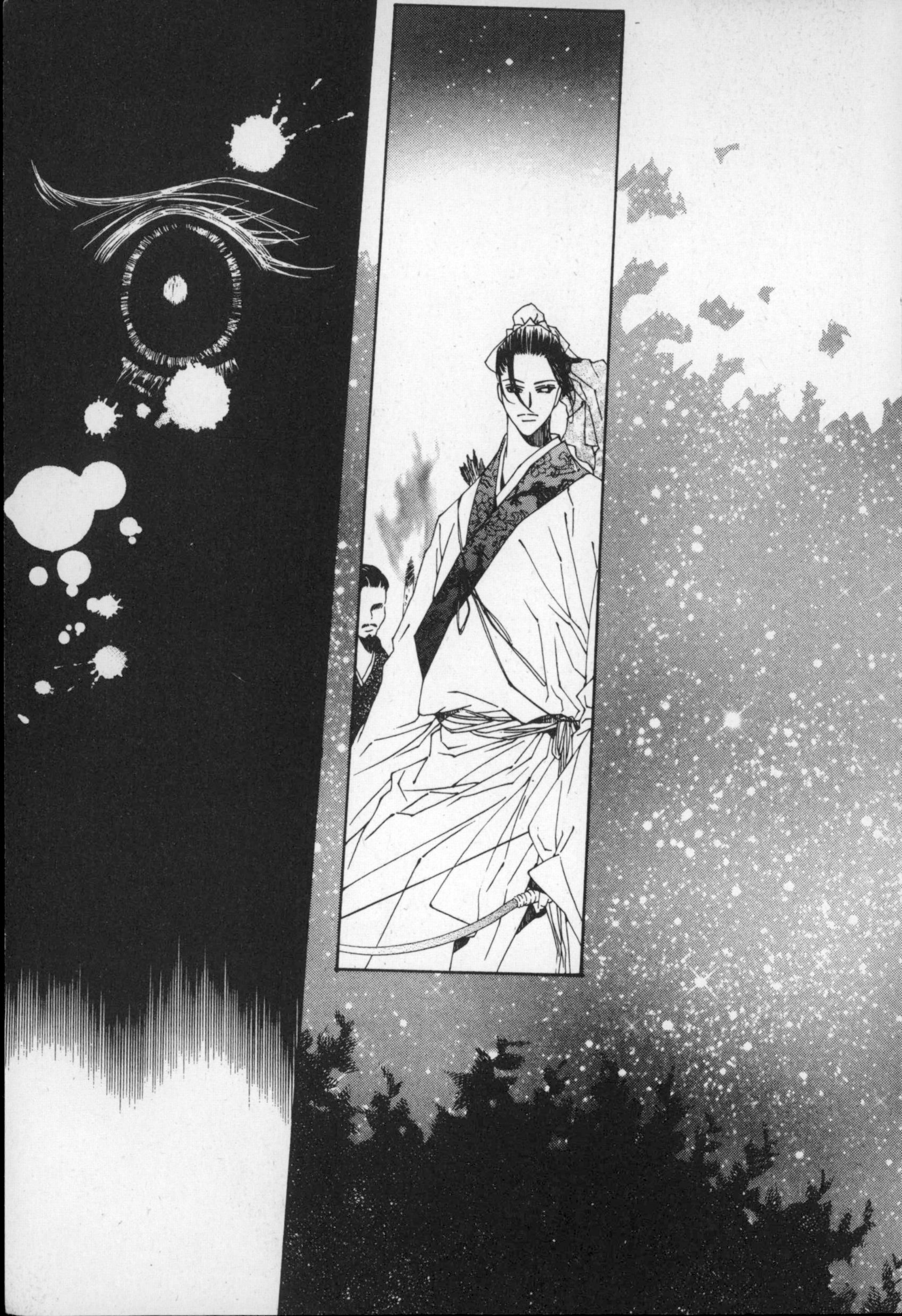

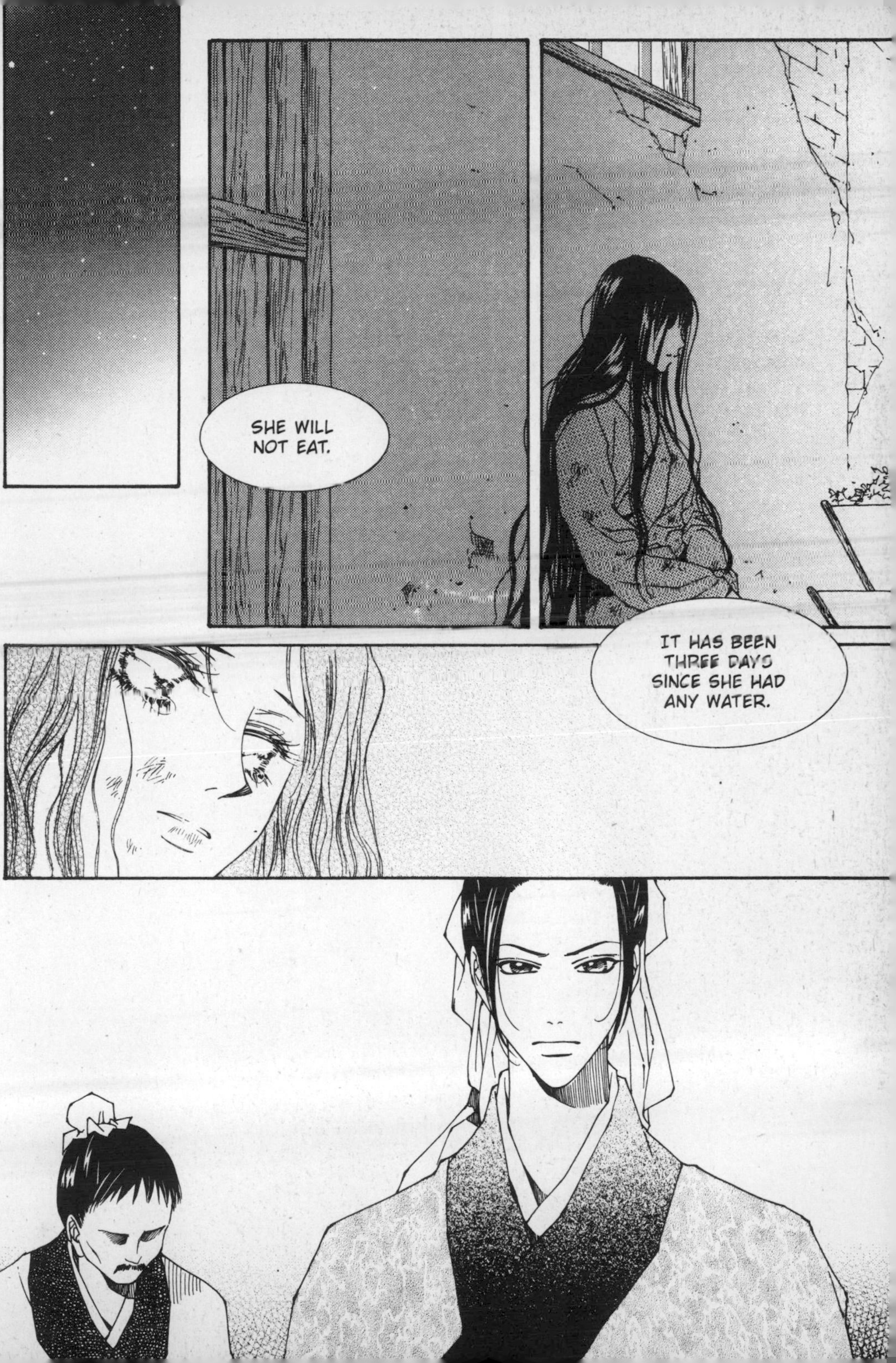
SHE WILL NOT EAT.
IT HAS BEEN THREE DAYS SINCE SHE HAD ANY WATER.

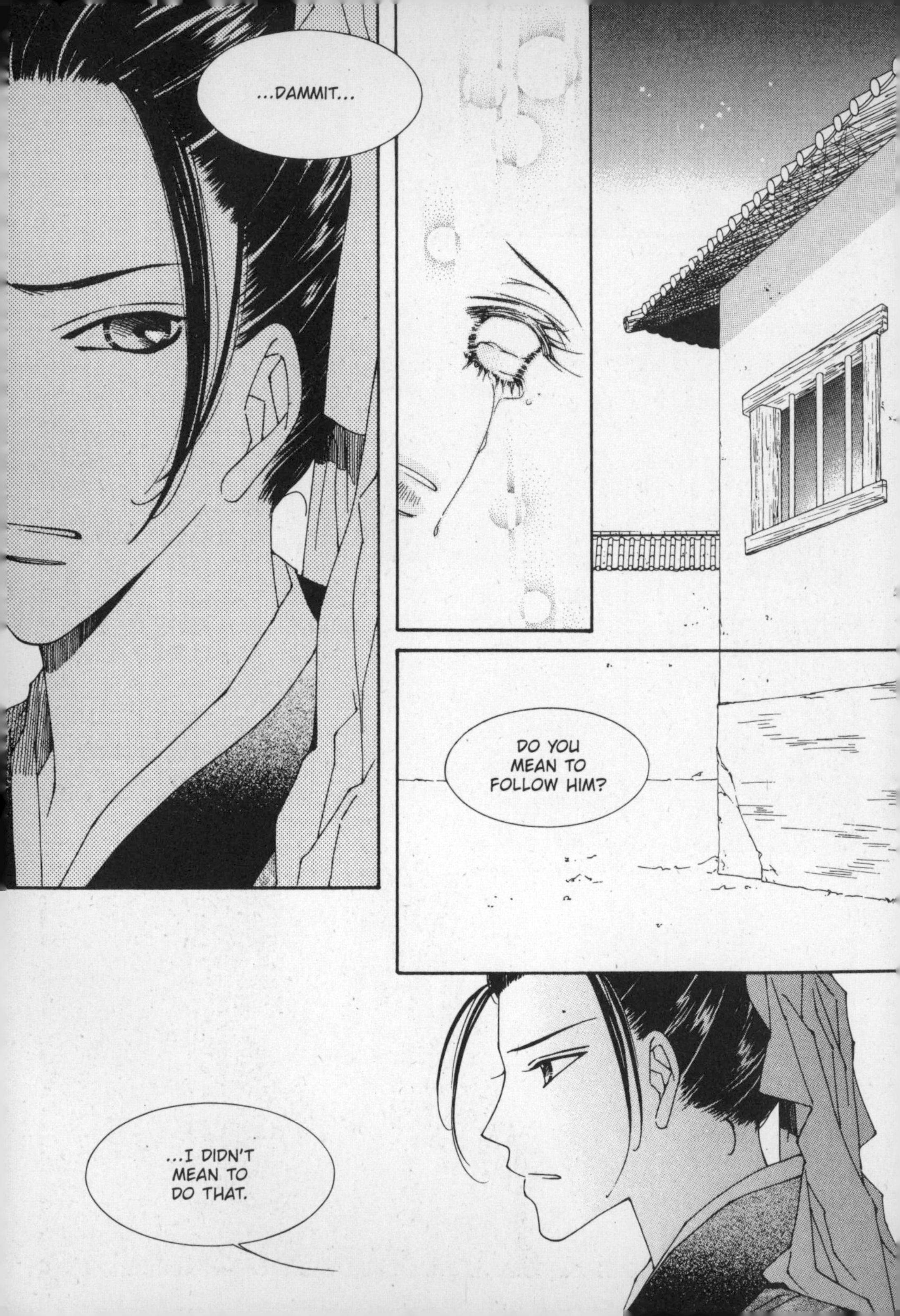
...DAMMIT...
DO YOU MEAN TO FOLLOW HIM?
...I DIDN'T MEAN TO DO THAT.

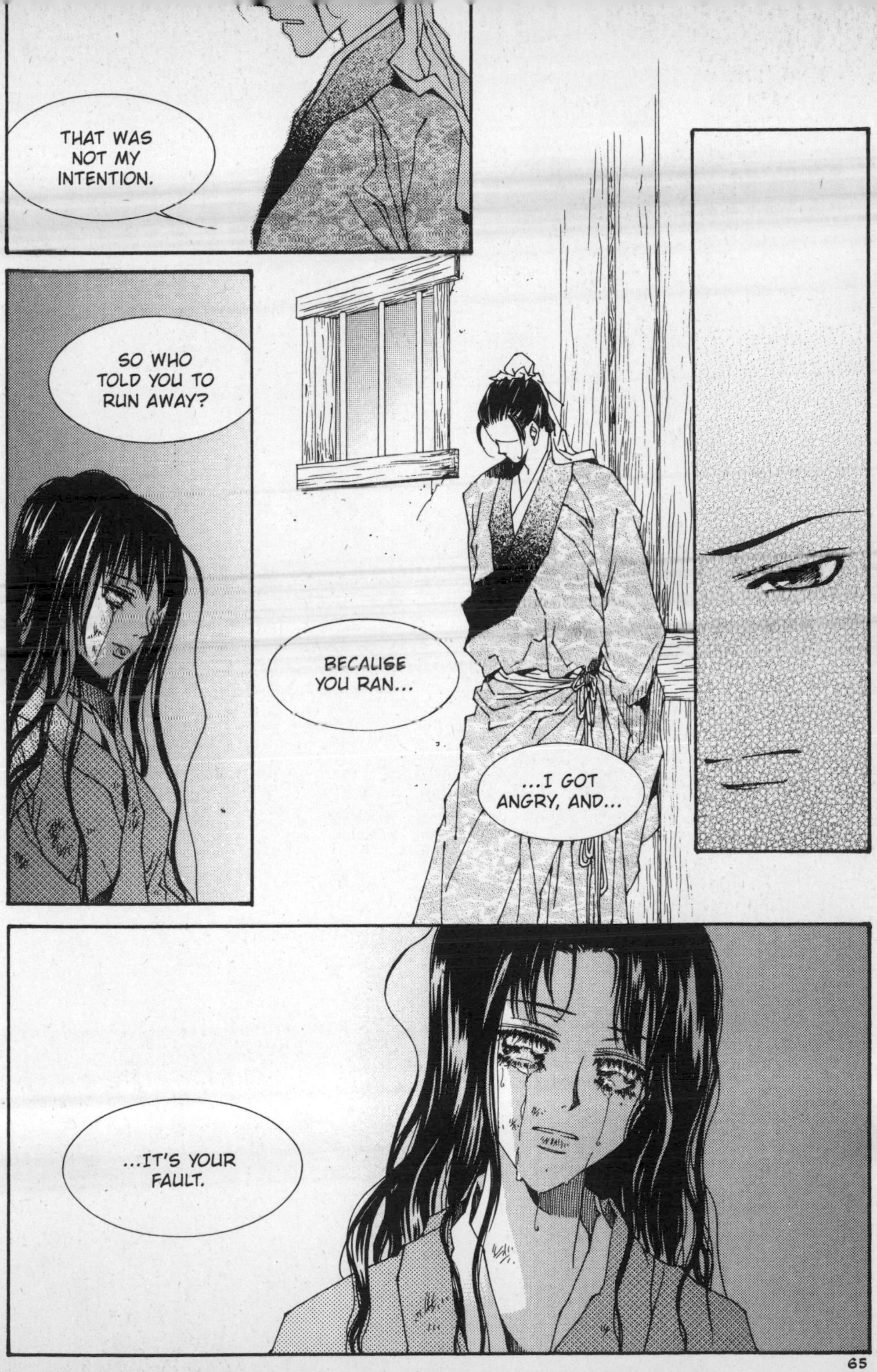
THAT WAS NOT MY INTENTION.
SO WHO TOLD YOU TO RUN AWAY?
BECAUSE YOU RAN...
...I GOT ANGRY, AND...
...IT'S YOUR FAULT.

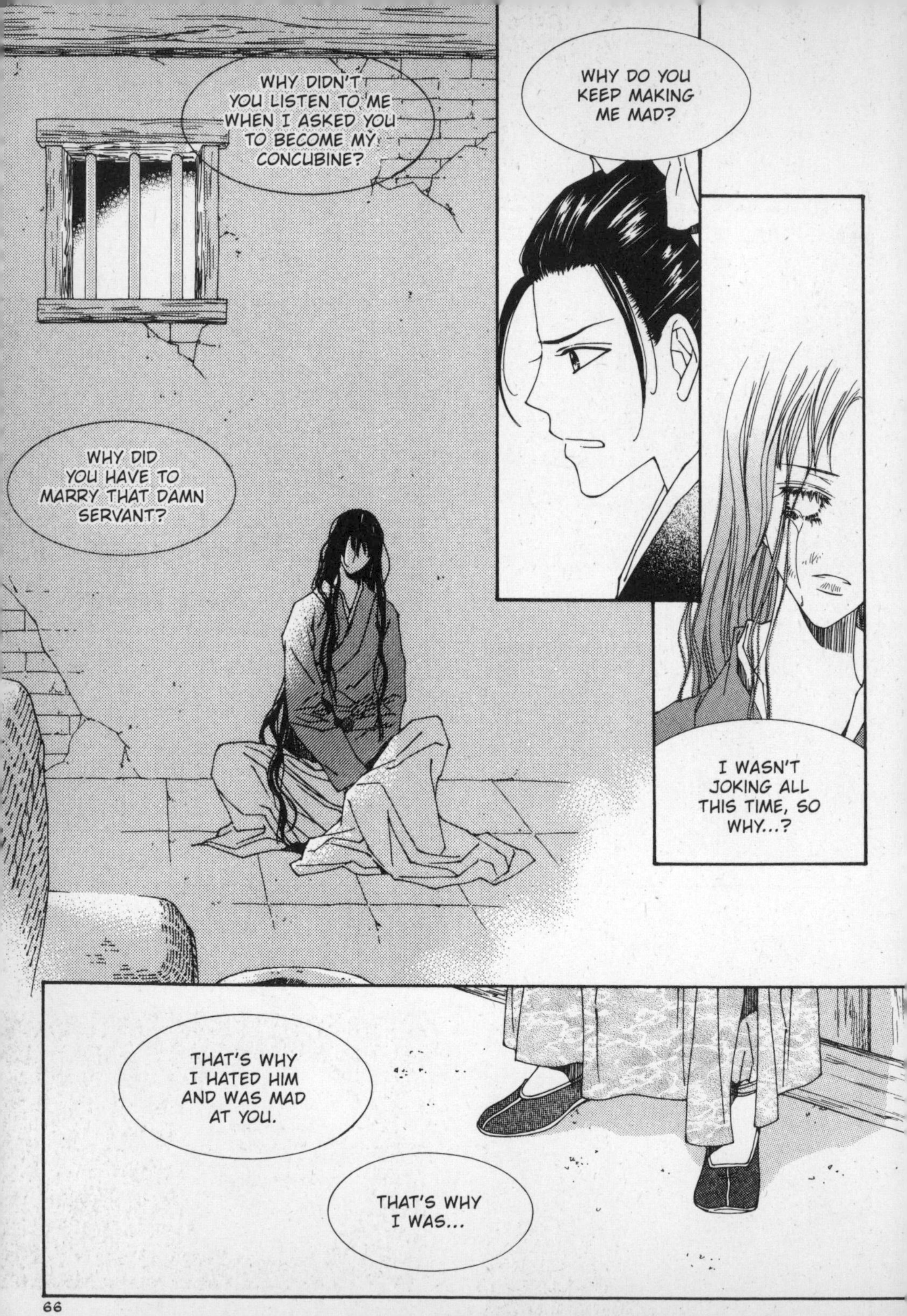
WHY DO YOU KEEP MAKING ME MAD?
WHY DIDN'T YOU LISTEN TO ME WHEN I ASKED YOU TO BECOME MY CONCUBINE?
WHY DID YOU HAVE TO MARRY THAT DAMN SERVANT?
I WASN'T JOKING ALL THIS TIME, SO WHY...?
THAT'S WHY I HATED HIM AND WAS MAD AT YOU.
THAT'S WHY I WAS...

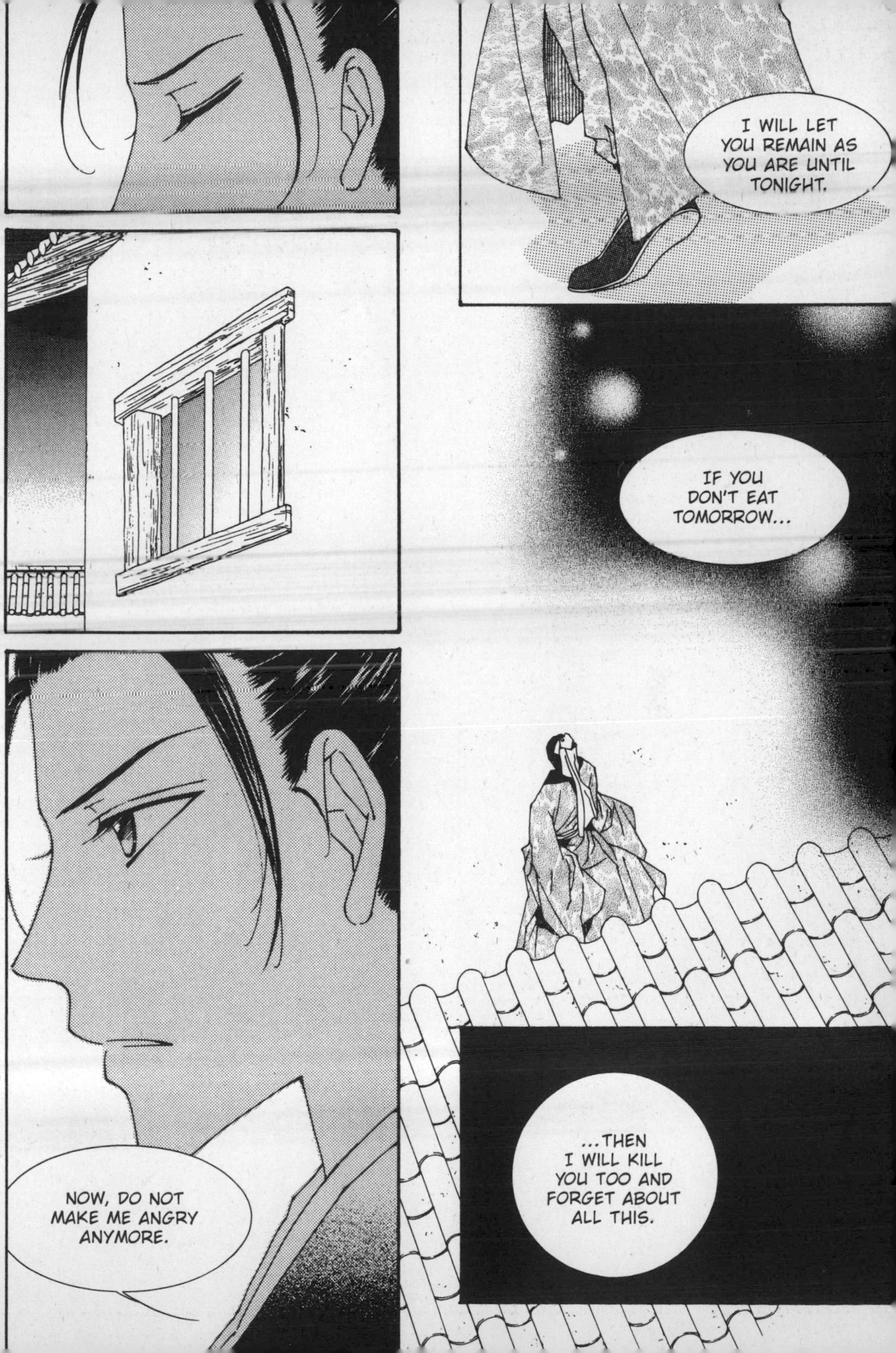
I WILL LET YOU REMAIN AS YOU ARE UNTIL TONIGHT.
IF YOU DON'T EAT TOMORROW...
...THEN I WILL KILL YOU TOO AND FORGET ABOUT ALL THIS.
NOW, DO NOT MAKE ME ANGRY ANYMORE.

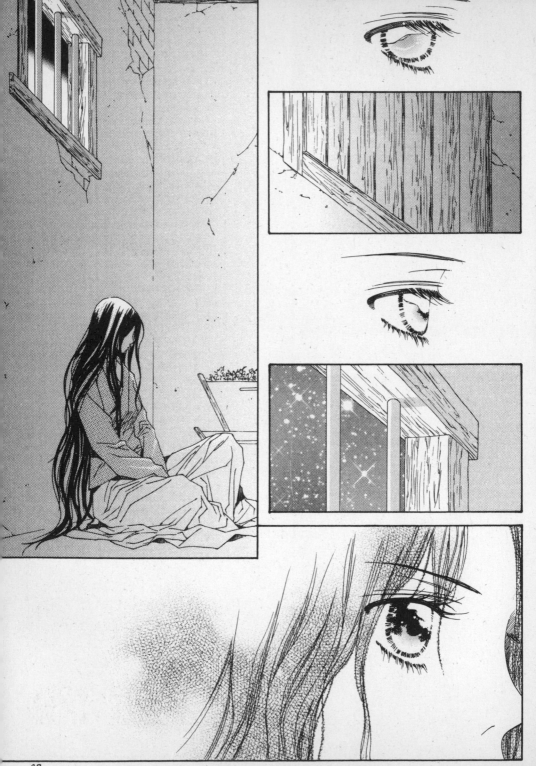

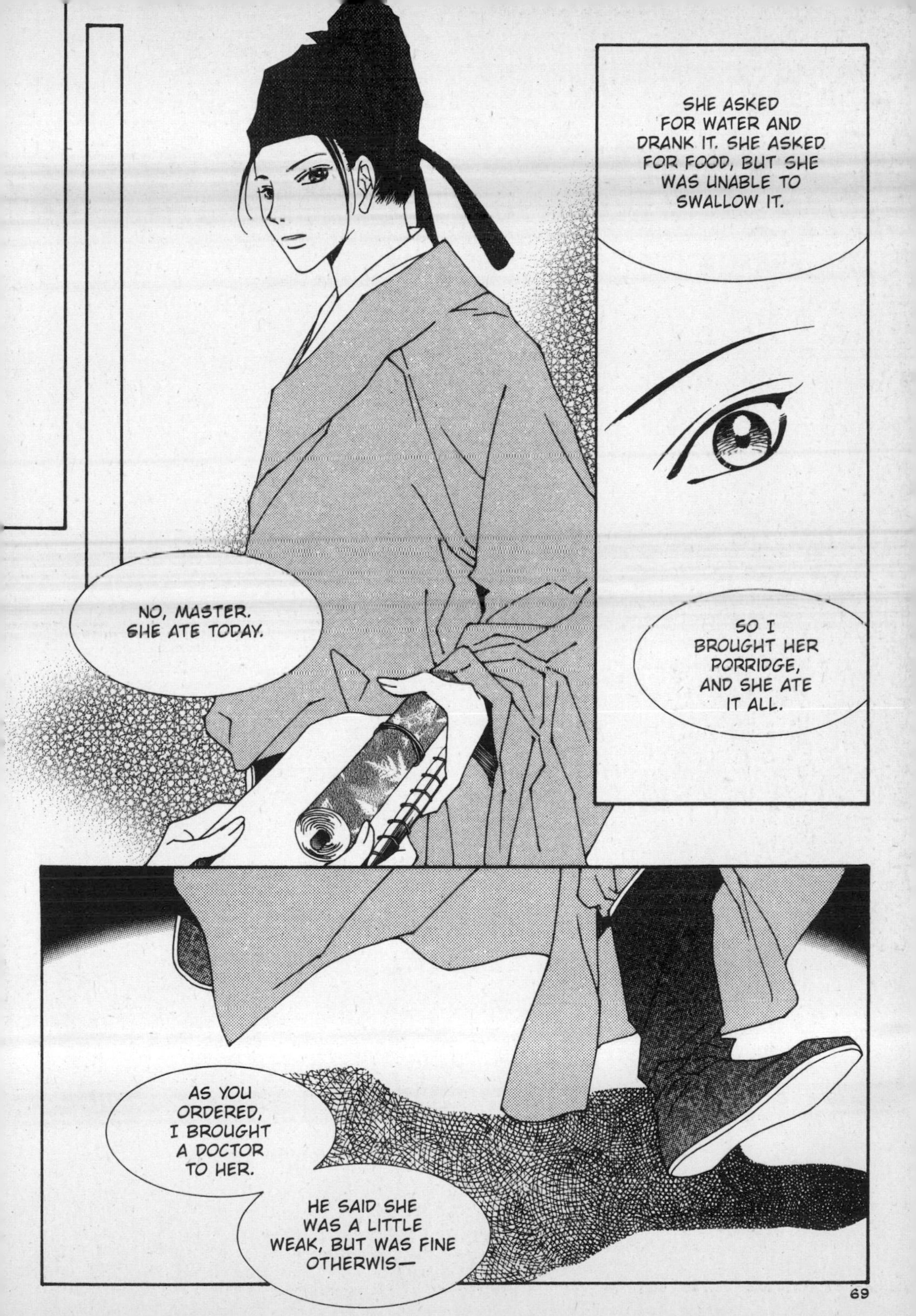
SHE ASKED FOR WATER AND DRANK IT. SHE ASKED FOR FOOD, BUT SHE WAS UNABLE TO SWALLOW IT.
NO, MASTER. SHE ATE TODAY.
SO I BROUGHT HER PORRIDGE, AND SHE ATE IT ALL.
AS YOU ORDERED, I BROUGHT A DOCTOR TO HER.
HE SAID SHE WAS A LITTLE WEAK, BUT WAS FINE OTHERWIS—

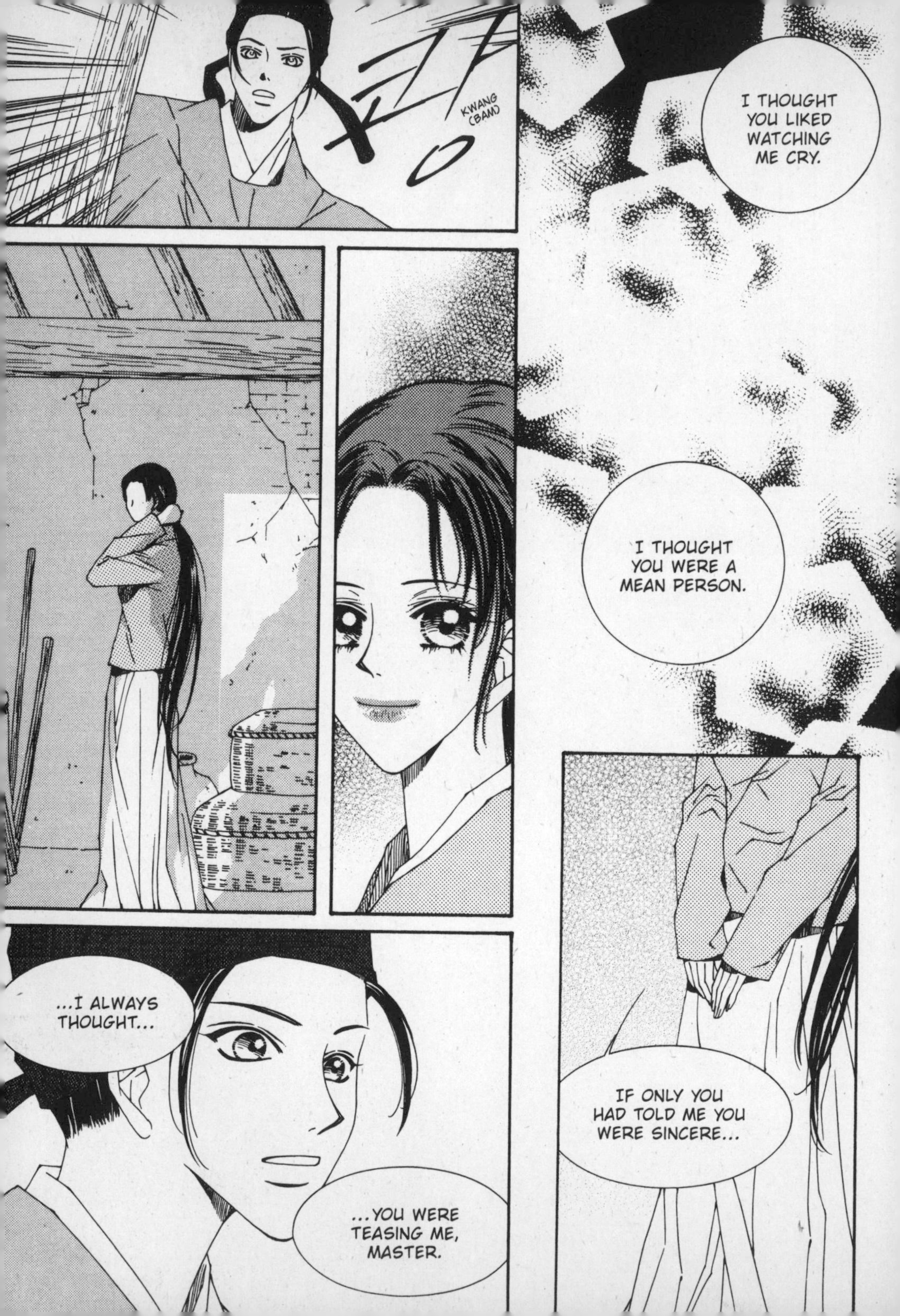
KWANG (BAM)
I THOUGHT YOU LIKED WATCHING ME CRY.
I THOUGHT YOU WERE A MEAN PERSON.
...I ALWAYS THOUGHT...
...YOU WERE TEASING ME, MASTER.
IF ONLY YOU HAD TOLD ME YOU WERE SINCERE...

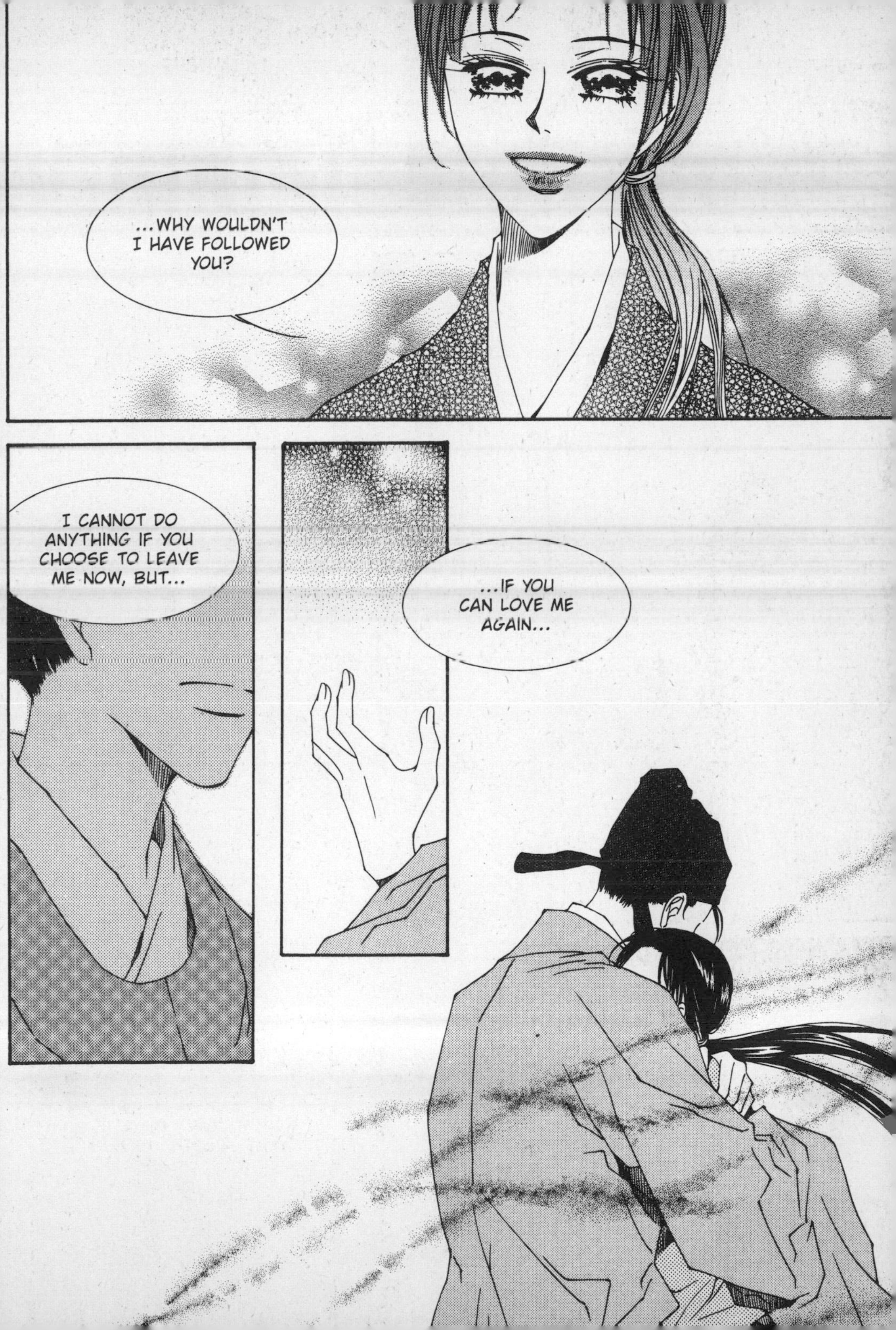
...WHY WOULDN'T I HAVE FOLLOWED YOU?
I CANNOT DO ANYTHING IF YOU CHOOSE TO LEAVE ME NOW, BUT...
...IF YOU CAN LOVE ME AGAIN...

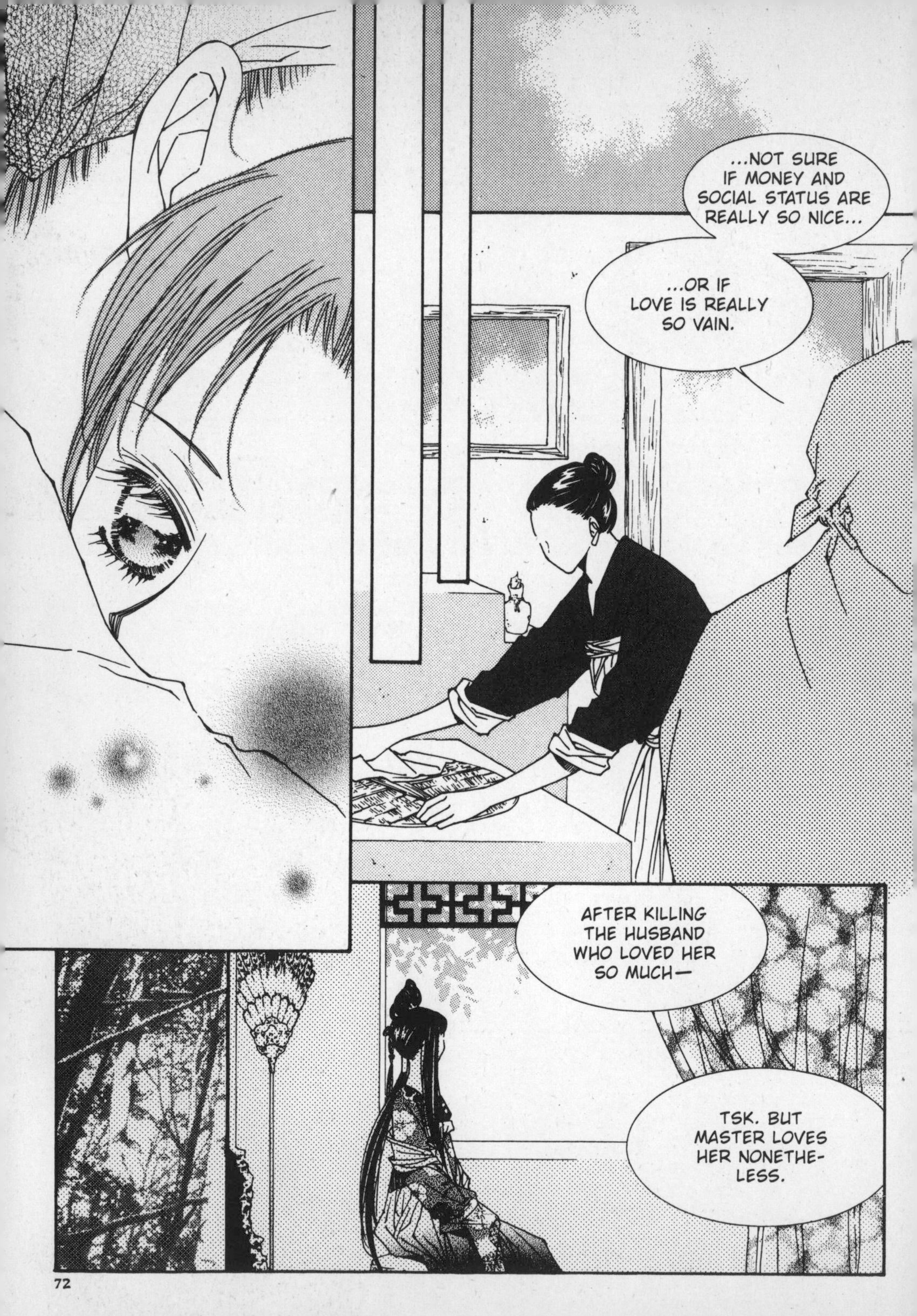
...NOT SURE IF MONEY AND SOCIAL STATUS ARE REALLY SO NICE...
...OR IF LOVE IS REALLY SO VAIN.
AFTER KILLING THE HUSBAND WHO LOVED HER SO MUCH—
TSK. BUT MASTER LOVES HER NONETHE-LESS.

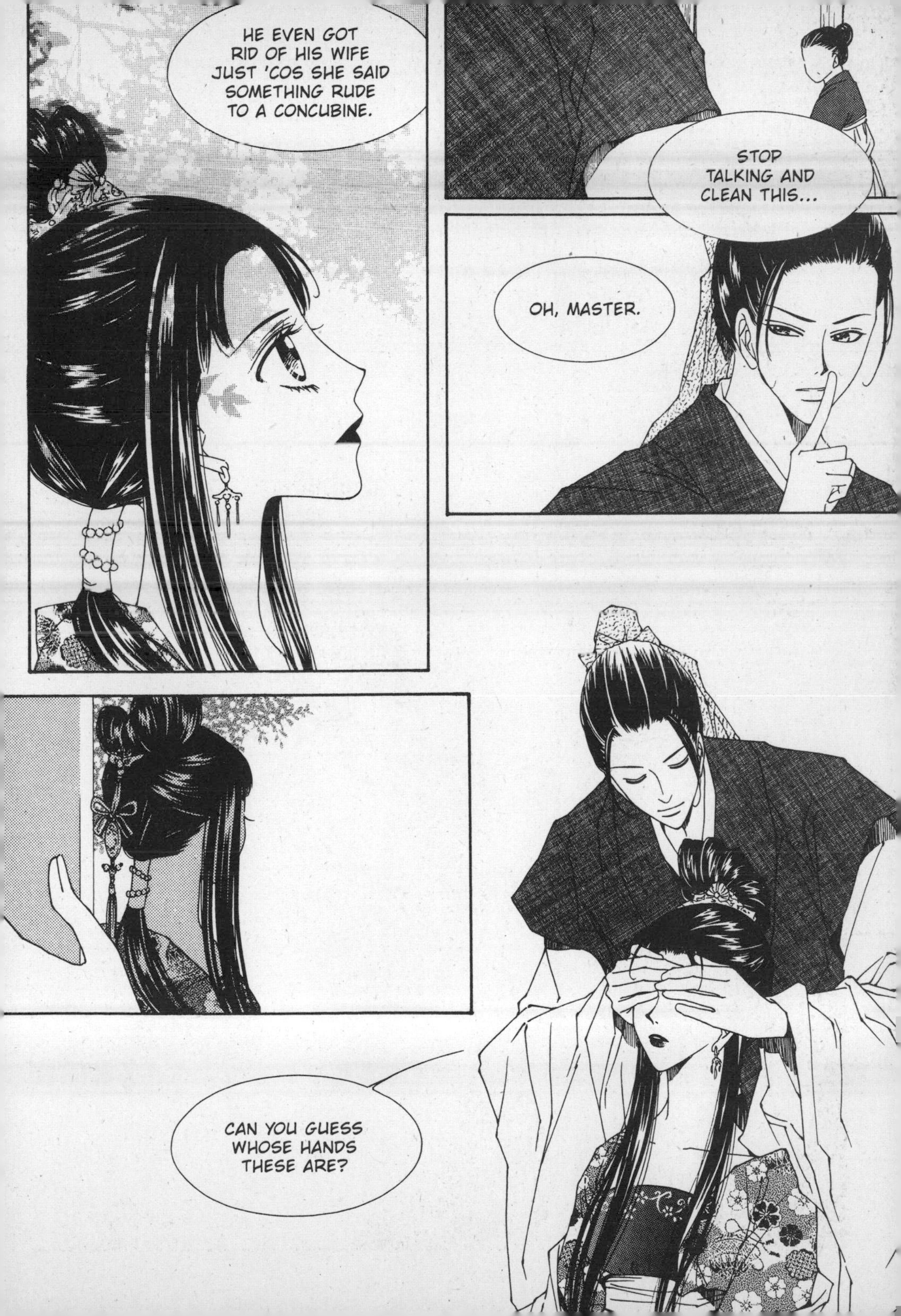
HE EVEN GOT RID OF HIS WIFE JUST 'COS SHE SAID SOMETHING RUDE TO A CONCUBINE.
STOP TALKING AND CLEAN THIS...
OH, MASTER.
CAN YOU GUESS WHOSE HANDS THESE ARE?

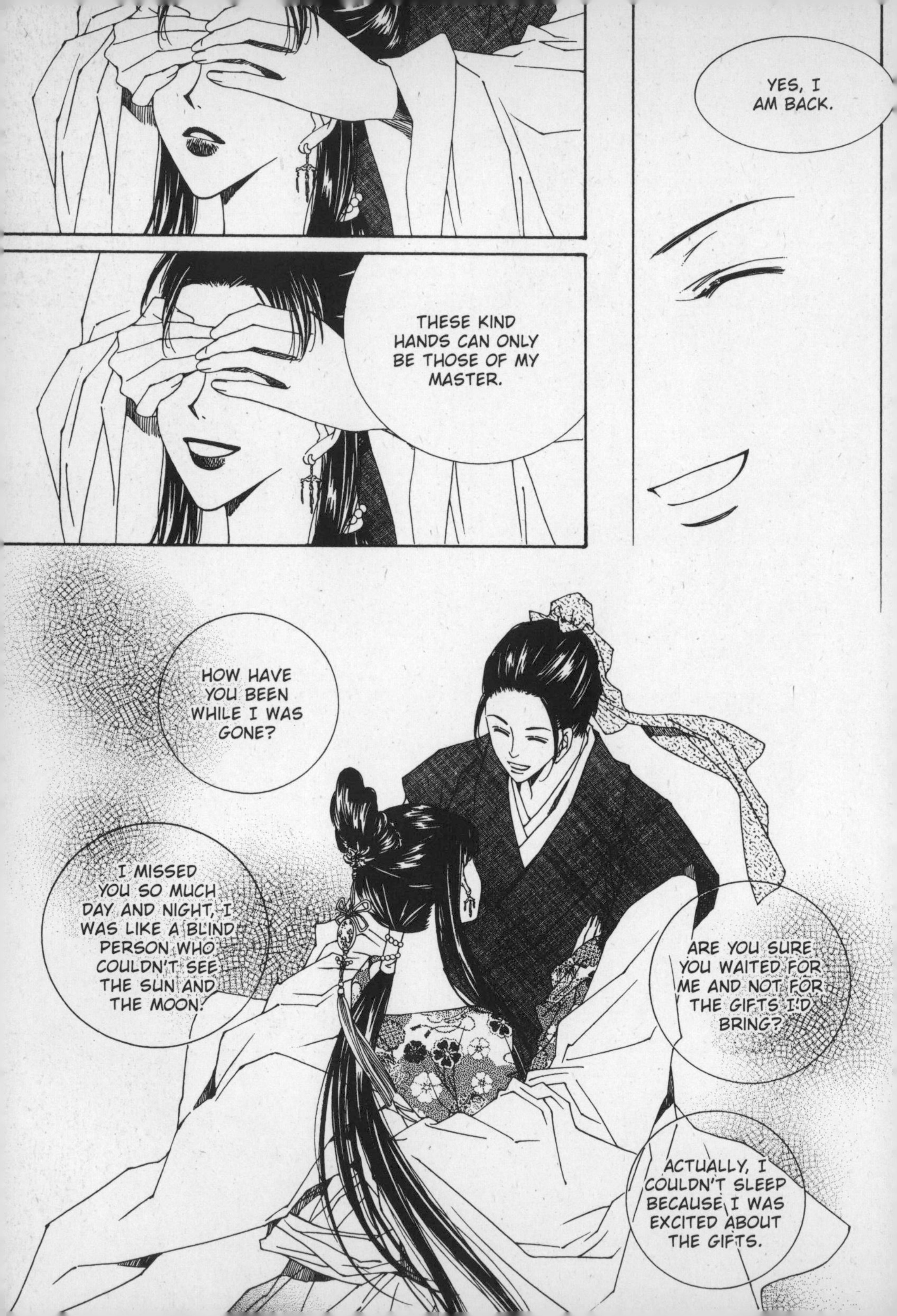

YES, I AM BACK.
THESE KIND HANDS CAN ONLY BE THOSE OF MY MASTER.
HOW HAVE YOU BEEN WHILE I WAS GONE?
I MISSED YOU SO MUCH DAY AND NIGHT, I WAS LIKE A BLIND PERSON WHO COULDN'T SEE THE SUN AND THE MOON.
ARE YOU SURE YOU WAITED FOR ME AND NOT FOR THE GIFTS I'D BRING?
ACTUALLY, I COULDN'T SLEEP BECAUSE I WAS EXCITED ABOUT THE GIFTS.

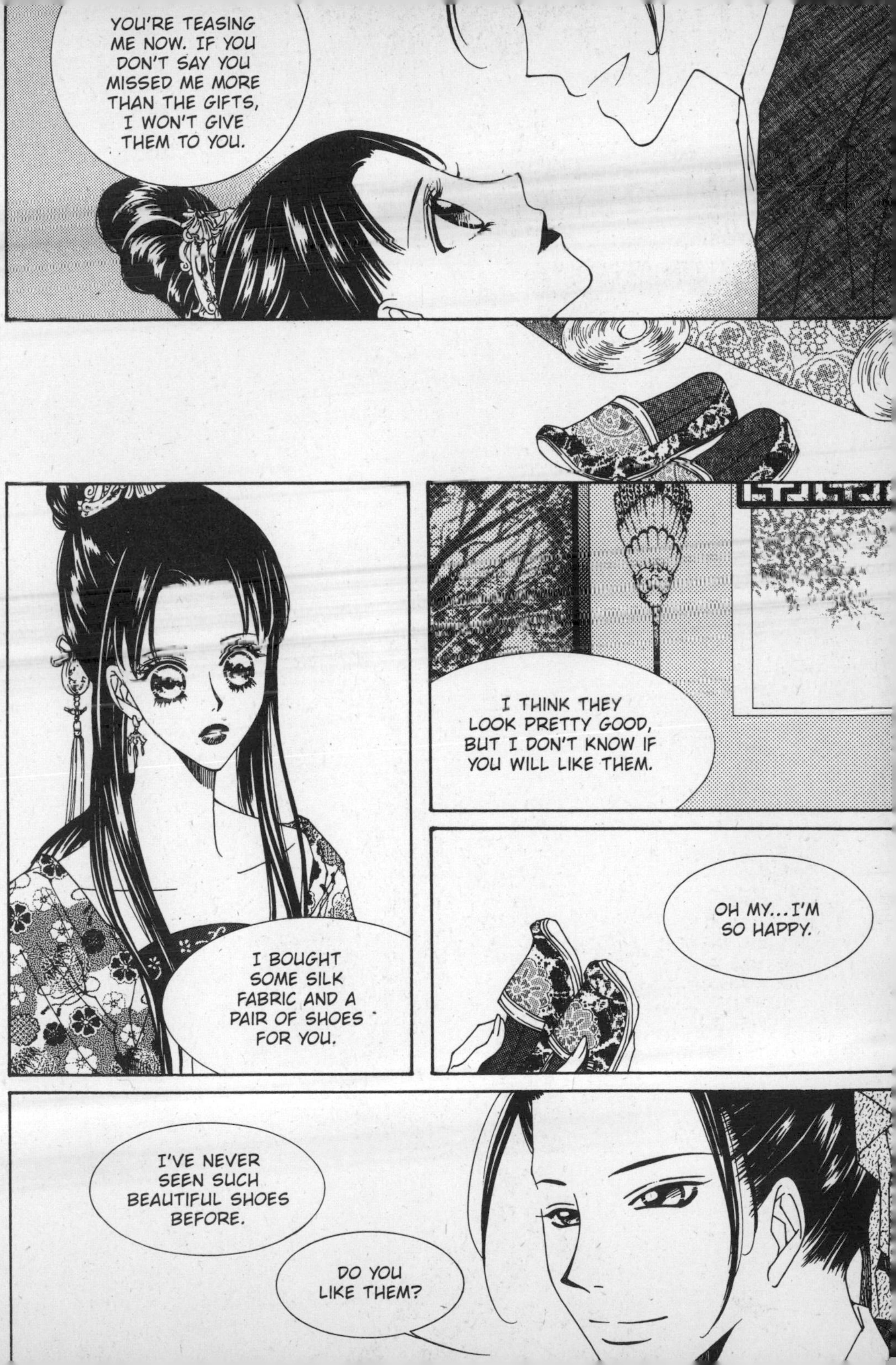
YOU'RE TEASING ME NOW. IF YOU DON'T SAY YOU MISSED ME MORE THAN THE GIFTS, I WON'T GIVE THEM TO YOU.
I BOUGHT SOME SILK FABRIC AND A PAIR OF SHOES FOR YOU.
I THINK THEY LOOK PRETTY GOOD, BUT I DON'T KNOW IF YOU WILL LIKE THEM.
OH MY... I'M SO HAPPY.
I'VE NEVER SEEN SUCH BEAUTIFUL SHOES BEFORE.
DO YOU LIKE THEM?

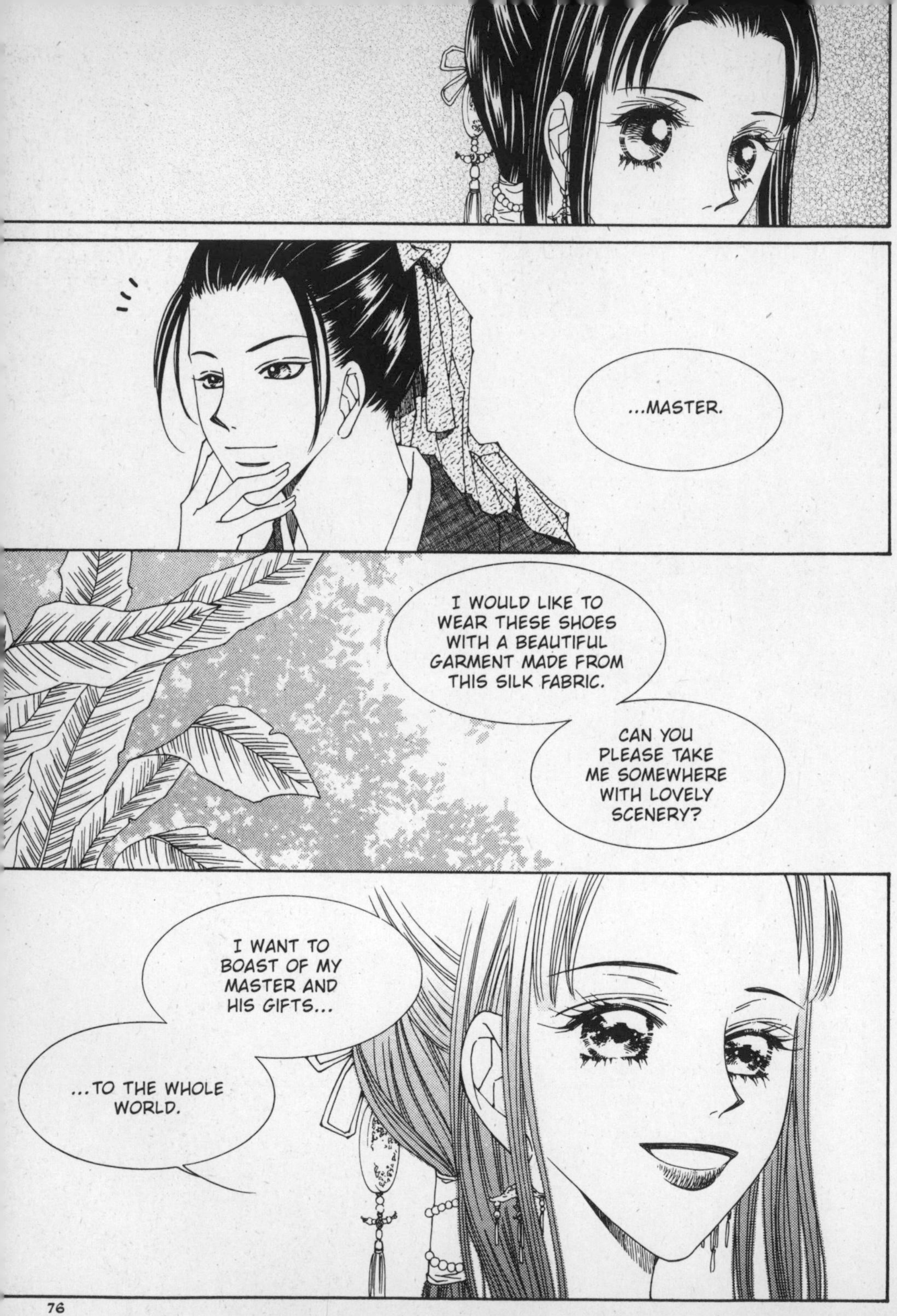
...MASTER.
I WOULD LIKE TO WEAR THESE SHOES WITH A BEAUTIFUL GARMENT MADE FROM THIS SILK FABRIC.
CAN YOU PLEASE TAKE ME SOMEWHERE WITH LOVELY SCENERY?
I WANT TO BOAST OF MY MASTER AND HIS GIFTS...
...TO THE WHOLE WORLD.

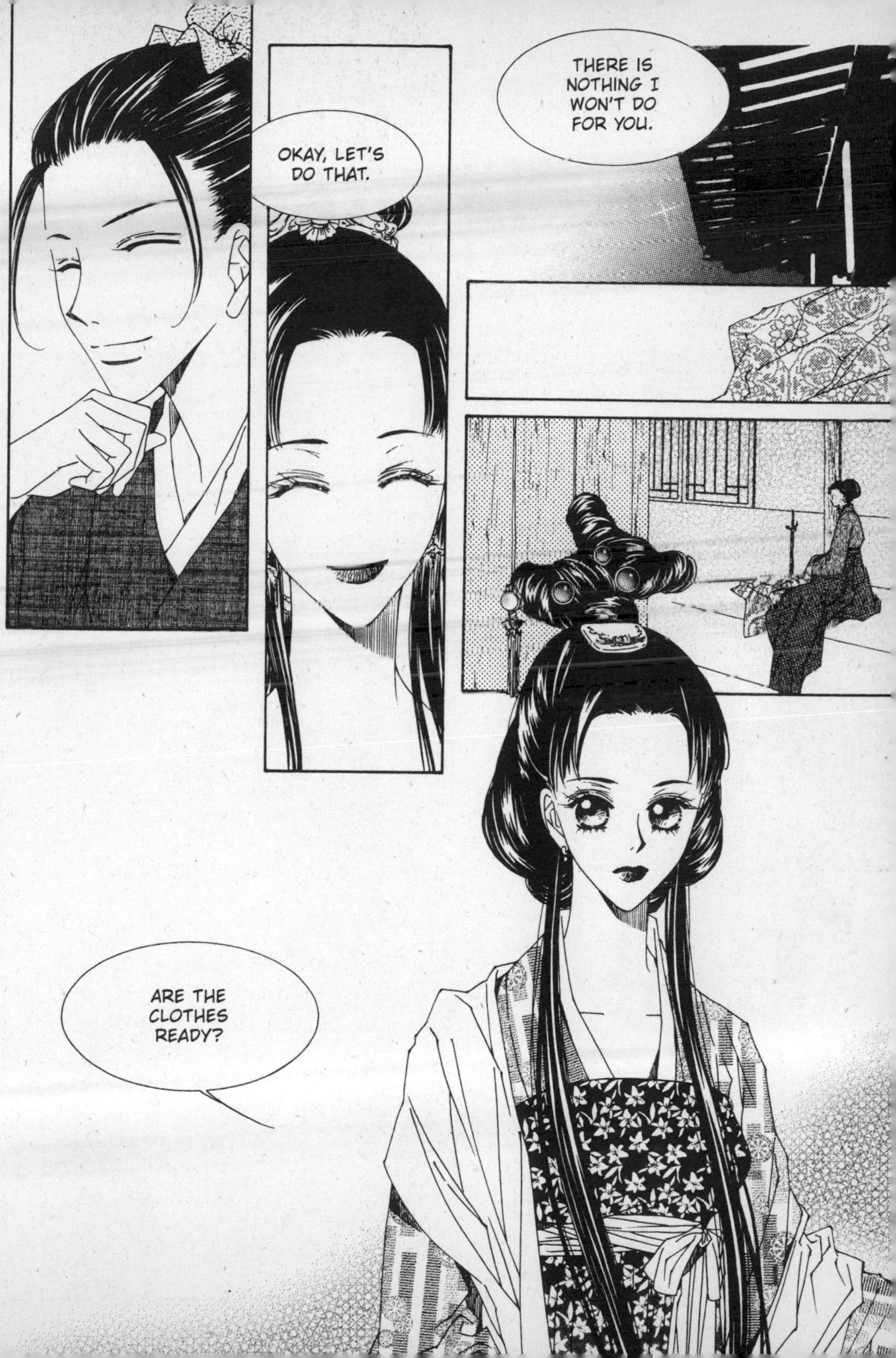
THERE IS NOTHING I WON'T DO FOR YOU.
OKAY, LET'S DO THAT.
ARE THE CLOTHES READY?

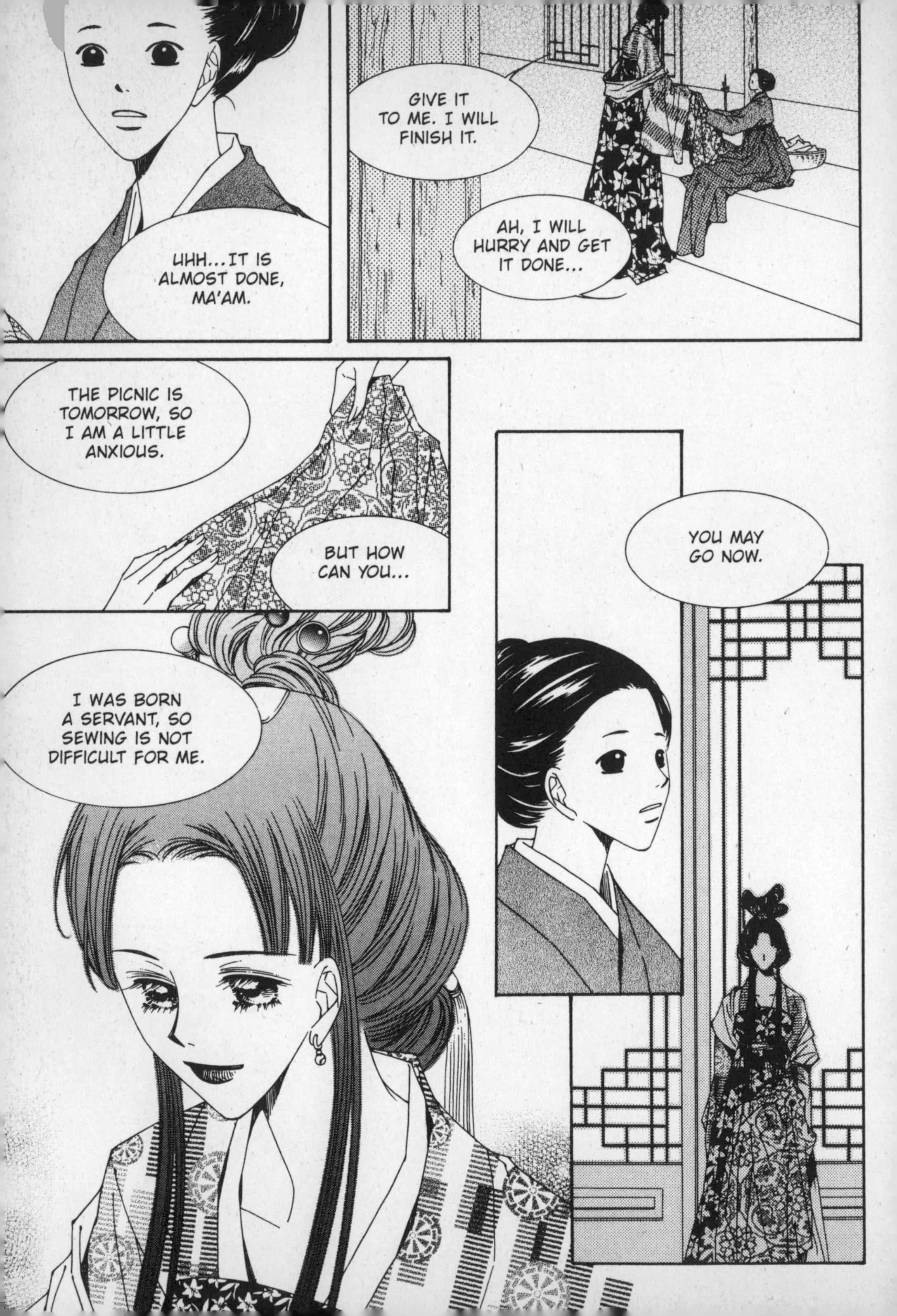
UHH...IT IS ALMOST DONE, MA'AM.
GIVE IT TO ME. I WILL FINISH IT.
AH, I WILL HURRY AND GET IT DONE...
THE PICNIC IS TOMORROW, SO I AM A LITTLE ANXIOUS.
BUT HOW CAN YOU...
YOU MAY GO NOW.
I WAS BORN A SERVANT, SO SEWING IS NOT DIFFICULT FOR ME.

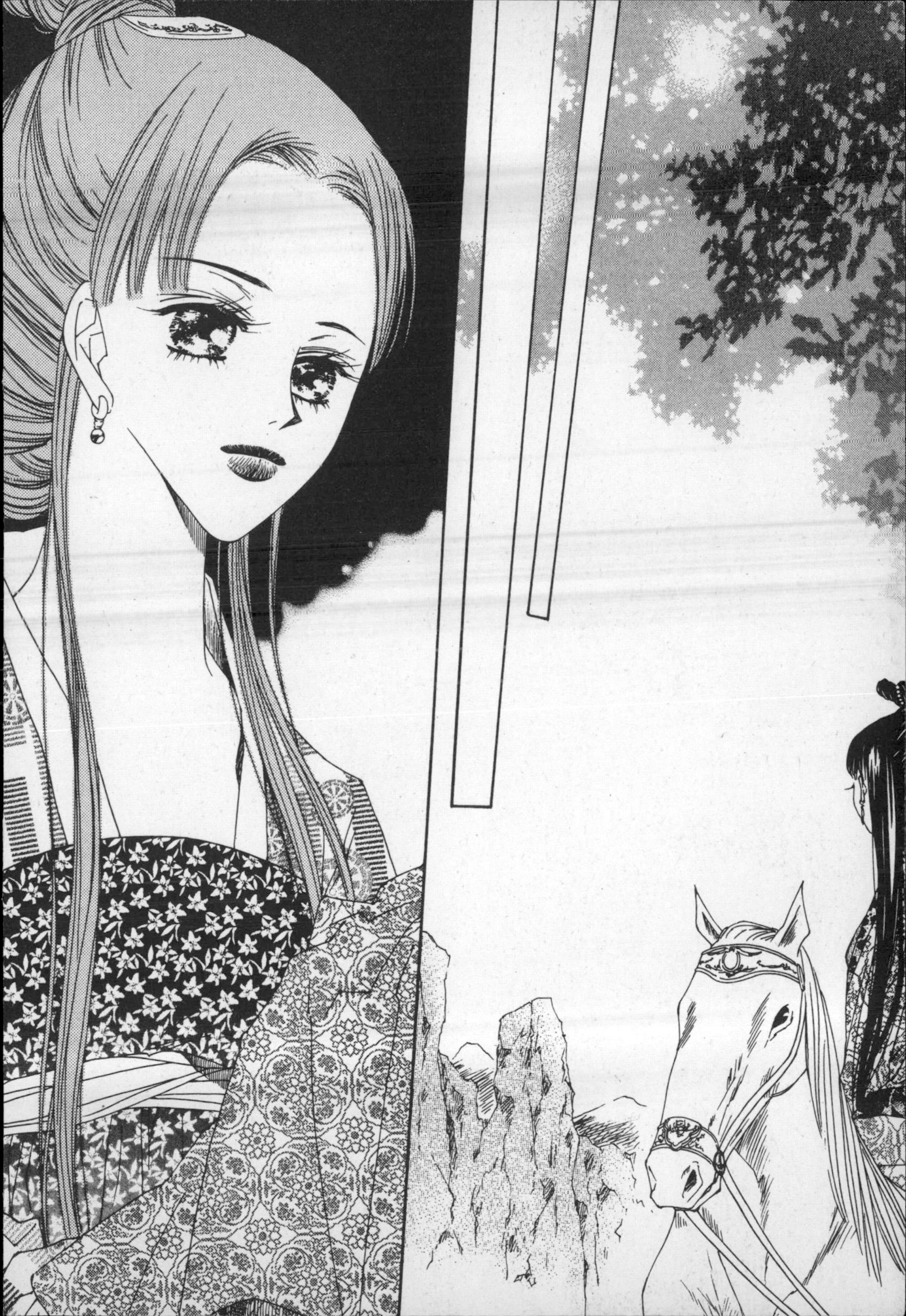

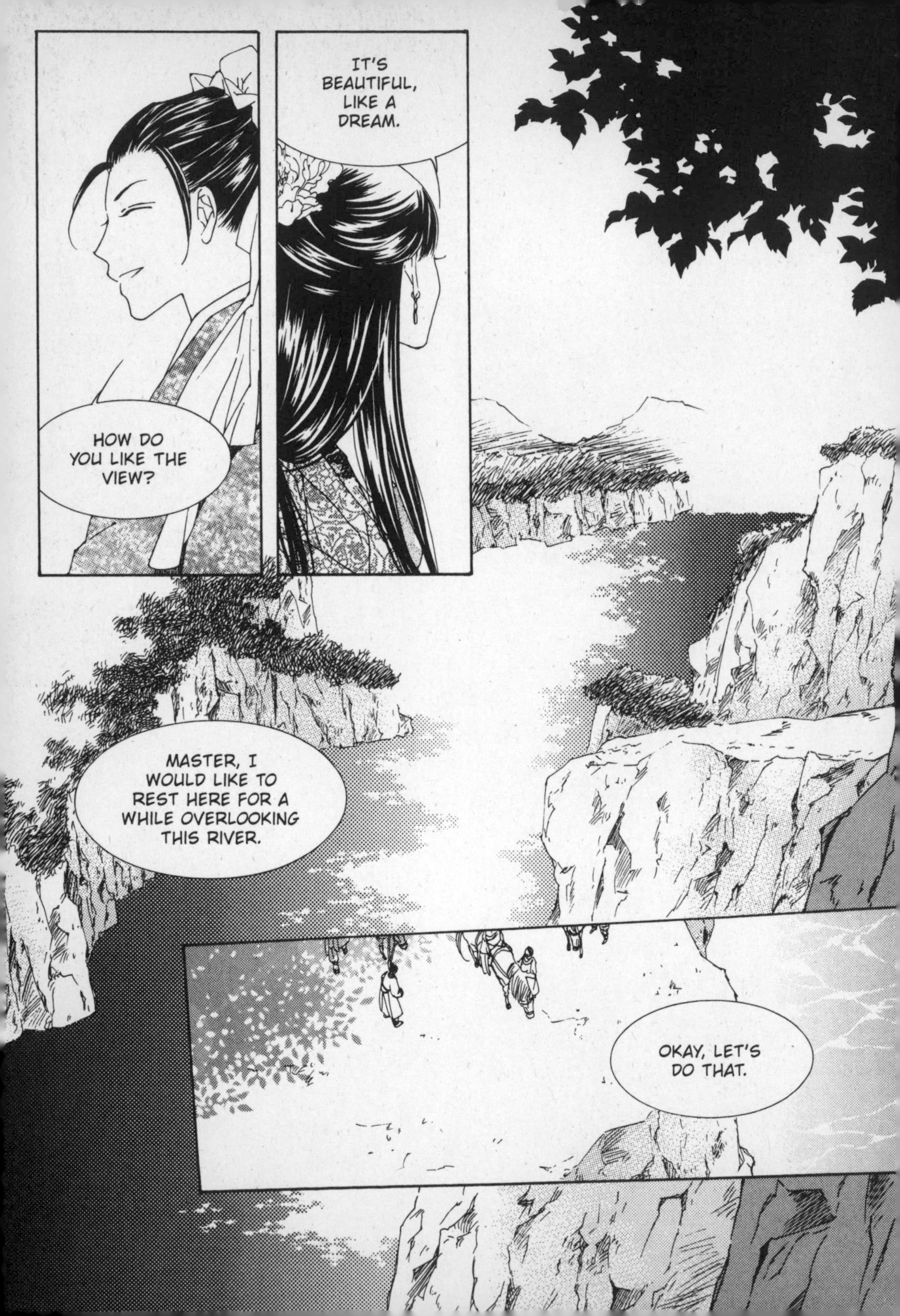

IT'S BEAUTIFUL, LIKE A DREAM.
HOW DO YOU LIKE THE VIEW?
MASTER, I WOULD LIKE TO REST HERE FOR A WHILE OVERLOOKING THIS RIVER.
OKAY, LET'S DO THAT.

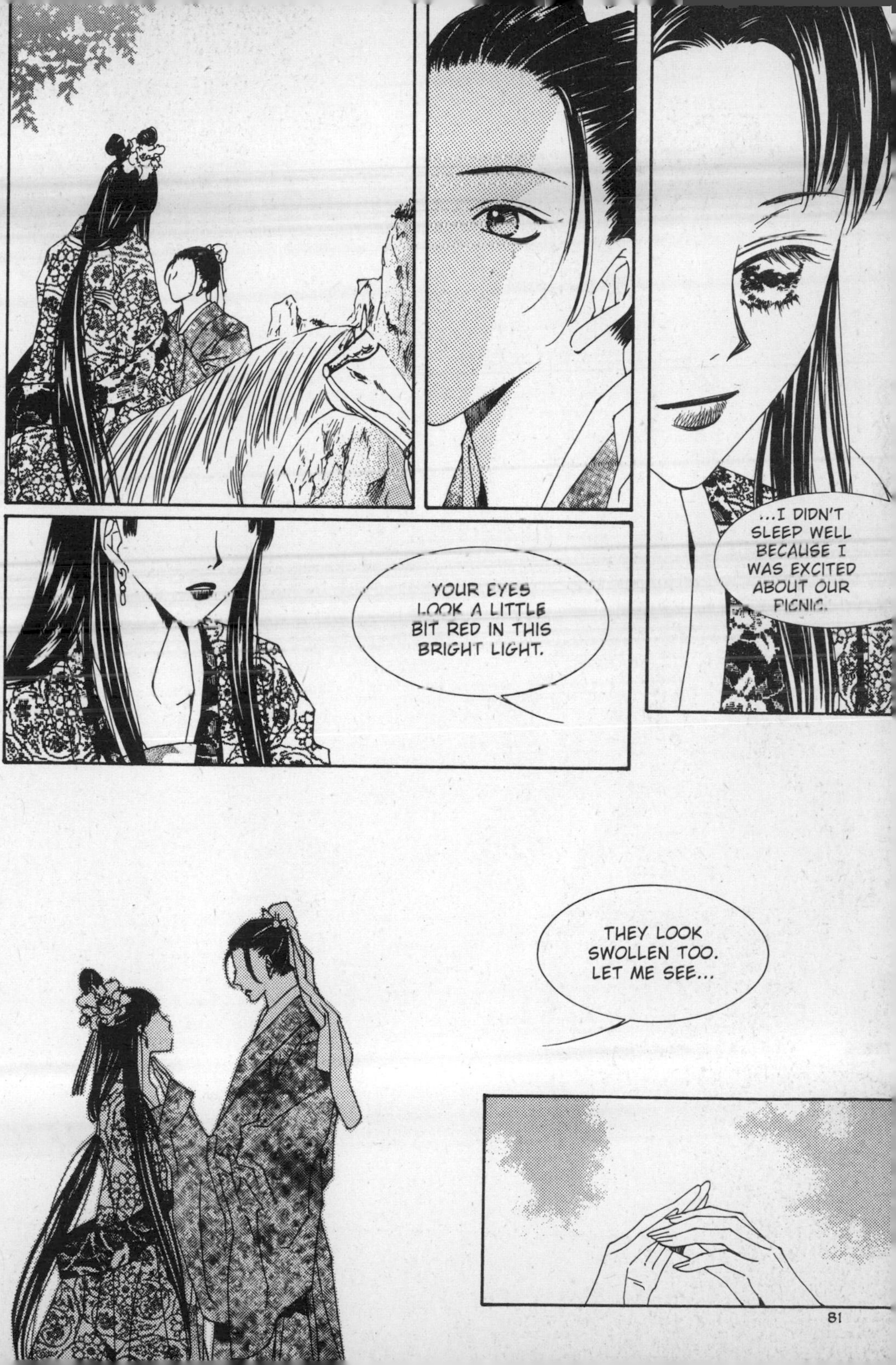
YOUR EYES LOOK A LITTLE BIT RED IN THIS BRIGHT LIGHT.
...I DIDN'T SLEEP WELL BECAUSE I WAS EXCITED ABOUT OUR PICNIC.
THEY LOOK SWOLLEN TOO. LET ME SEE...

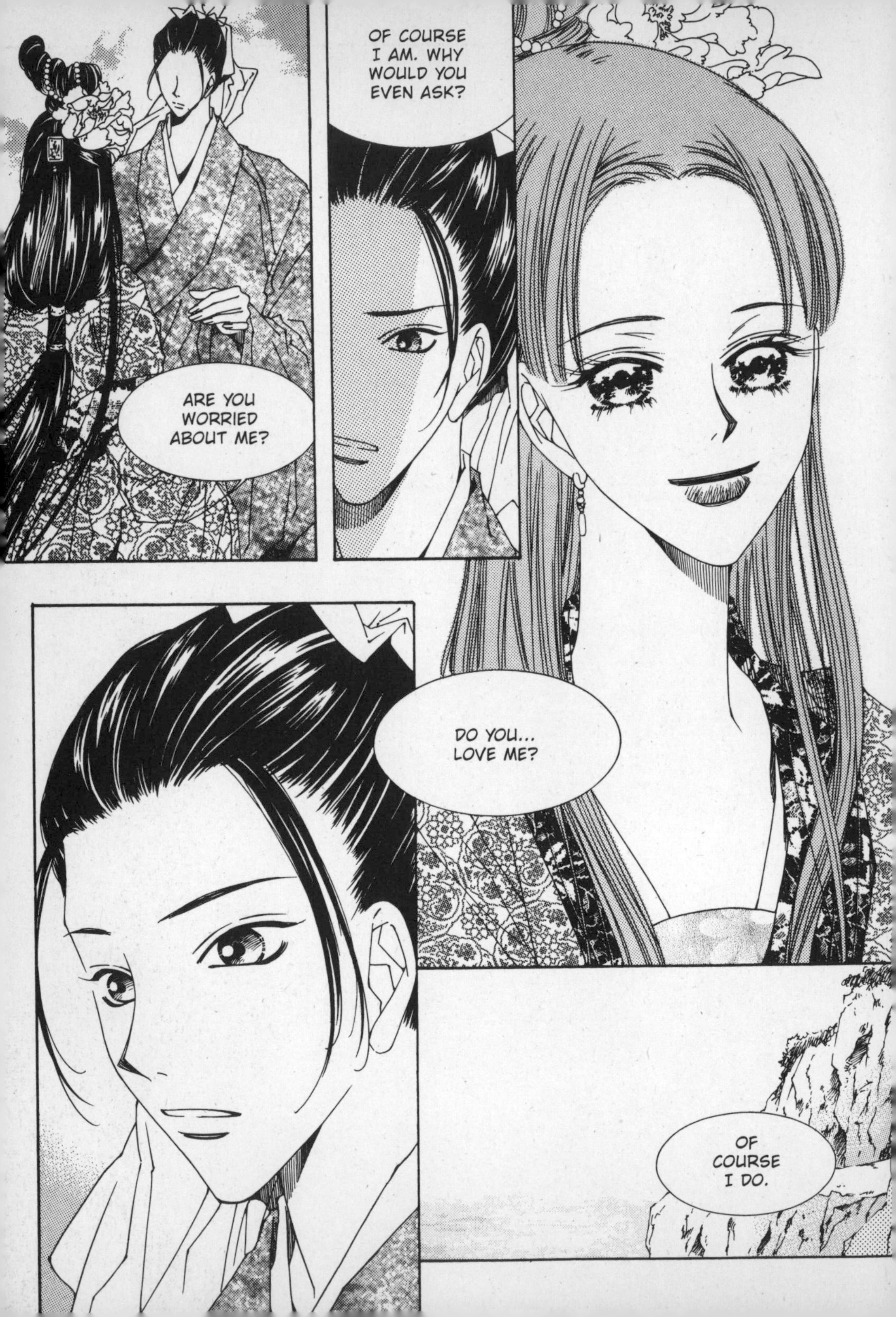
ARE YOU WORRIED ABOUT ME?
OF COURSE I AM. WHY WOULD YOU EVEN ASK?
DO YOU... LOVE ME?
OF COURSE I DO.

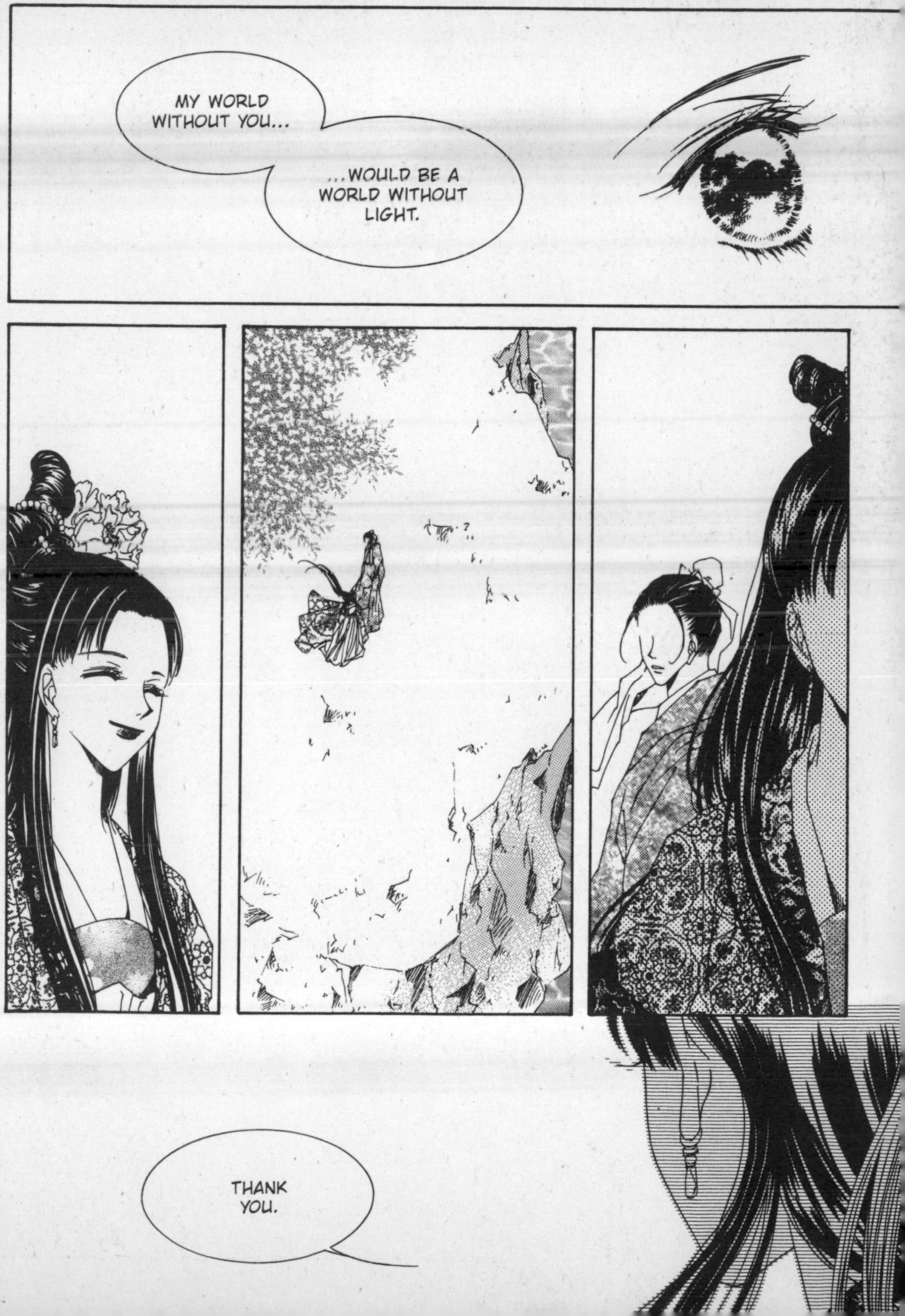
MY WORLD WITHOUT YOU...
...WOULD BE A WORLD WITHOUT LIGHT.
THANK YOU.

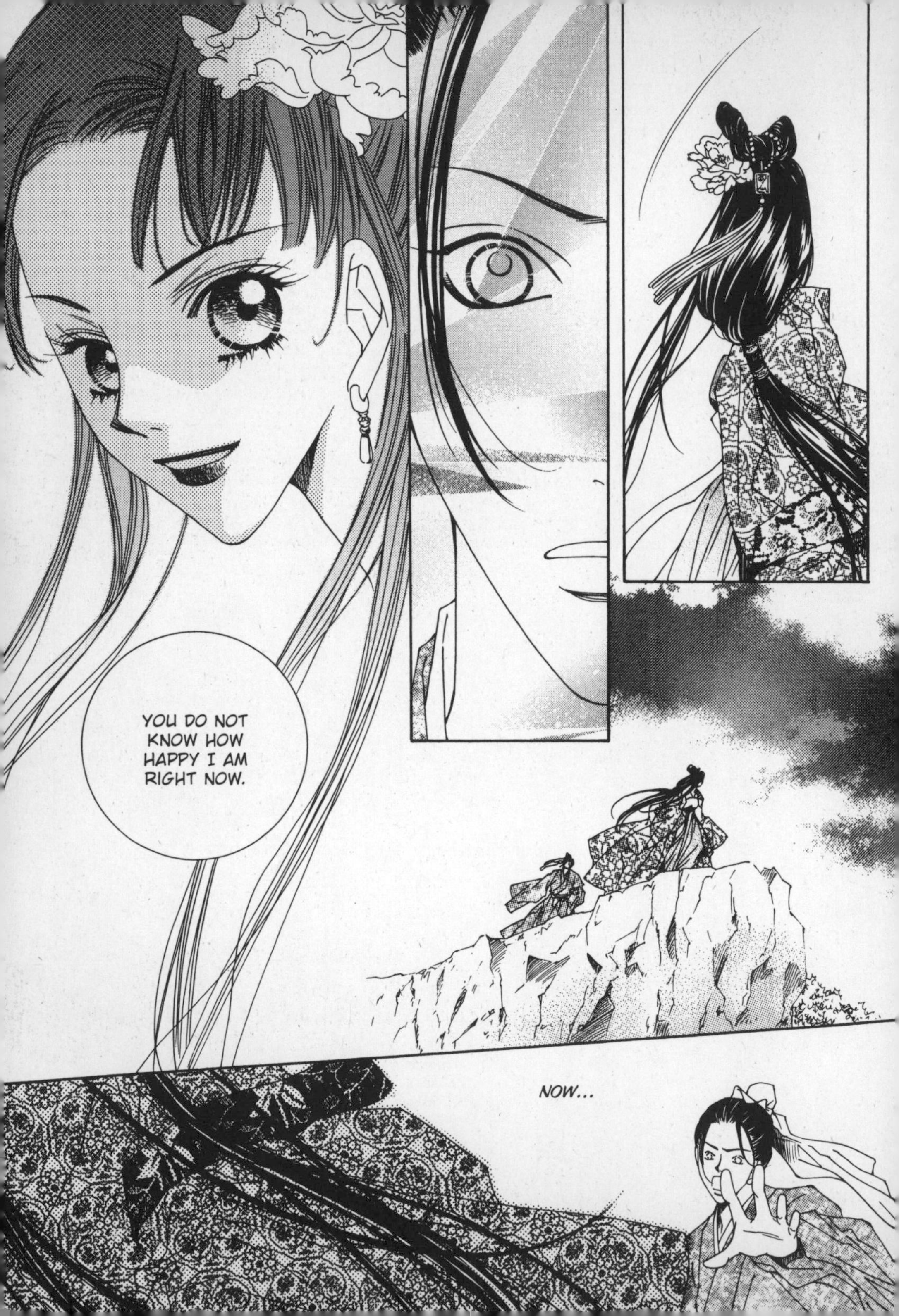
YOU DO NOT KNOW HOW HAPPY I AM RIGHT NOW.
NOW...

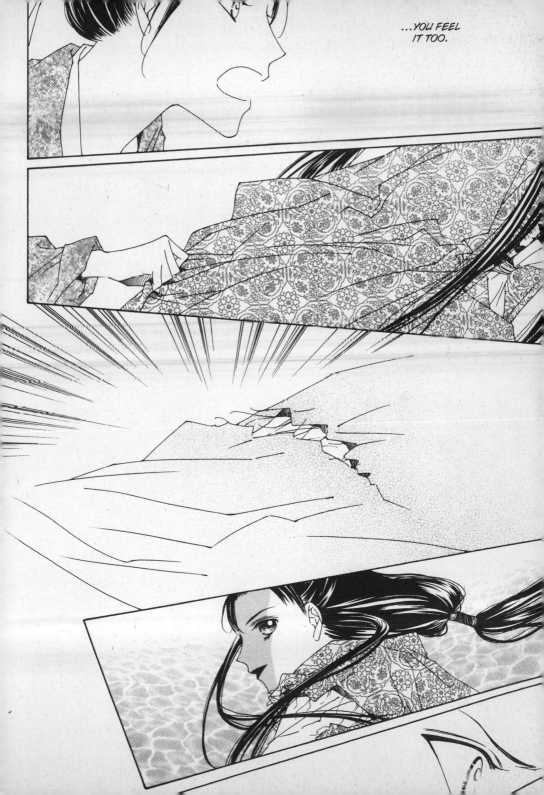

...YOU FEEL IT TOO.

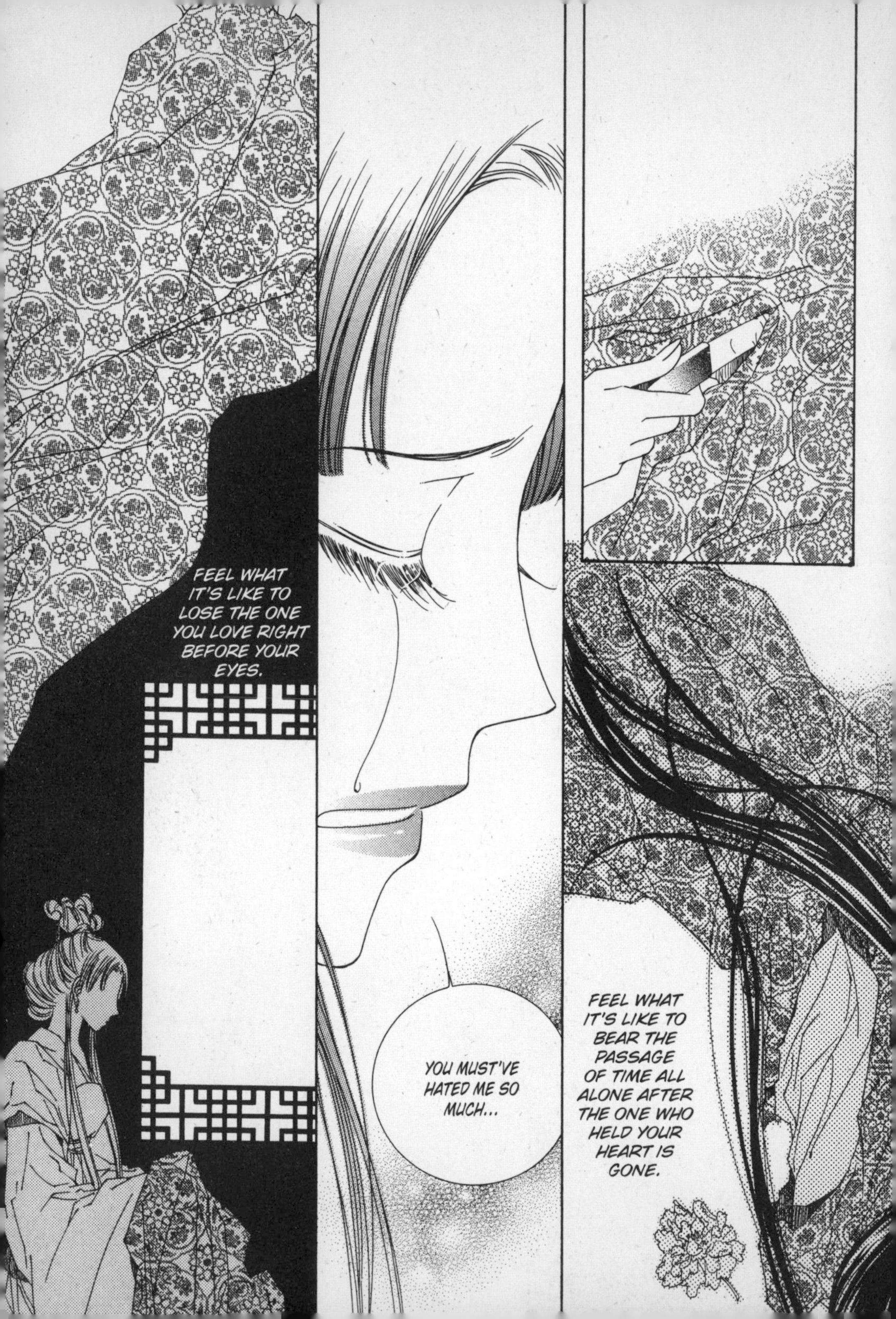

FEEL WHAT IT'S LIKE TO BEAR THE PASSAGE OF TIME ALL ALONE AFTER THE ONE WHO HELD YOUR HEART IS GONE.
YOU MUST'VE HATED ME SO MUCH...
FEEL WHAT IT'S LIKE TO LOSE THE ONE YOU LOVE RIGHT BEFORE YOUR EYES.

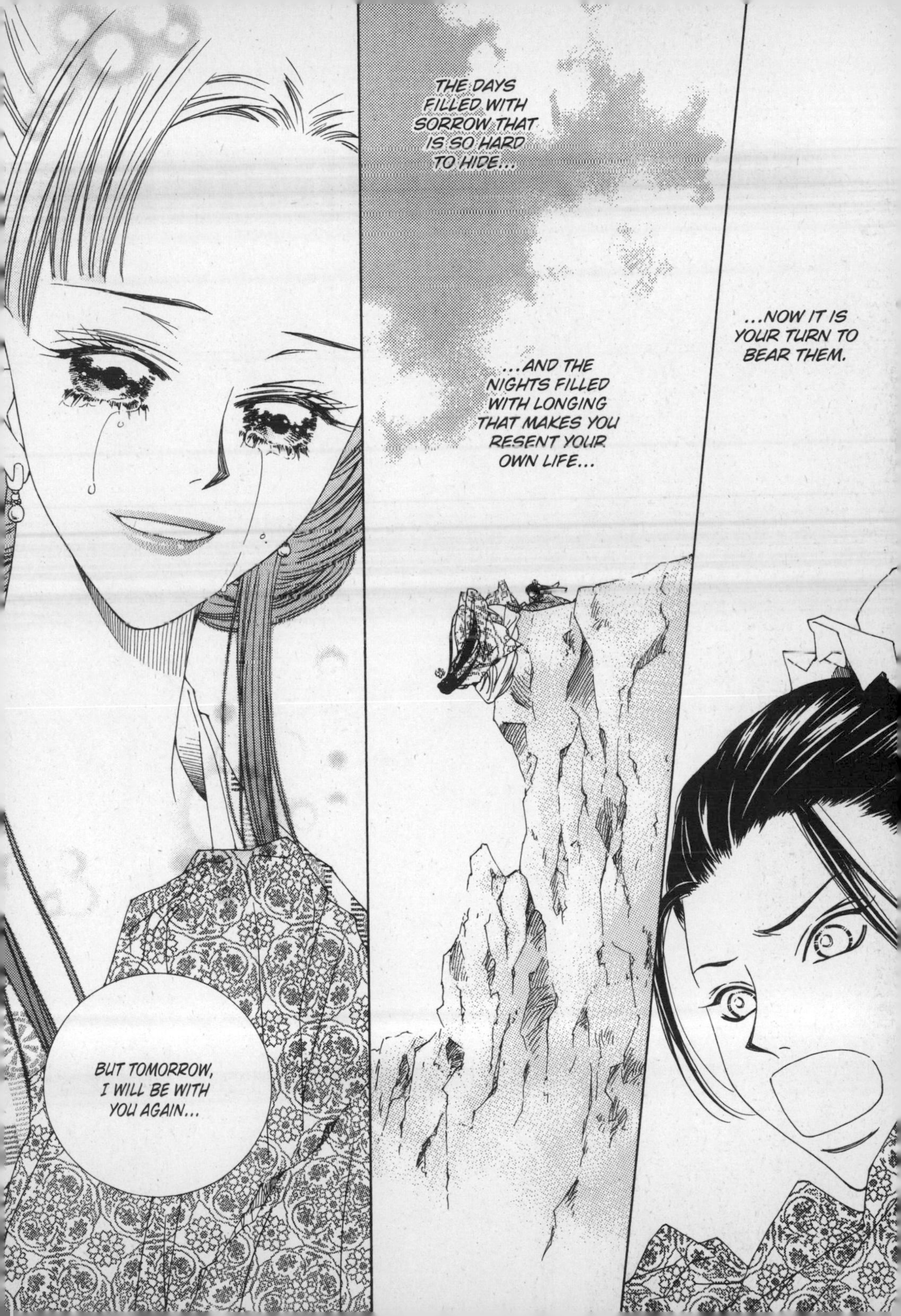
THE DAYS FILLED WITH SORROW THAT IS SO HARD TO HIDE...
...AND THE NIGHTS FILLED WITH LONGING THAT MAKES YOU RESENT YOUR OWN LIFE...
...NOW IT IS YOUR TURN TO BEAR THEM.
BUT TOMORROW, I WILL BE WITH YOU AGAIN...

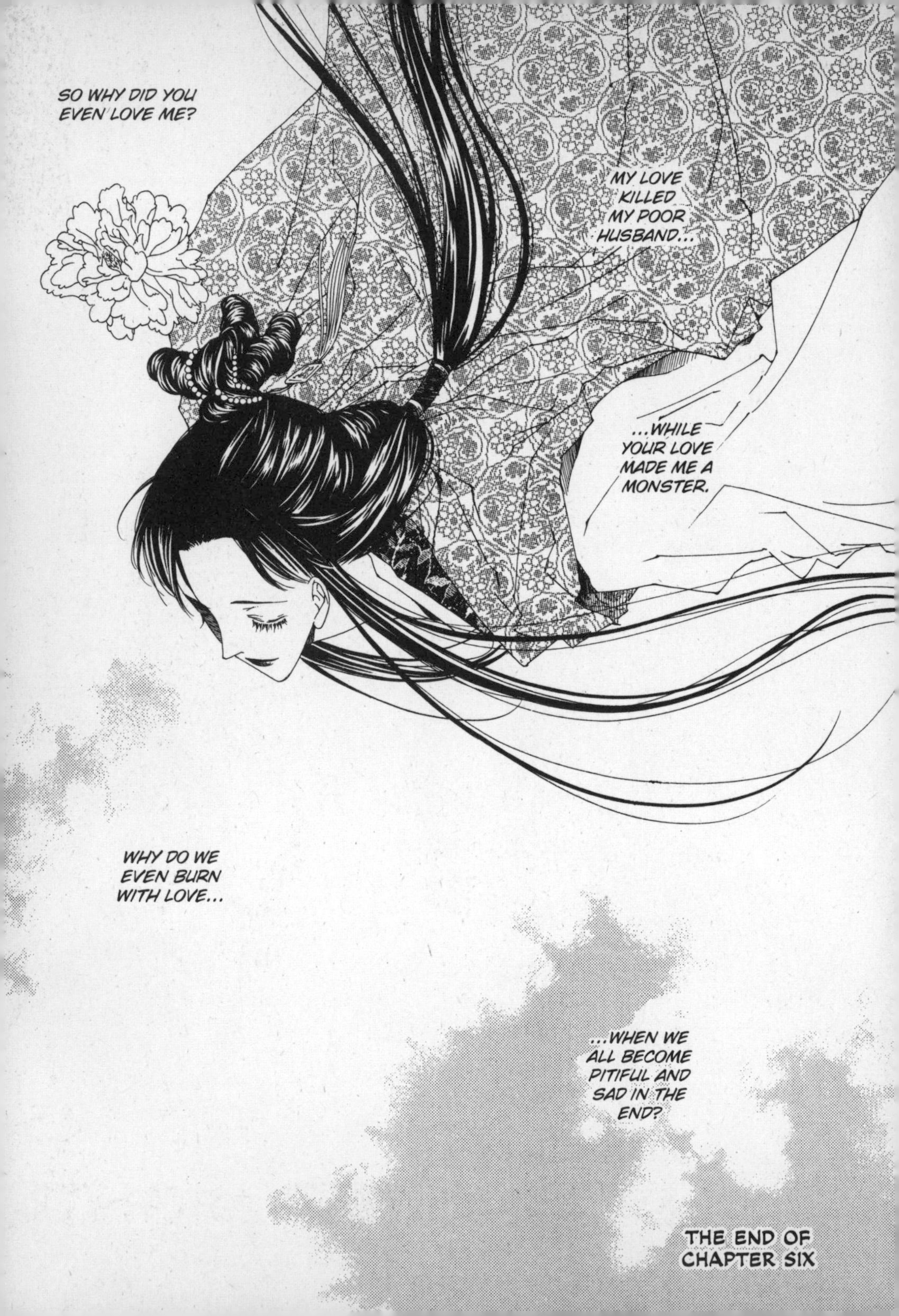
SO WHY DID YOU EVEN LOVE ME?
MY LOVE KILLED MY POOR HUSBAND...
...WHILE YOUR LOVE MADE ME A MONSTER.
WHY DO WE EVEN BURN WITH LOVE...
...WHEN WE ALL BECOME PITIFUL AND SAD IN THE END?
THE END OF CHAPTER SIX

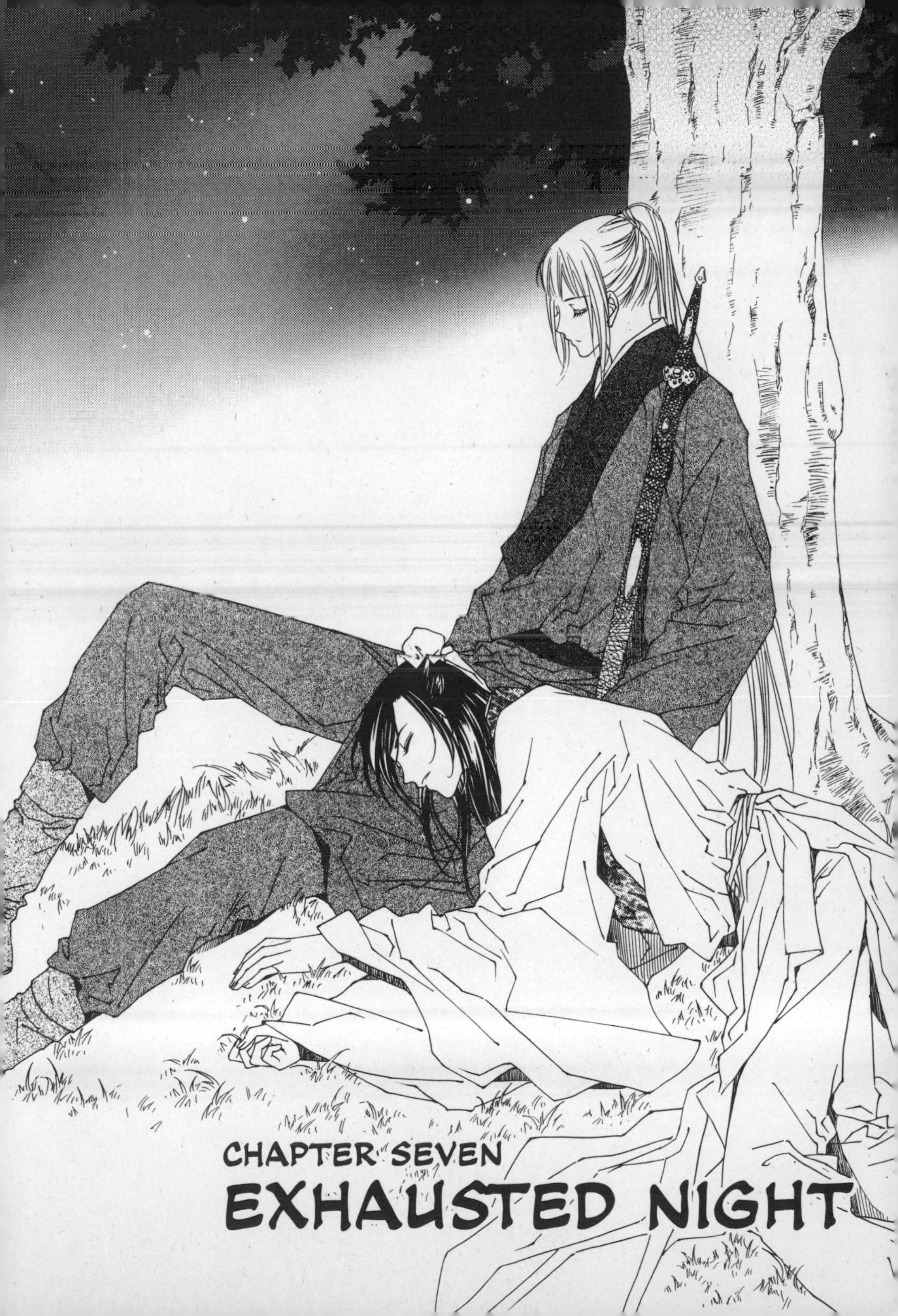
CHAPTER SEVEN
EXHAUSTED NIGHT

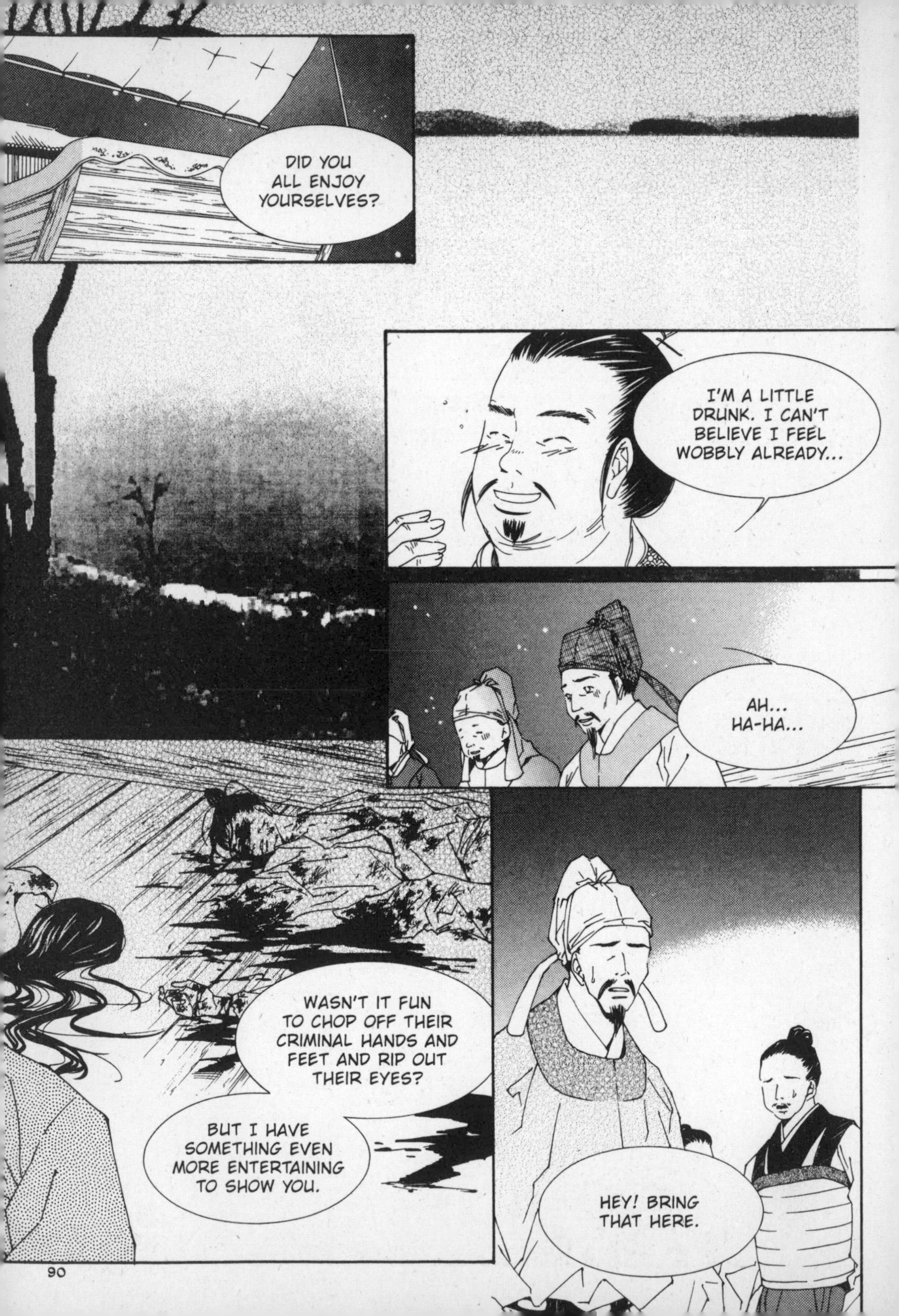
DID YOU ALL ENJOY YOURSELVES?
I'M A LITTLE DRUNK. I CAN'T BELIEVE I FEEL WOBBLY ALREADY...
AH... HA-HA...
WASN'T IT FUN TO CHOP OFF THEIR CRIMINAL HANDS AND FEET AND RIP OUT THEIR EYES?
BUT I HAVE SOMETHING EVEN MORE ENTERTAINING TO SHOW YOU.
HEY! BRING THAT HERE.

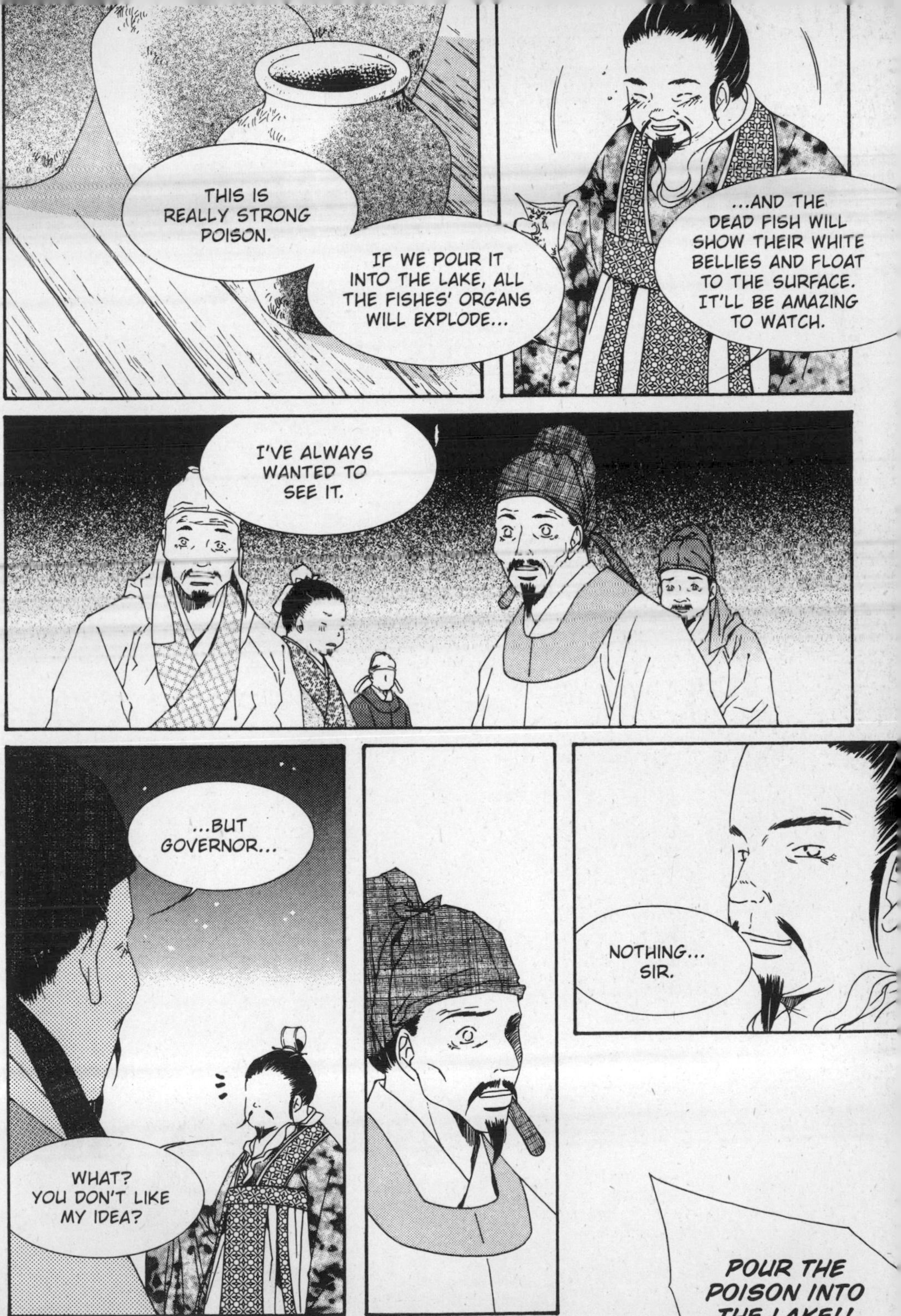
THIS IS REALLY STRONG POISON.
IF WE POUR IT INTO THE LAKE, ALL THE FISHES' ORGANS WILL EXPLODE...
...AND THE DEAD FISH WILL SHOW THEIR WHITE BELLIES AND FLOAT TO THE SURFACE. IT'LL BE AMAZING TO WATCH.
I'VE ALWAYS WANTED TO SEE IT.
...BUT GOVERNOR...
WHAT? YOU DON'T LIKE MY IDEA?
NOTHING... SIR.
POUR THE POISON INTO THE LAKE!!

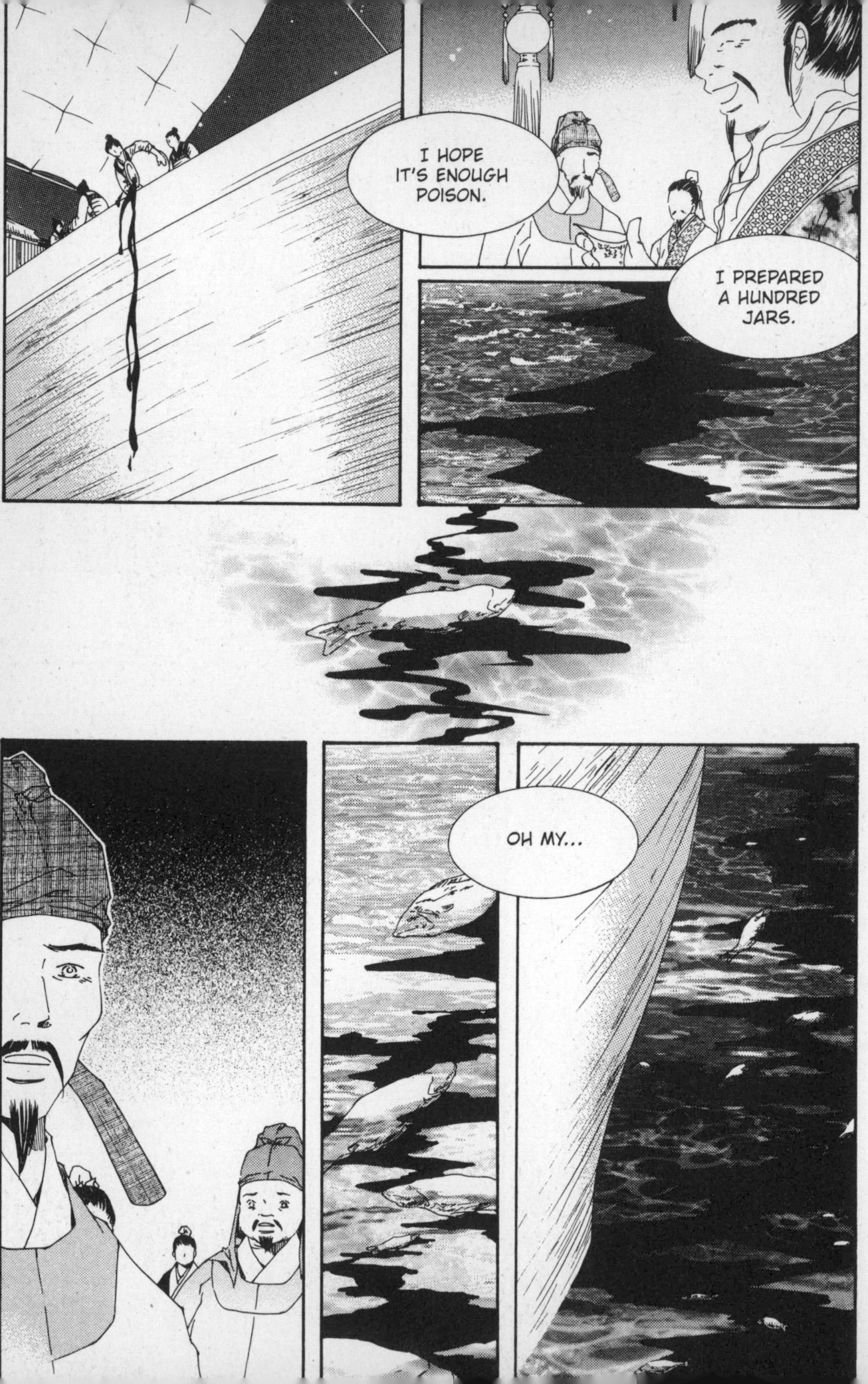
I HOPE IT'S ENOUGH POISON.
I PREPARED A HUNDRED JARS.
OH MY...

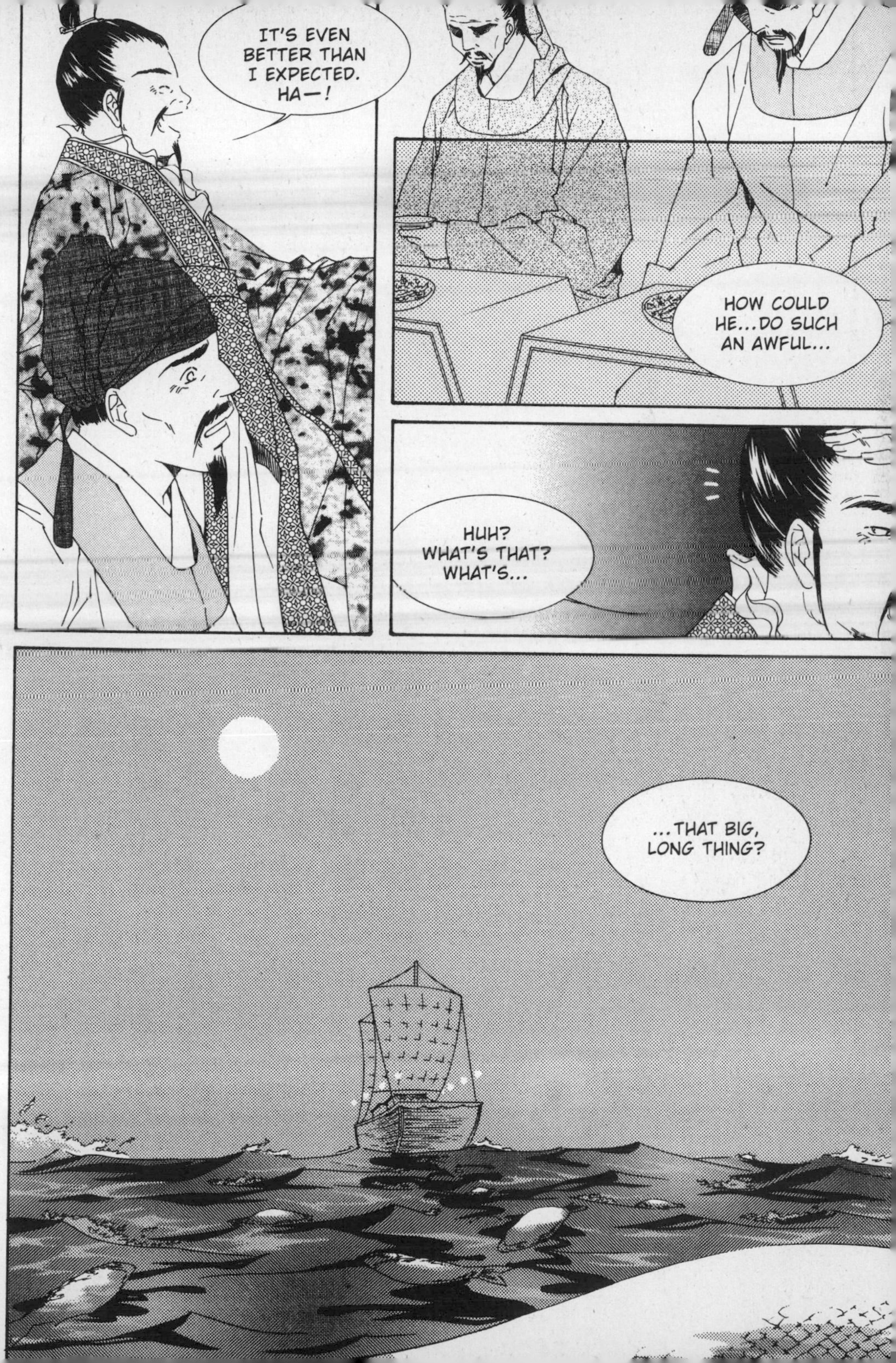
IT'S EVEN BETTER THAN I EXPECTED. HA—!
HOW COULD HE...DO SUCH AN AWFUL...
HUH? WHAT'S THAT? WHAT'S...
...THAT BIG, LONG THING?

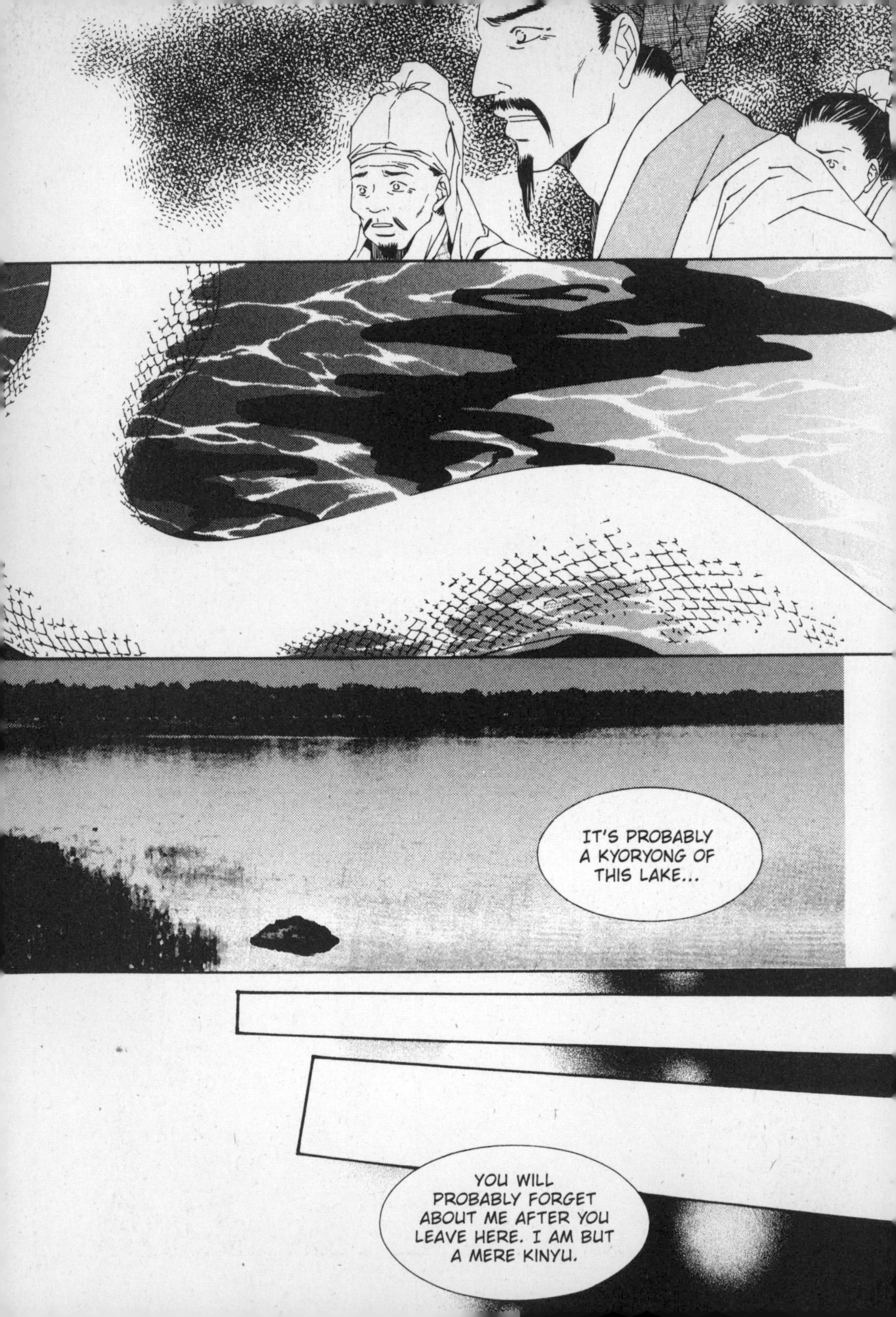
IT'S PROBABLY A KYORYONG OF THIS LAKE...
YOU WILL PROBABLY FORGET ABOUT ME AFTER YOU LEAVE HERE. I AM BUT A MERE KINYU.

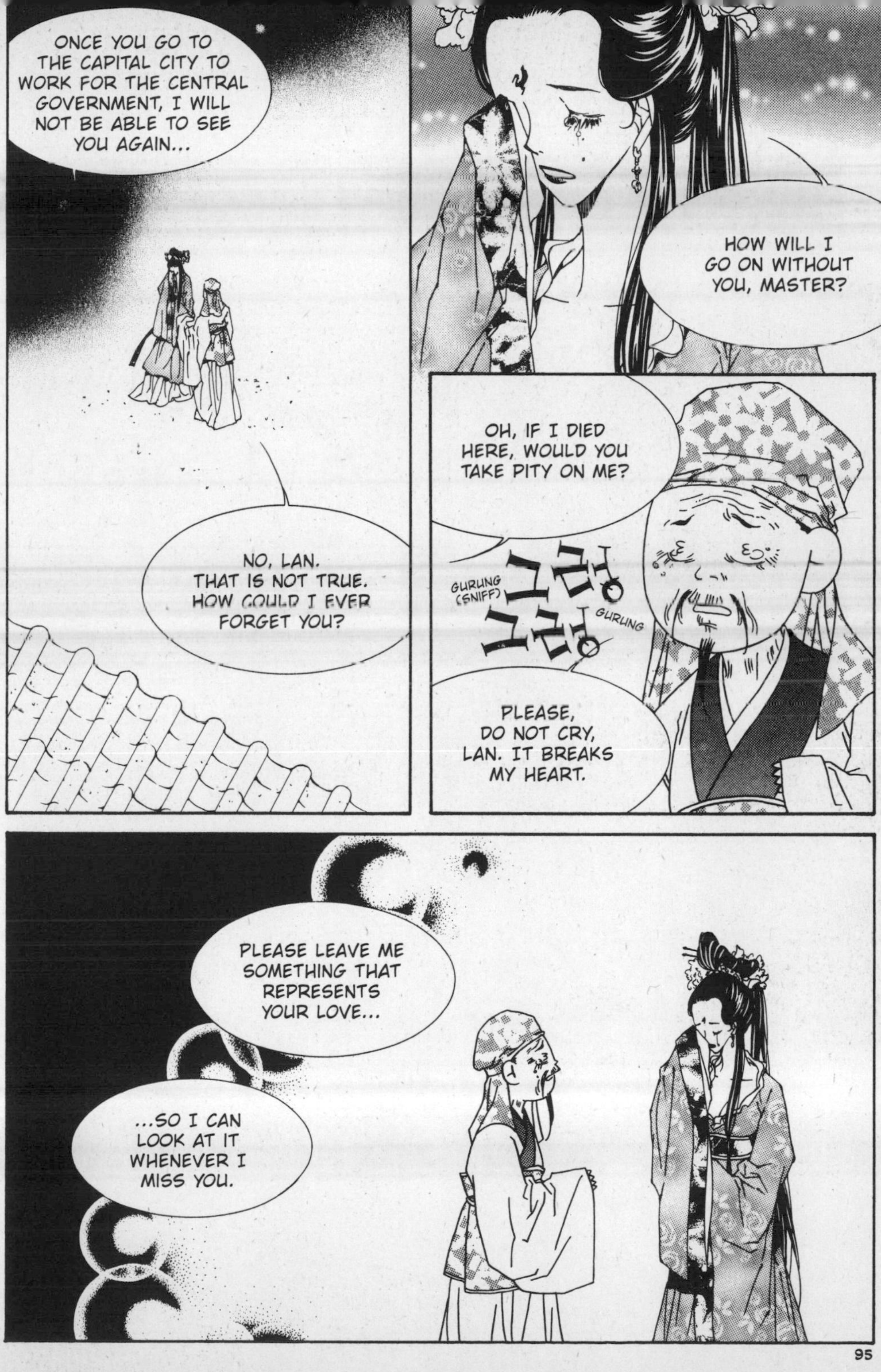
ONCE YOU GO TO THE CAPITAL CITY TO WORK FOR THE CENTRAL GOVERNMENT, I WILL NOT BE ABLE TO SEE YOU AGAIN...
HOW WILL I GO ON WITHOUT YOU, MASTER?
NO, LAN. THAT IS NOT TRUE. HOW COULD I EVER FORGET YOU?
OH, IF I DIED HERE, WOULD YOU TAKE PITY ON ME?
그렁 그렁
GURUNG (SNIFF)
GURUNG
PLEASE, DO NOT CRY, LAN. IT BREAKS MY HEART.
PLEASE LEAVE ME SOMETHING THAT REPRESENTS YOUR LOVE...
...SO I CAN LOOK AT IT WHENEVER I MISS YOU.

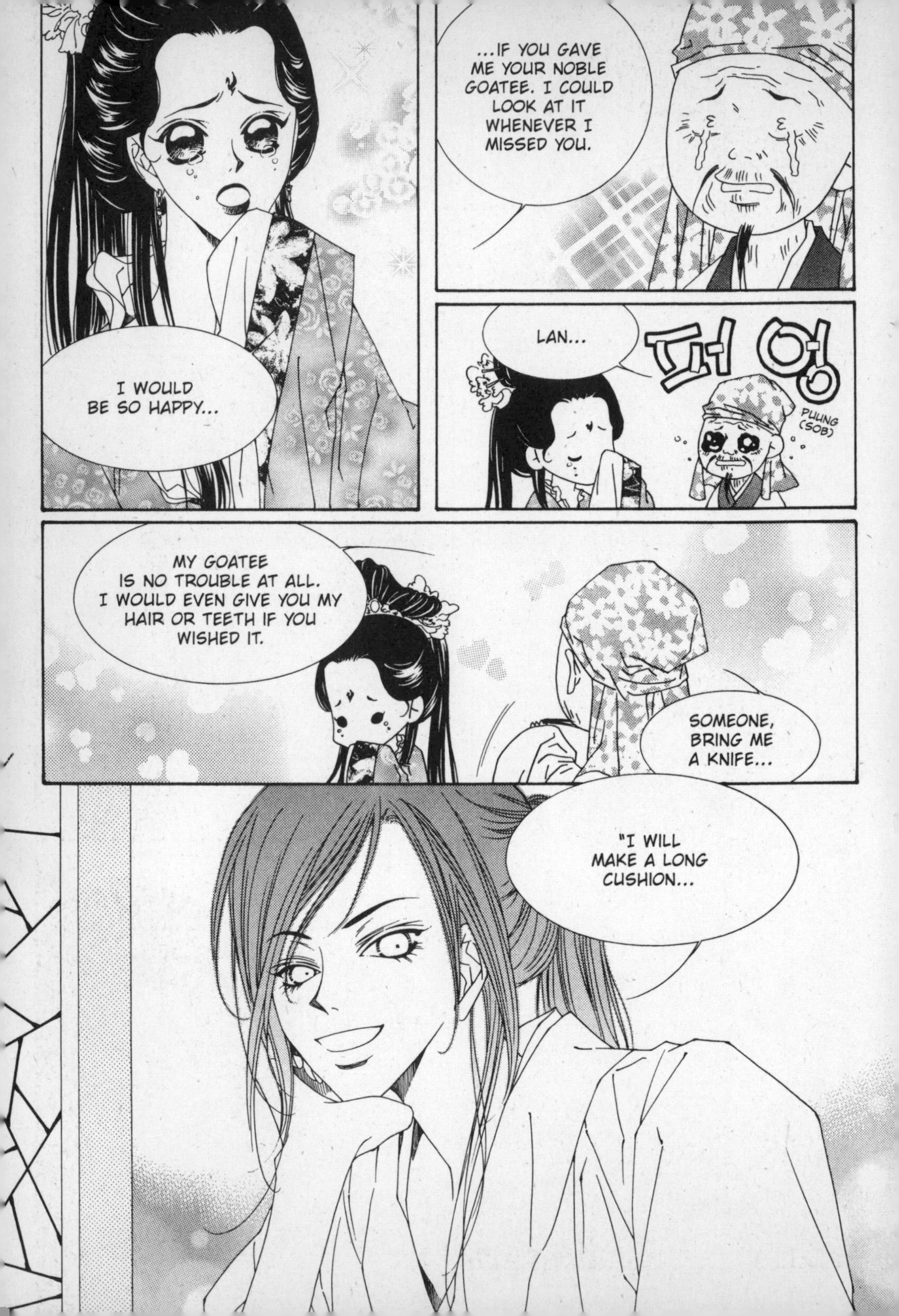

I WOULD BE SO HAPPY...
...IF YOU GAVE ME YOUR NOBLE GOATEE. I COULD LOOK AT IT WHENEVER I MISSED YOU.
LAN...
퍼엉
PUUNG (SOB)
MY GOATEE IS NO TROUBLE AT ALL. I WOULD EVEN GIVE YOU MY HAIR OR TEETH IF YOU WISHED IT.
SOMEONE, BRING ME A KNIFE...
"I WILL MAKE A LONG CUSHION...

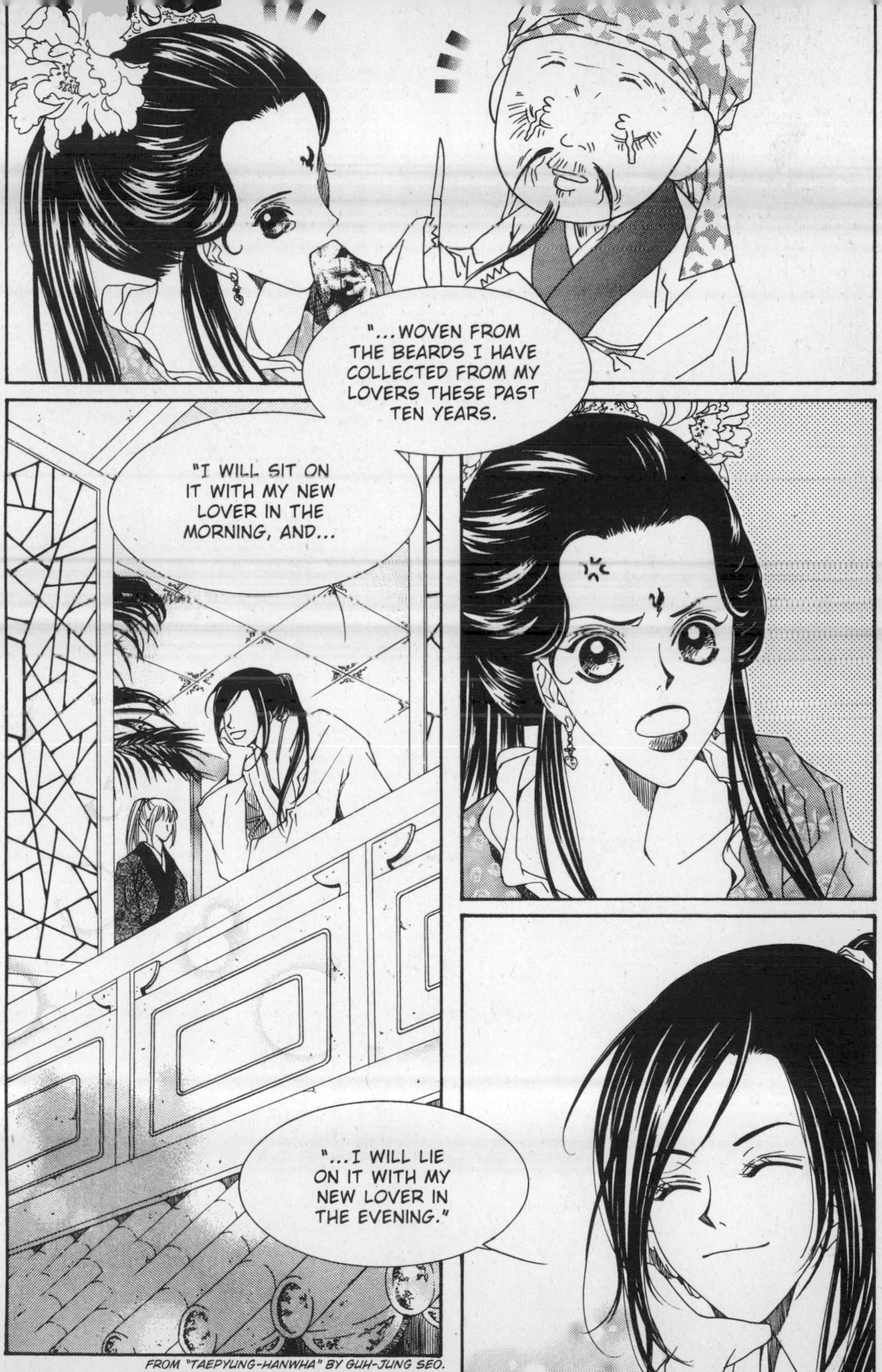
"...WOVEN FROM THE BEARDS I HAVE COLLECTED FROM MY LOVERS THESE PAST TEN YEARS.
"I WILL SIT ON IT WITH MY NEW LOVER IN THE MORNING, AND...
"...I WILL LIE ON IT WITH MY NEW LOVER IN THE EVENING."

FROM "TAEPYUNG-HANWHA" BY GUH-JUNG SEO.

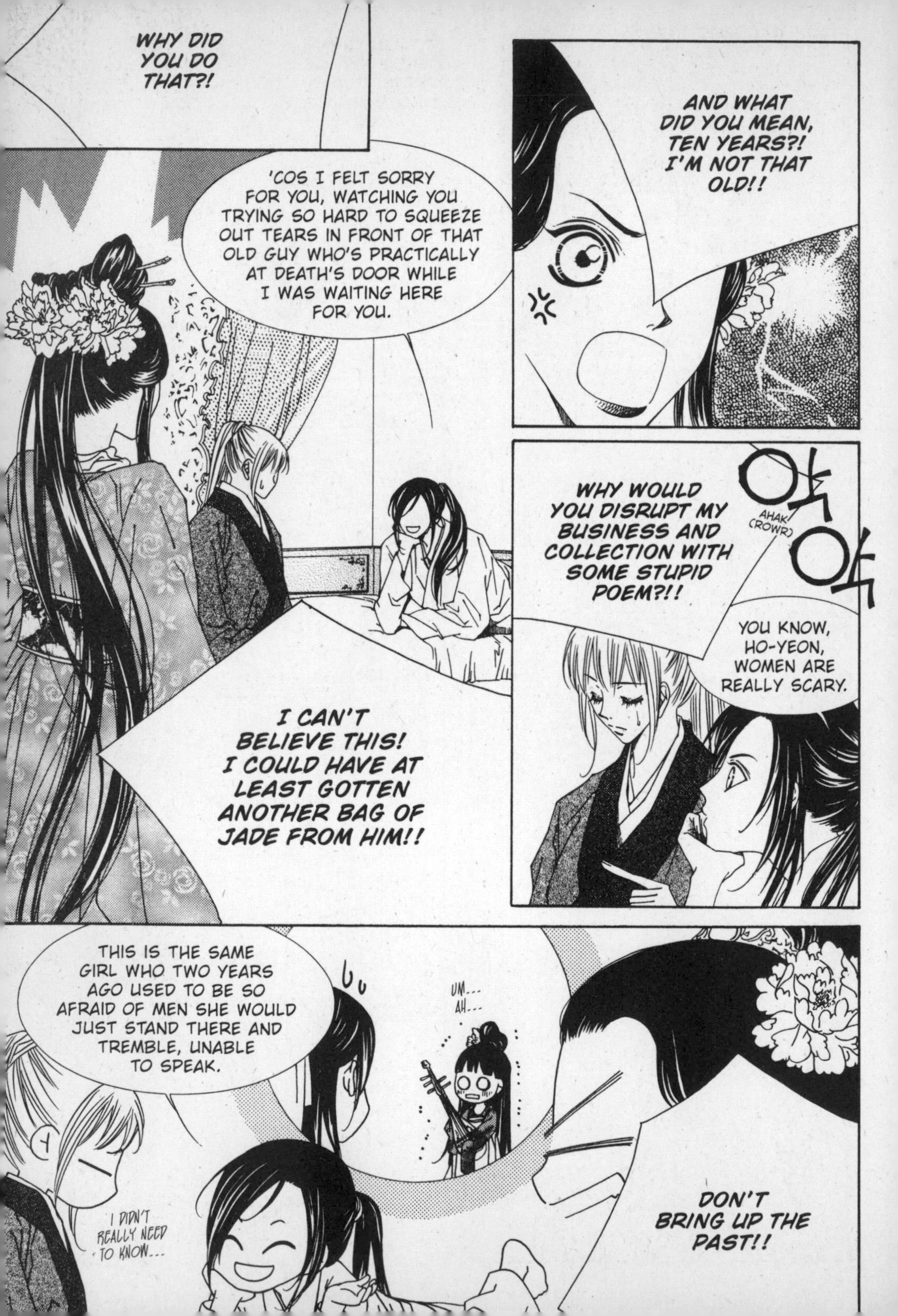

WHY DID YOU DO THAT?!
'COS I FELT SORRY FOR YOU, WATCHING YOU TRYING SO HARD TO SQUEEZE OUT TEARS IN FRONT OF THAT OLD GUY WHO'S PRACTICALLY AT DEATH'S DOOR WHILE I WAS WAITING HERE FOR YOU.
AND WHAT DID YOU MEAN, TEN YEARS?! I'M NOT THAT OLD!!
I CAN'T BELIEVE THIS! I COULD HAVE AT LEAST GOTTEN ANOTHER BAG OF JADE FROM HIM!!
WHY WOULD YOU DISRUPT MY BUSINESS AND COLLECTION WITH SOME STUPID POEM?!!
AHAK (ROWR)
YOU KNOW, HO-YEON, WOMEN ARE REALLY SCARY.
THIS IS THE SAME GIRL WHO TWO YEARS AGO USED TO BE SO AFRAID OF MEN SHE WOULD JUST STAND THERE AND TREMBLE, UNABLE TO SPEAK.
UM... AH...
I DIDN'T REALLY NEED TO KNOW...
DON'T BRING UP THE PAST!!

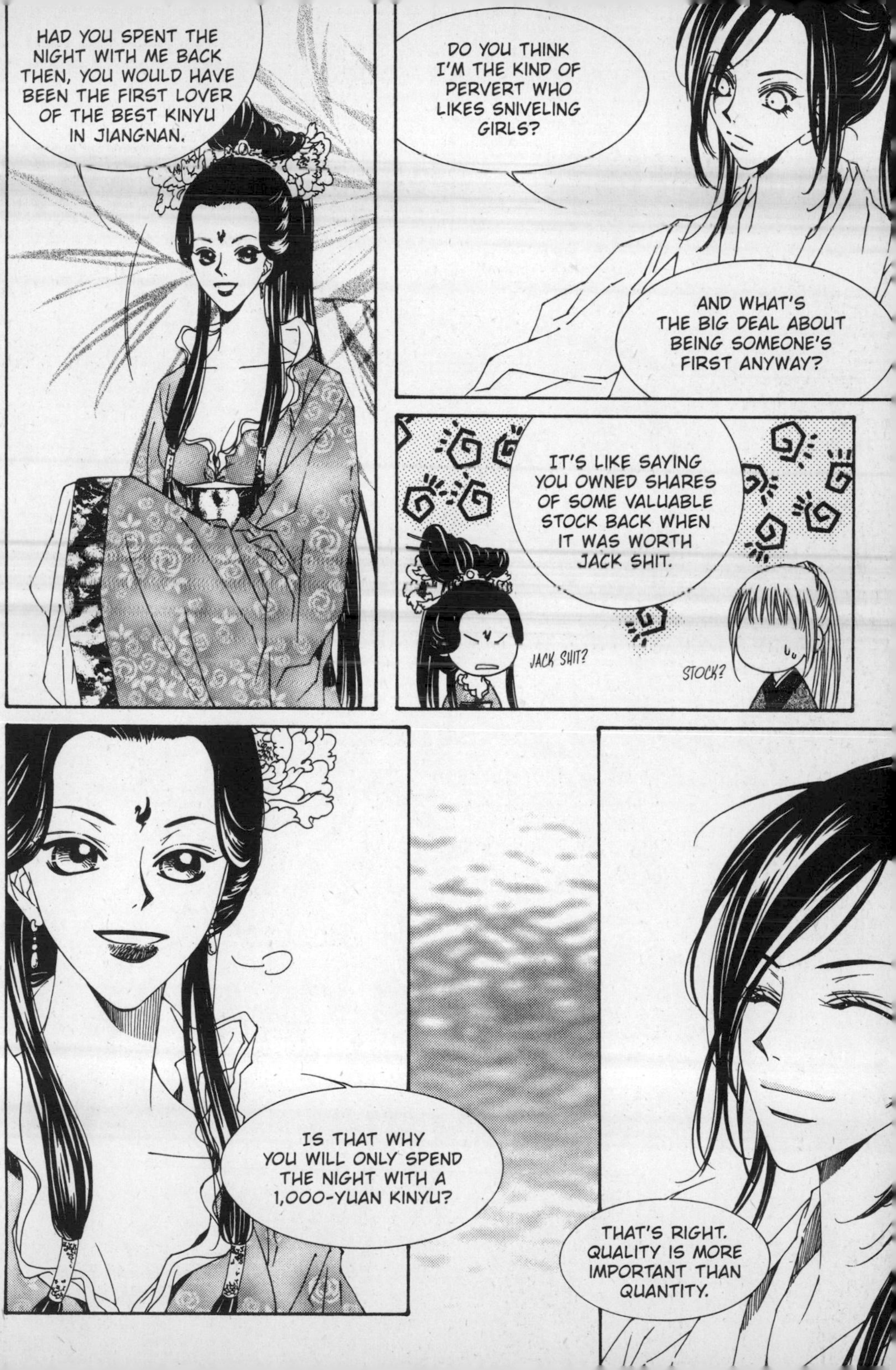
HAD YOU SPENT THE NIGHT WITH ME BACK THEN, YOU WOULD HAVE BEEN THE FIRST LOVER OF THE BEST KINYU IN JIANGNAN.
DO YOU THINK I'M THE KIND OF PERVERT WHO LIKES SNIVELING GIRLS?
AND WHAT'S THE BIG DEAL ABOUT BEING SOMEONE'S FIRST ANYWAY?
IT'S LIKE SAYING YOU OWNED SHARES OF SOME VALUABLE STOCK BACK WHEN IT WAS WORTH JACK SHIT.
JACK SHIT?
STOCK?
IS THAT WHY YOU WILL ONLY SPEND THE NIGHT WITH A 1,000-YUAN KINYU?
THAT'S RIGHT. QUALITY IS MORE IMPORTANT THAN QUANTITY.

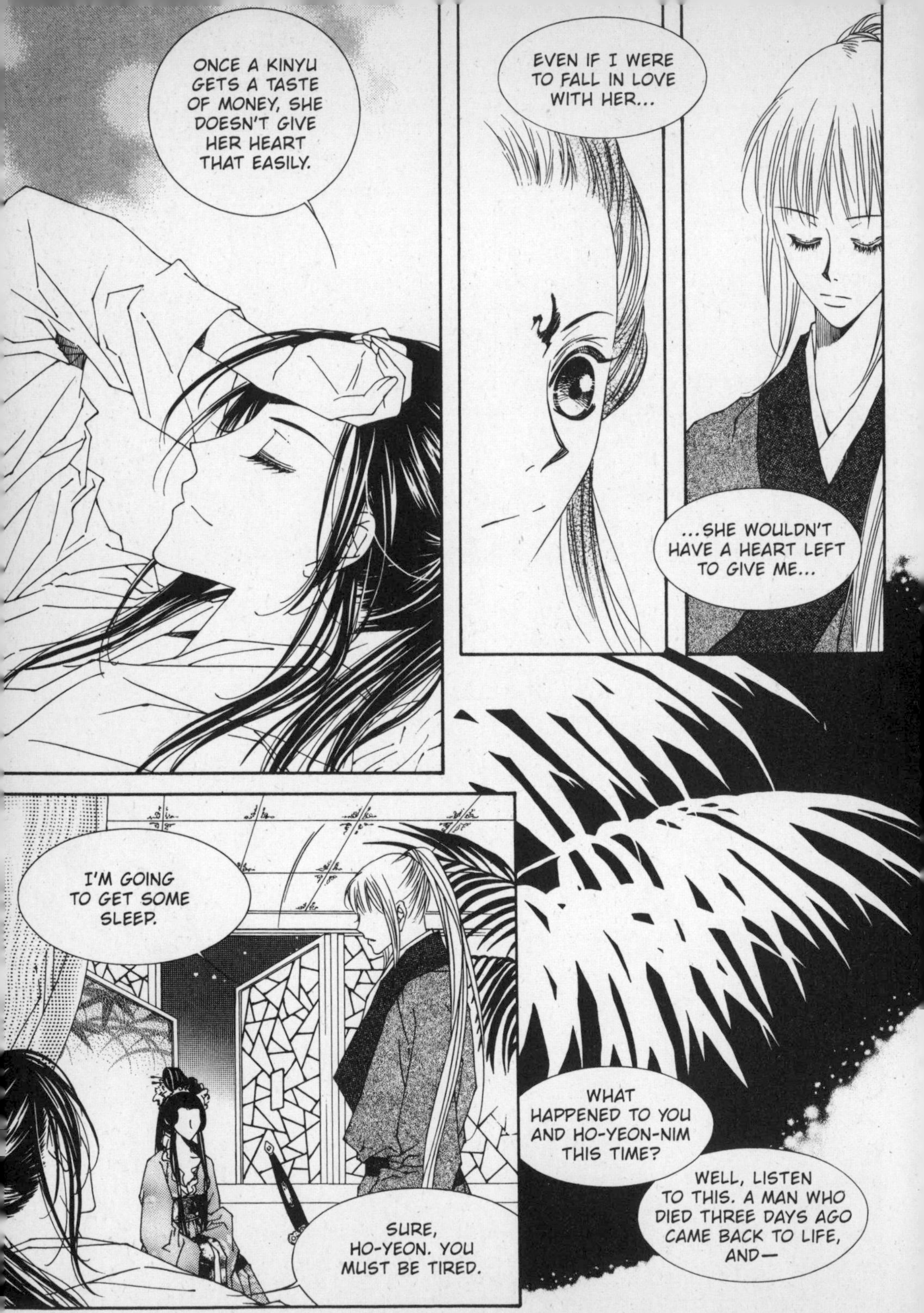
ONCE A KINYU GETS A TASTE OF MONEY, SHE DOESN'T GIVE HER HEART THAT EASILY.
EVEN IF I WERE TO FALL IN LOVE WITH HER...
...SHE WOULDN'T HAVE A HEART LEFT TO GIVE ME...
I'M GOING TO GET SOME SLEEP.
SURE, HO-YEON. YOU MUST BE TIRED.
WHAT HAPPENED TO YOU AND HO-YEON-NIM THIS TIME?
WELL, LISTEN TO THIS. A MAN WHO DIED THREE DAYS AGO CAME BACK TO LIFE, AND—

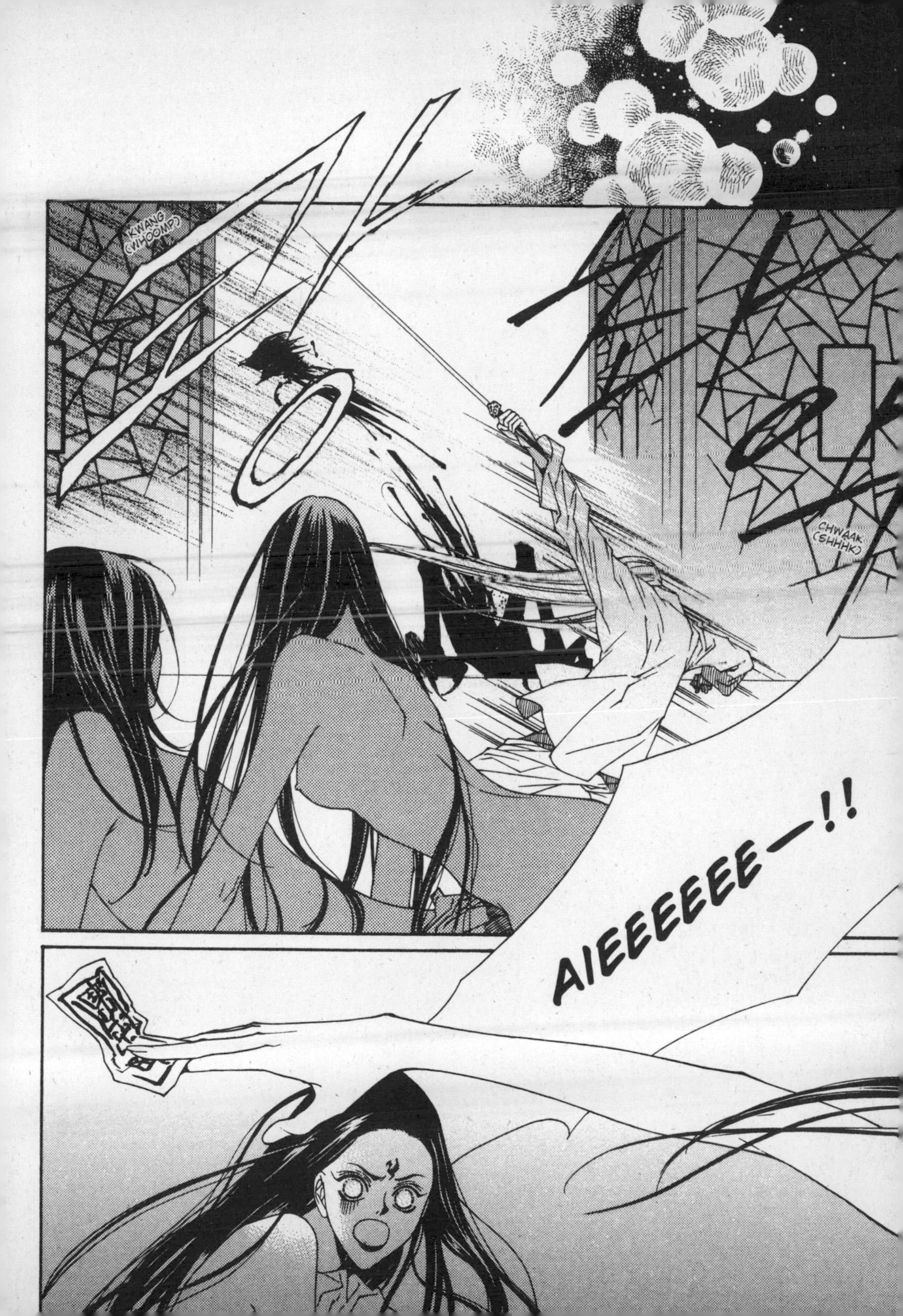
KWANG (WHOOMP)
CHWAAK (SHHHK)
AIEEEEEE—!!

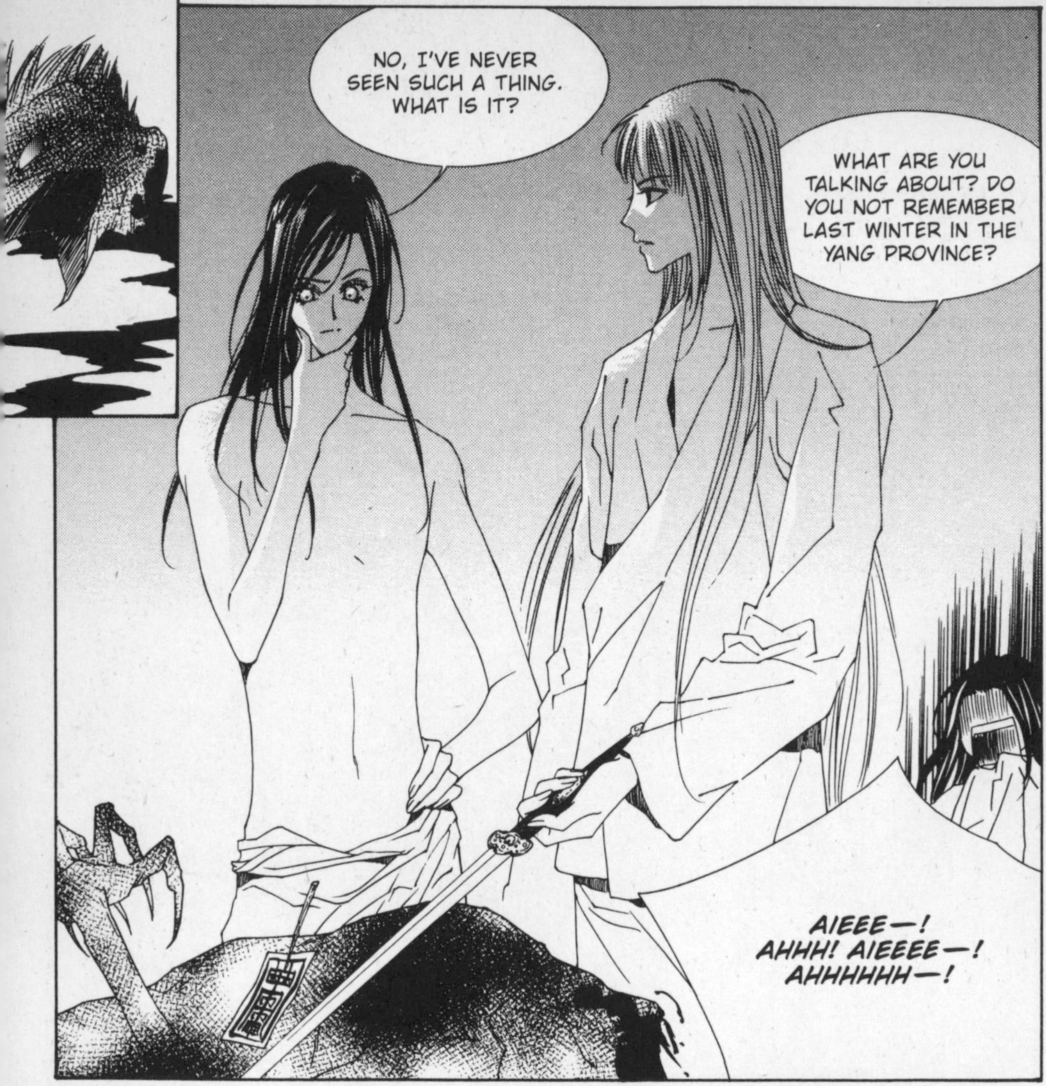
NO, I'VE NEVER SEEN SUCH A THING. WHAT IS IT?
WHAT ARE YOU TALKING ABOUT? DO YOU NOT REMEMBER LAST WINTER IN THE YANG PROVINCE?
AIEEE—! AHHH! AIEEEE—! AHHHHHH—!

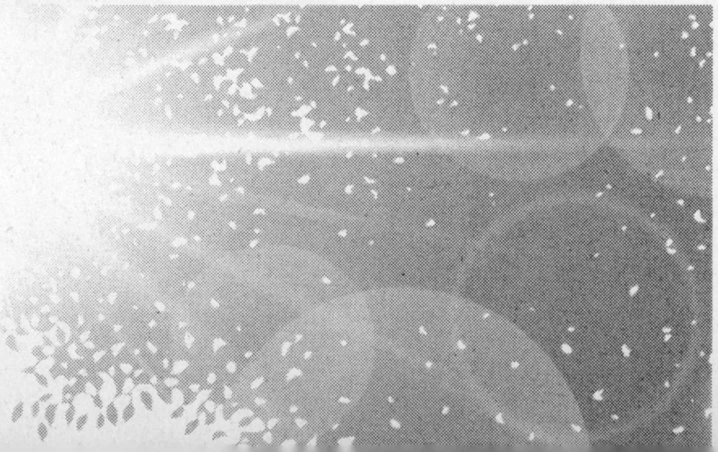

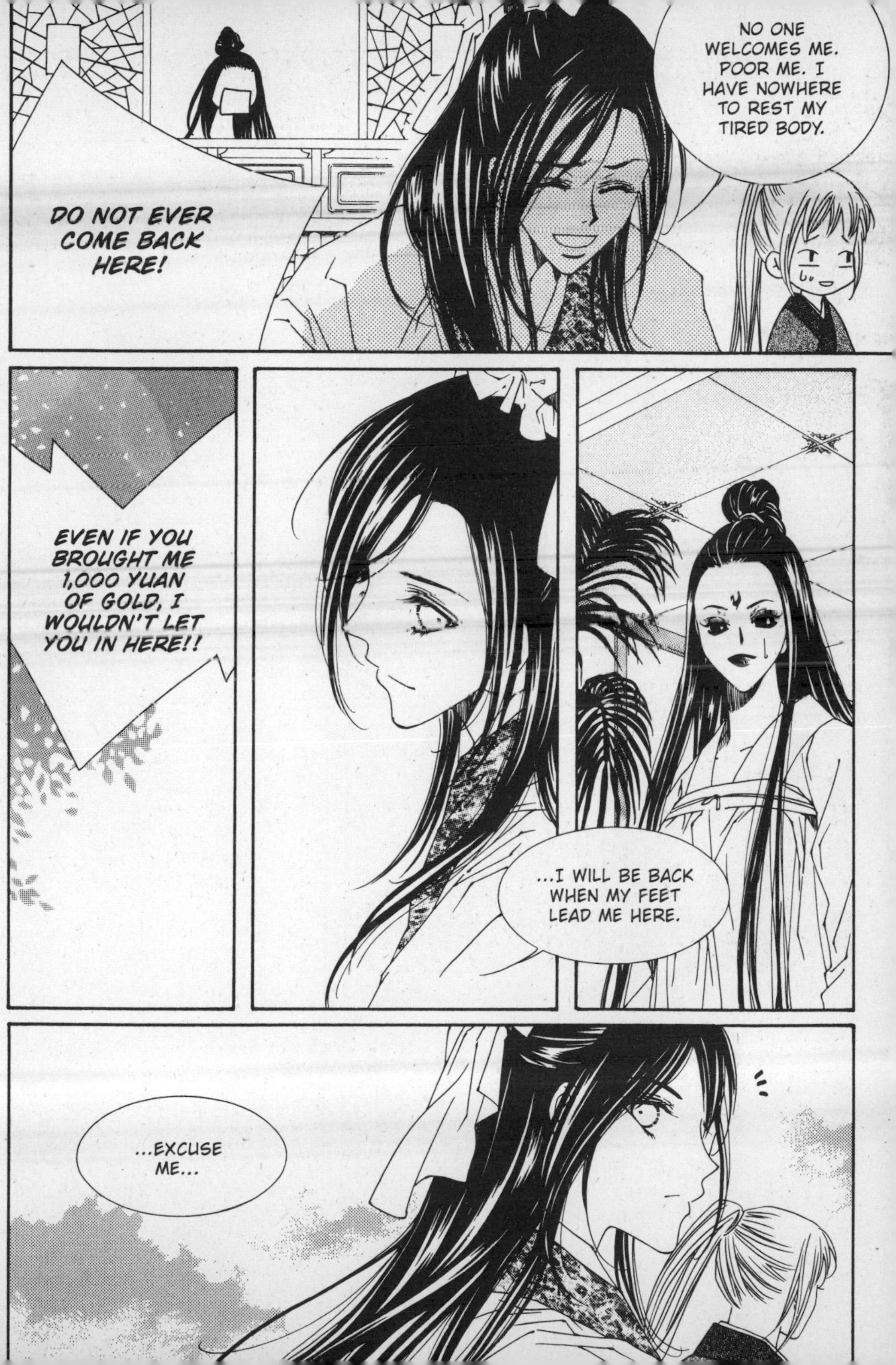
NO ONE WELCOMES ME. POOR ME. I HAVE NOWHERE TO REST MY TIRED BODY.
DO NOT EVER COME BACK HERE!
EVEN IF YOU BROUGHT ME 1,000 YUAN OF GOLD, I WOULDN'T LET YOU IN HERE!!
...I WILL BE BACK WHEN MY FEET LEAD ME HERE.
...EXCUSE ME...

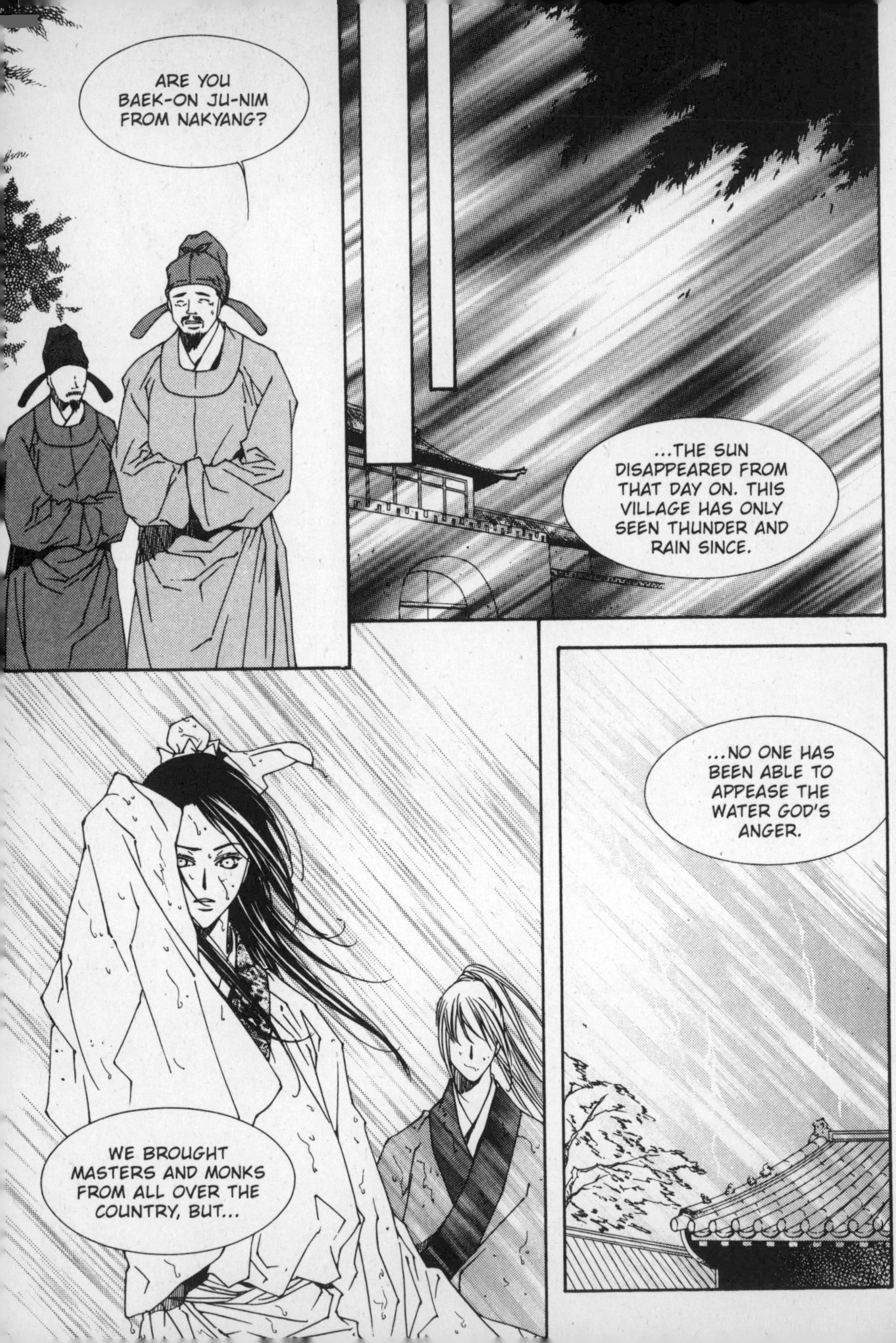
ARE YOU BAEK-ON JU-NIM FROM NAKYANG?
...THE SUN DISAPPEARED FROM THAT DAY ON. THIS VILLAGE HAS ONLY SEEN THUNDER AND RAIN SINCE.
WE BROUGHT MASTERS AND MONKS FROM ALL OVER THE COUNTRY, BUT...
...NO ONE HAS BEEN ABLE TO APPEASE THE WATER GOD'S ANGER.

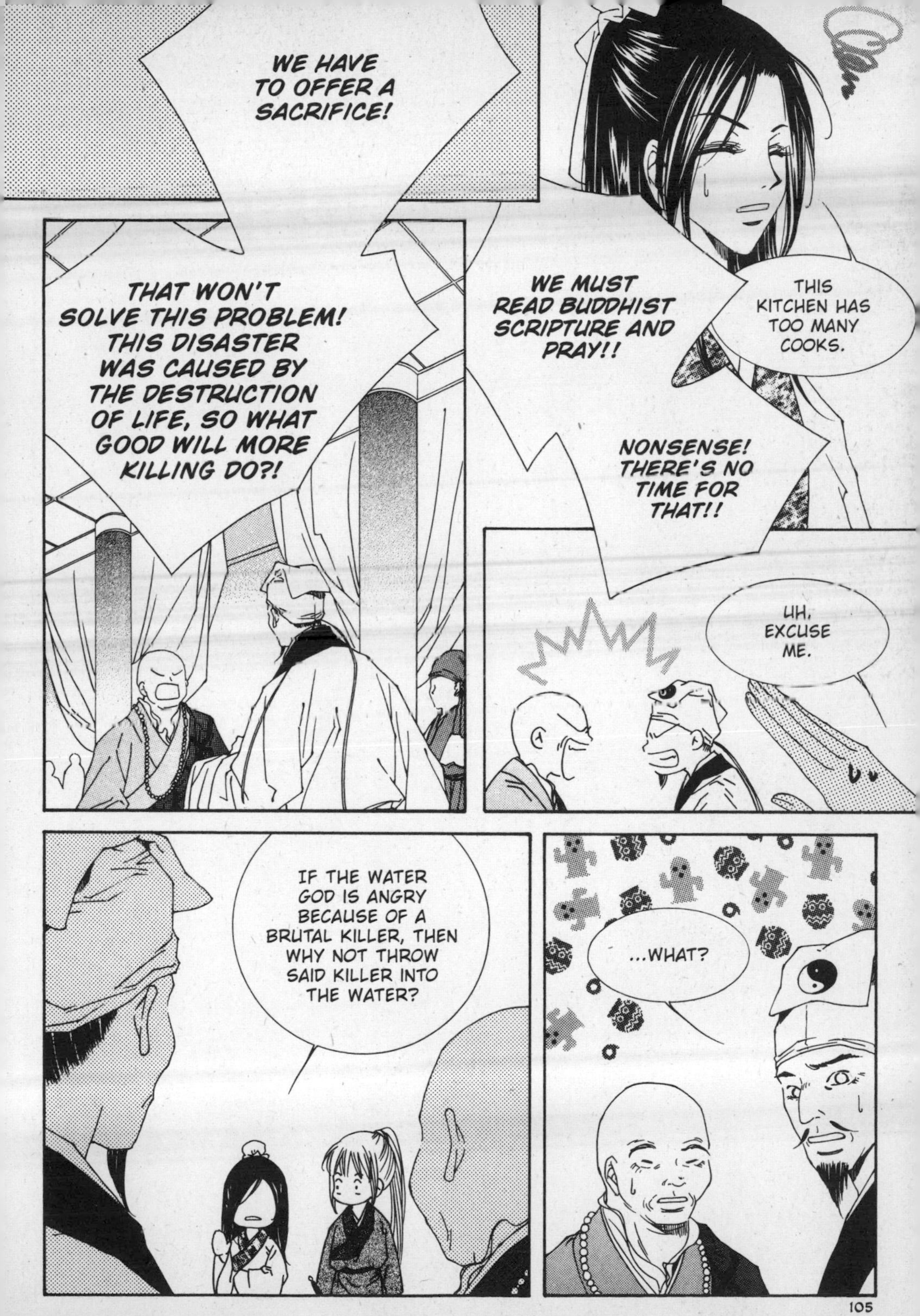
WE HAVE TO OFFER A SACRIFICE!
THIS KITCHEN HAS TOO MANY COOKS.
WE MUST READ BUDDHIST SCRIPTURE AND PRAY!!
THAT WON'T SOLVE THIS PROBLEM! THIS DISASTER WAS CAUSED BY THE DESTRUCTION OF LIFE, SO WHAT GOOD WILL MORE KILLING DO?!
NONSENSE! THERE'S NO TIME FOR THAT!!
UH, EXCUSE ME.
IF THE WATER GOD IS ANGRY BECAUSE OF A BRUTAL KILLER, THEN WHY NOT THROW SAID KILLER INTO THE WATER?
...WHAT?

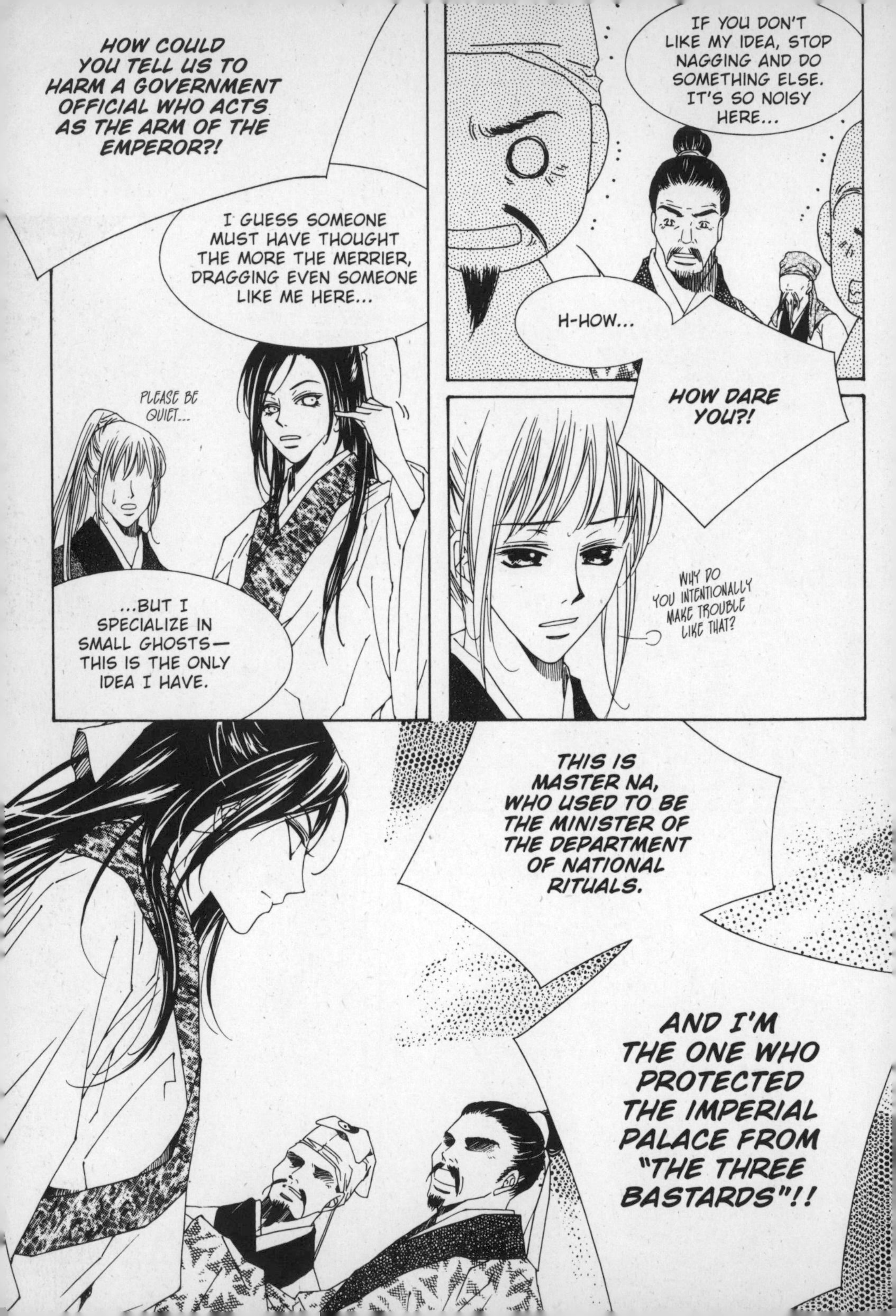
HOW COULD YOU TELL US TO HARM A GOVERNMENT OFFICIAL WHO ACTS AS THE ARM OF THE EMPEROR?!
I GUESS SOMEONE MUST HAVE THOUGHT THE MORE THE MERRIER, DRAGGING EVEN SOMEONE LIKE ME HERE...
PLEASE BE QUIET...
...BUT I SPECIALIZE IN SMALL GHOSTS—THIS IS THE ONLY IDEA I HAVE.
IF YOU DON'T LIKE MY IDEA, STOP NAGGING AND DO SOMETHING ELSE. IT'S SO NOISY HERE...
H-HOW...
HOW DARE YOU?!
WHY DO YOU INTENTIONALLY MAKE TROUBLE LIKE THAT?
THIS IS MASTER NA, WHO USED TO BE THE MINISTER OF THE DEPARTMENT OF NATIONAL RITUALS.
AND I'M THE ONE WHO PROTECTED THE IMPERIAL PALACE FROM "THE THREE BASTARDS"!!

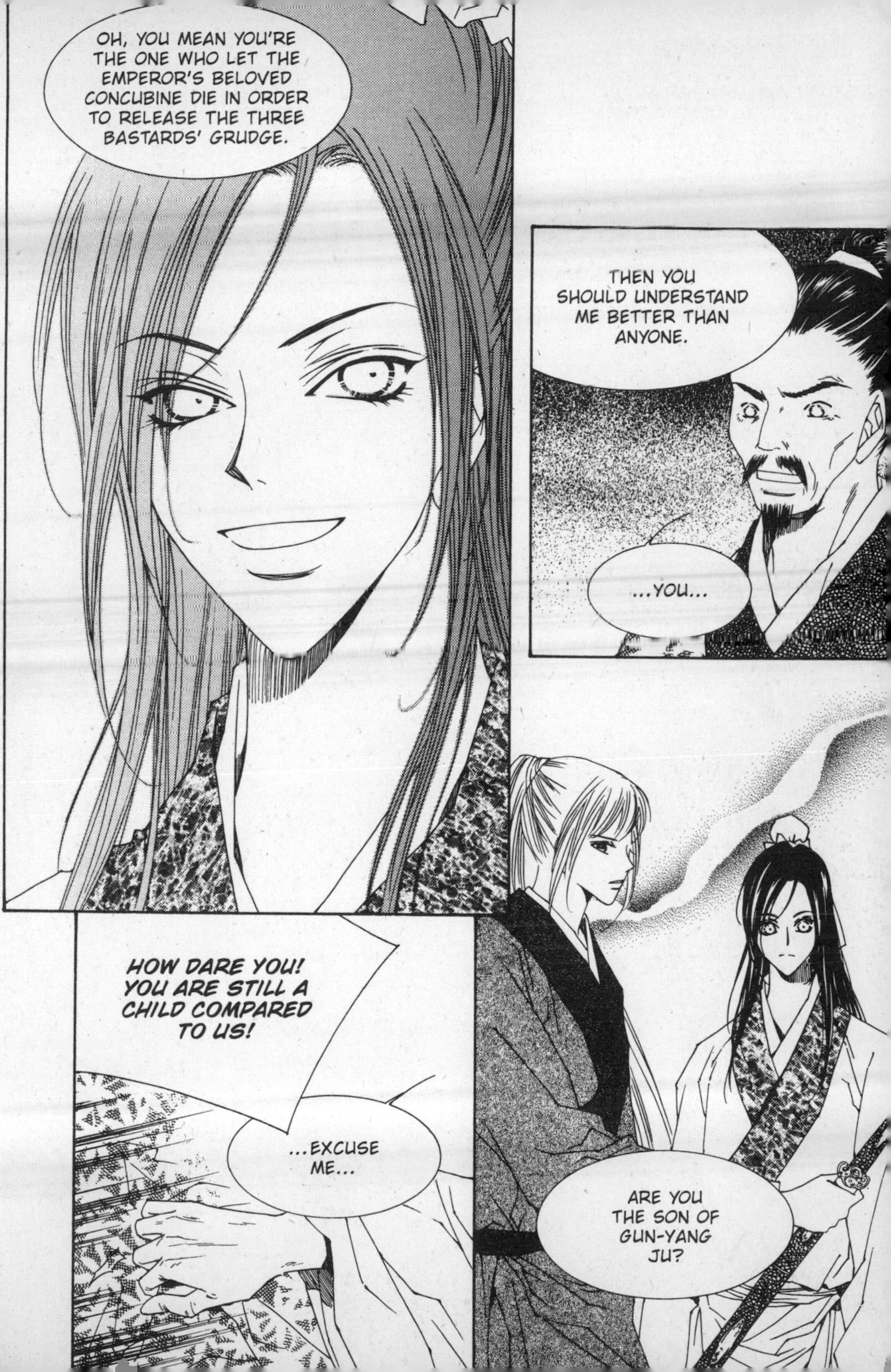
OH, YOU MEAN YOU'RE THE ONE WHO LET THE EMPEROR'S BELOVED CONCUBINE DIE IN ORDER TO RELEASE THE THREE BASTARDS' GRUDGE.
THEN YOU SHOULD UNDERSTAND ME BETTER THAN ANYONE.
...YOU...
HOW DARE YOU! YOU ARE STILL A CHILD COMPARED TO US!
...EXCUSE ME...
ARE YOU THE SON OF GUN-YANG JU?

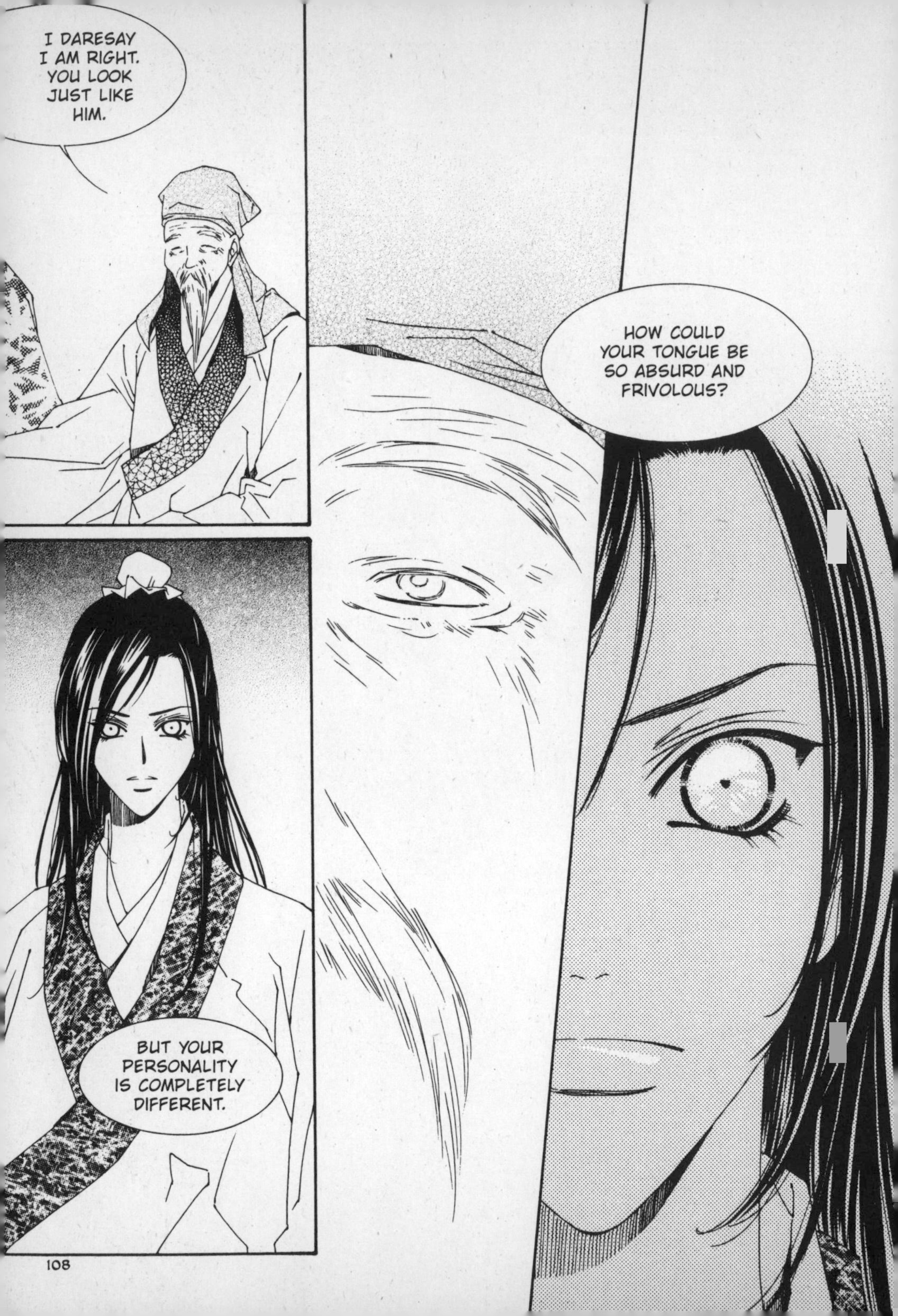
I DARESAY I AM RIGHT. YOU LOOK JUST LIKE HIM.
BUT YOUR PERSONALITY IS COMPLETELY DIFFERENT.
HOW COULD YOUR TONGUE BE SO ABSURD AND FRIVOLOUS?

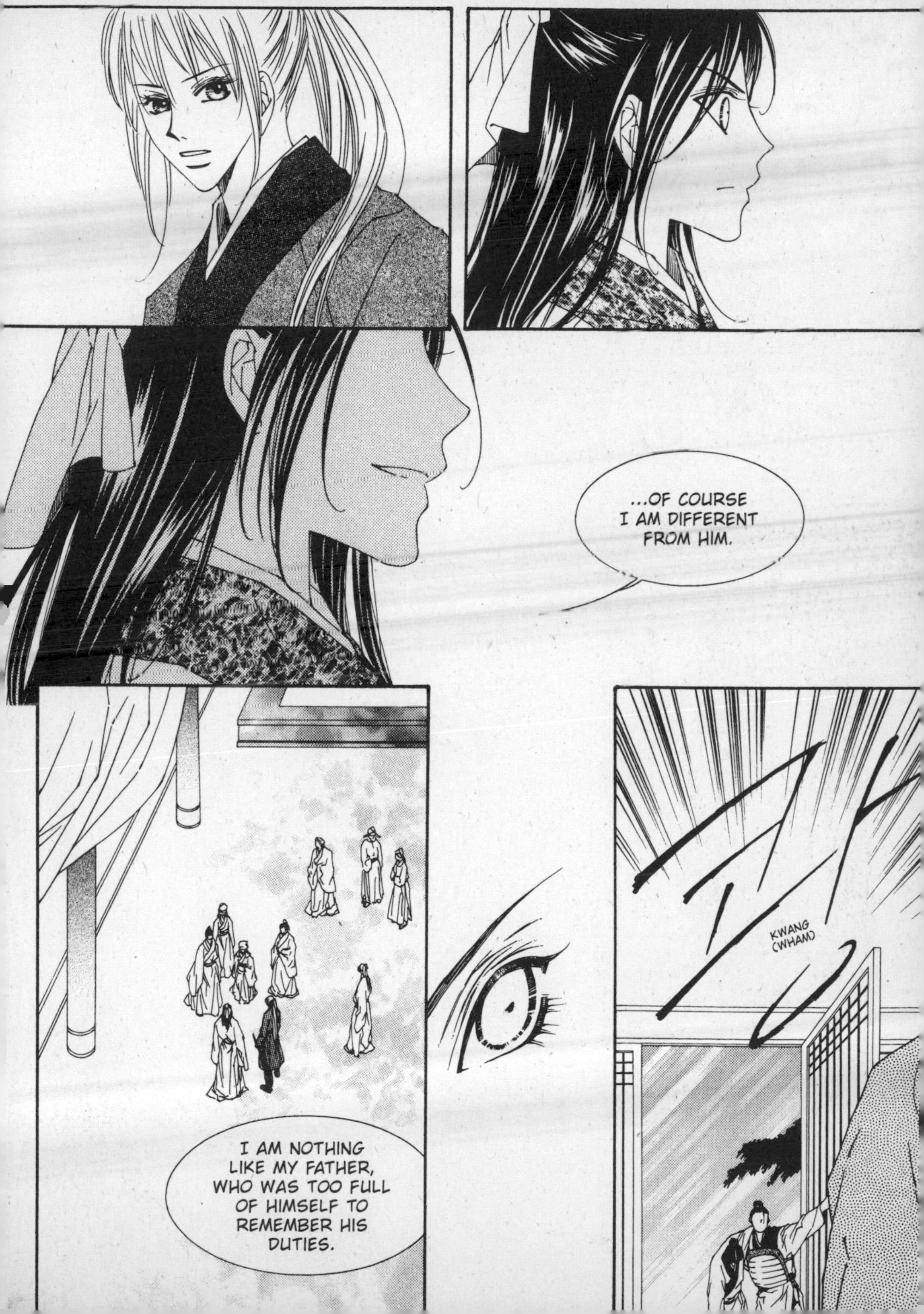
...OF COURSE I AM DIFFERENT FROM HIM.
I AM NOTHING LIKE MY FATHER, WHO WAS TOO FULL OF HIMSELF TO REMEMBER HIS DUTIES.
KWANG (WHAM)

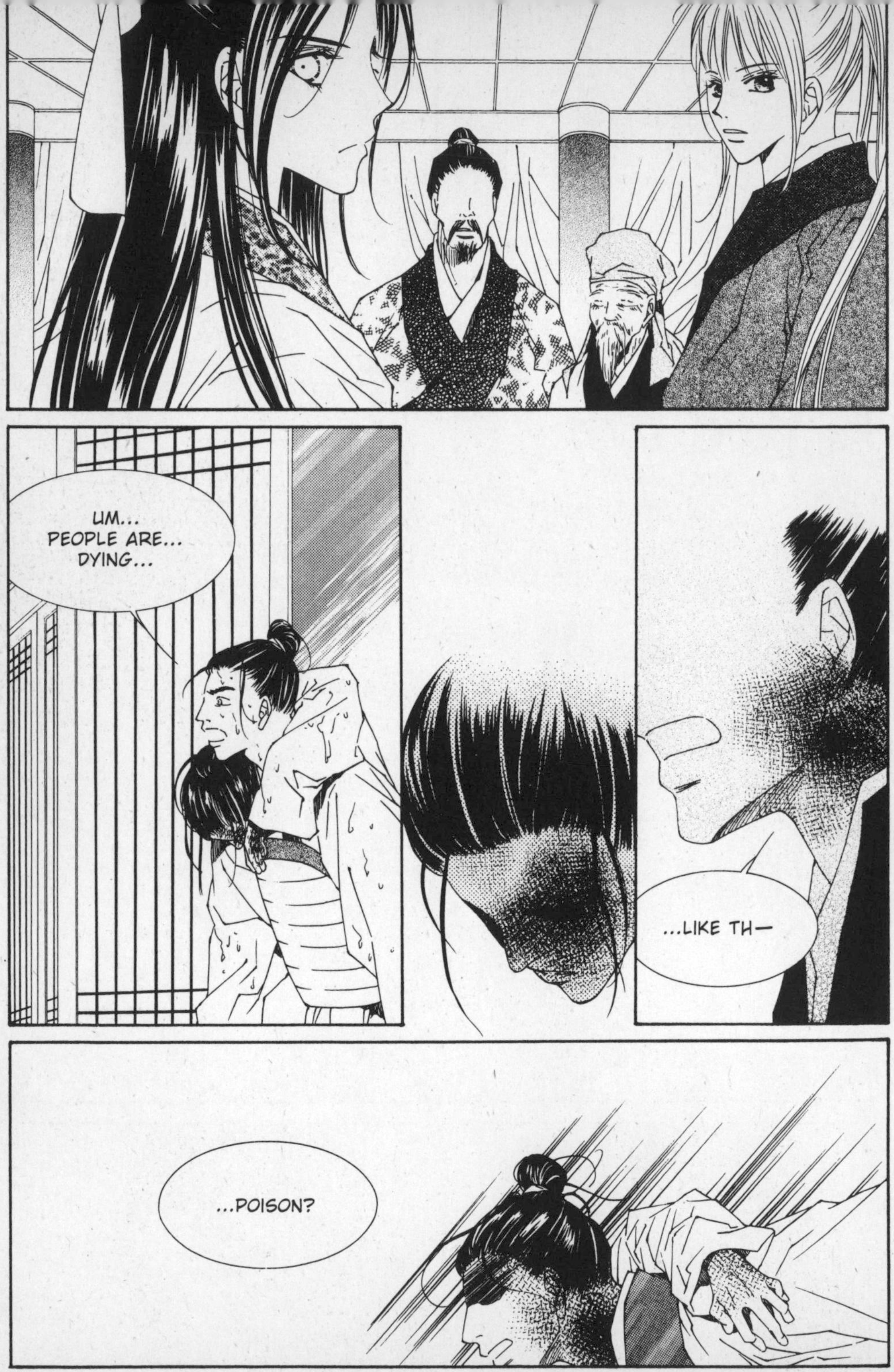
UM... PEOPLE ARE... DYING...
...LIKE TH—
...POISON?

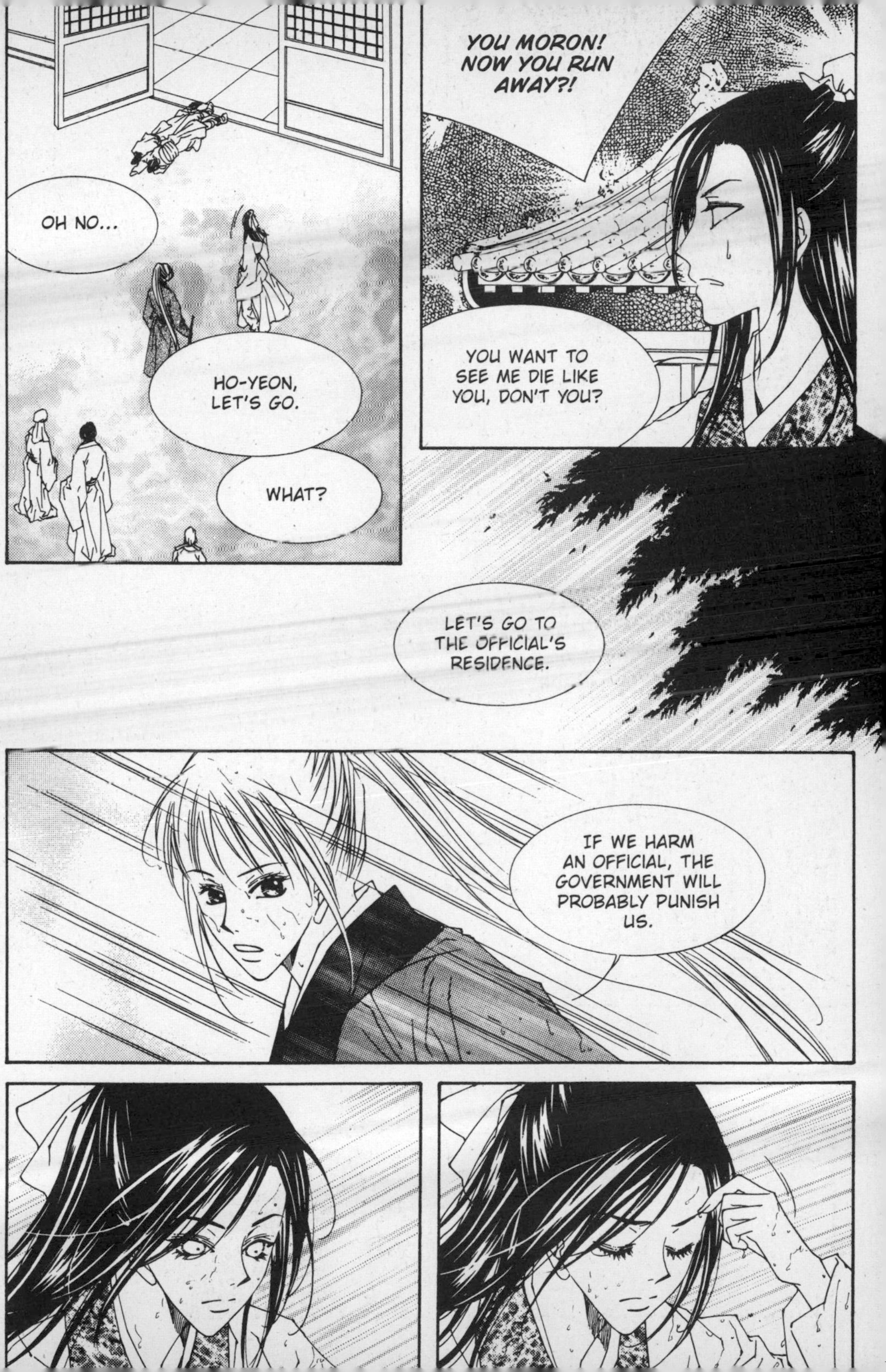
YOU MORON! NOW YOU RUN AWAY?!
YOU WANT TO SEE ME DIE LIKE YOU, DON'T YOU?
OH NO...
HO-YEON, LET'S GO.
WHAT?
LET'S GO TO THE OFFICIAL'S RESIDENCE.
IF WE HARM AN OFFICIAL, THE GOVERNMENT WILL PROBABLY PUNISH US.

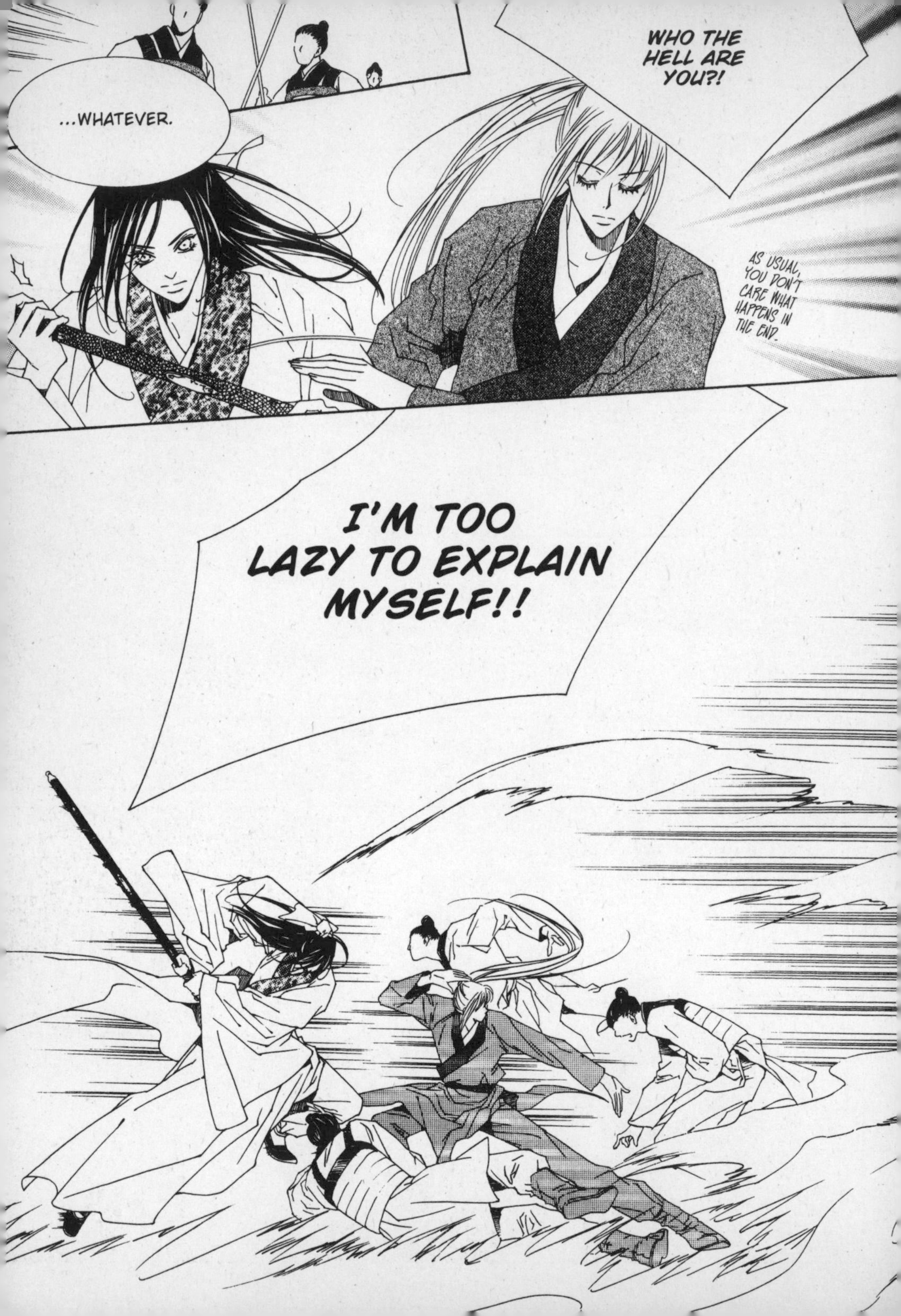
WHO THE HELL ARE YOU?!
...WHATEVER.
AS USUAL, YOU DON'T CARE WHAT HAPPENS IN THE END.
I'M TOO LAZY TO EXPLAIN MYSELF!!

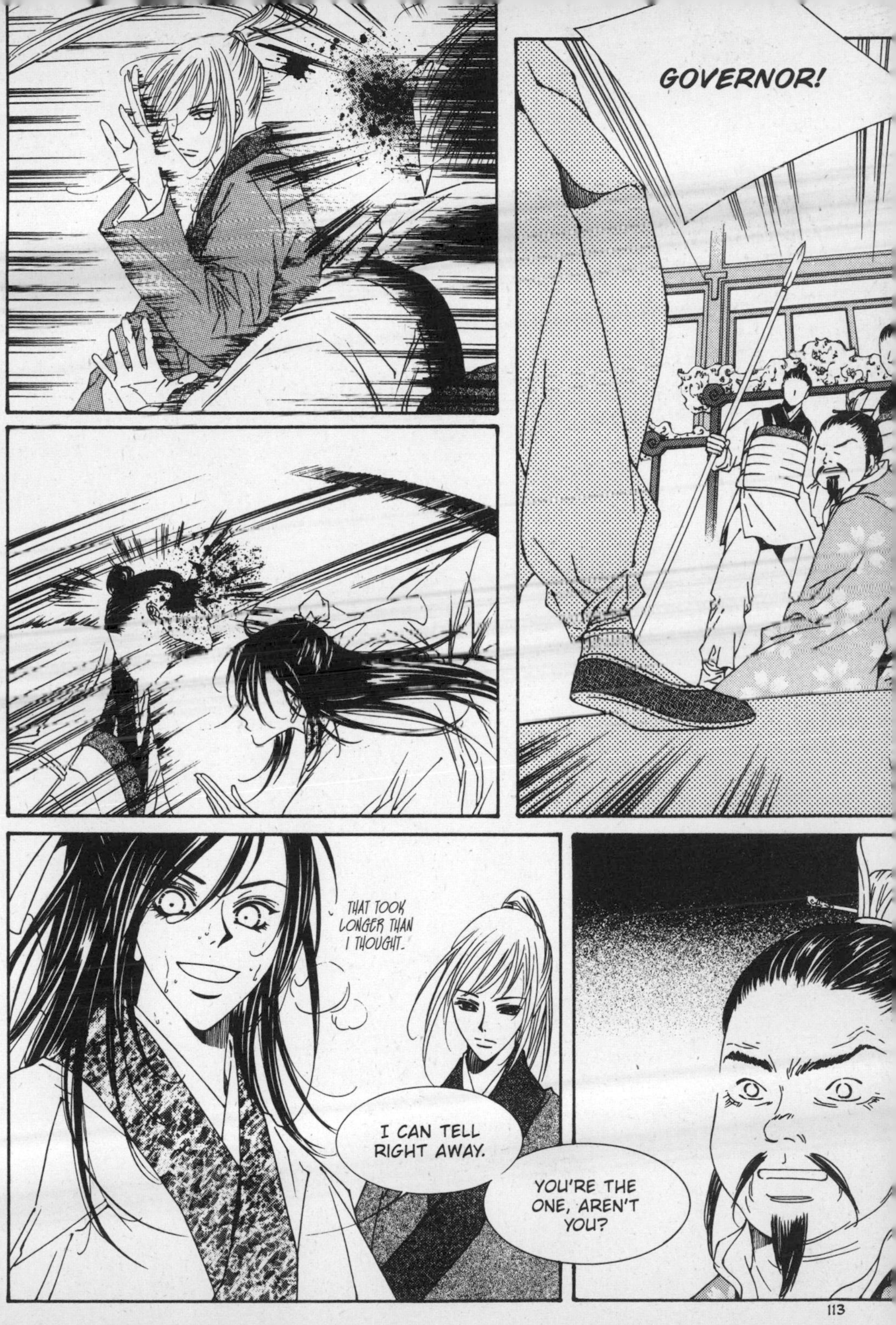

GOVERNOR!
THAT TOOK LONGER THAN I THOUGHT.
YOU'RE THE ONE, AREN'T YOU?
I CAN TELL RIGHT AWAY.

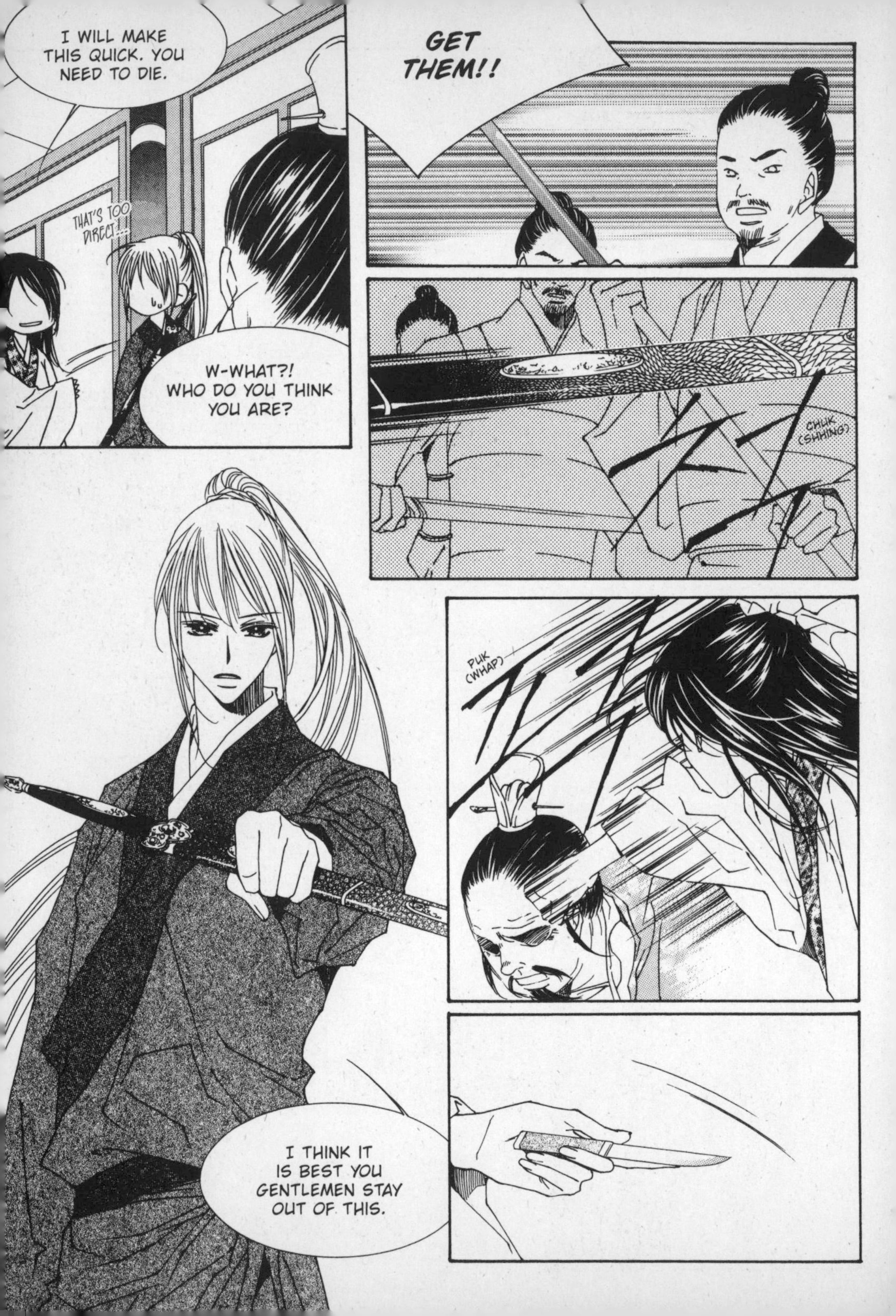
I WILL MAKE THIS QUICK. YOU NEED TO DIE.
THAT'S TOO DIRECT!...
W-WHAT?! WHO DO YOU THINK YOU ARE?
GET THEM!!
CHUK (SHHING)
PUK (WHAP)
I THINK IT IS BEST YOU GENTLEMEN STAY OUT OF THIS.

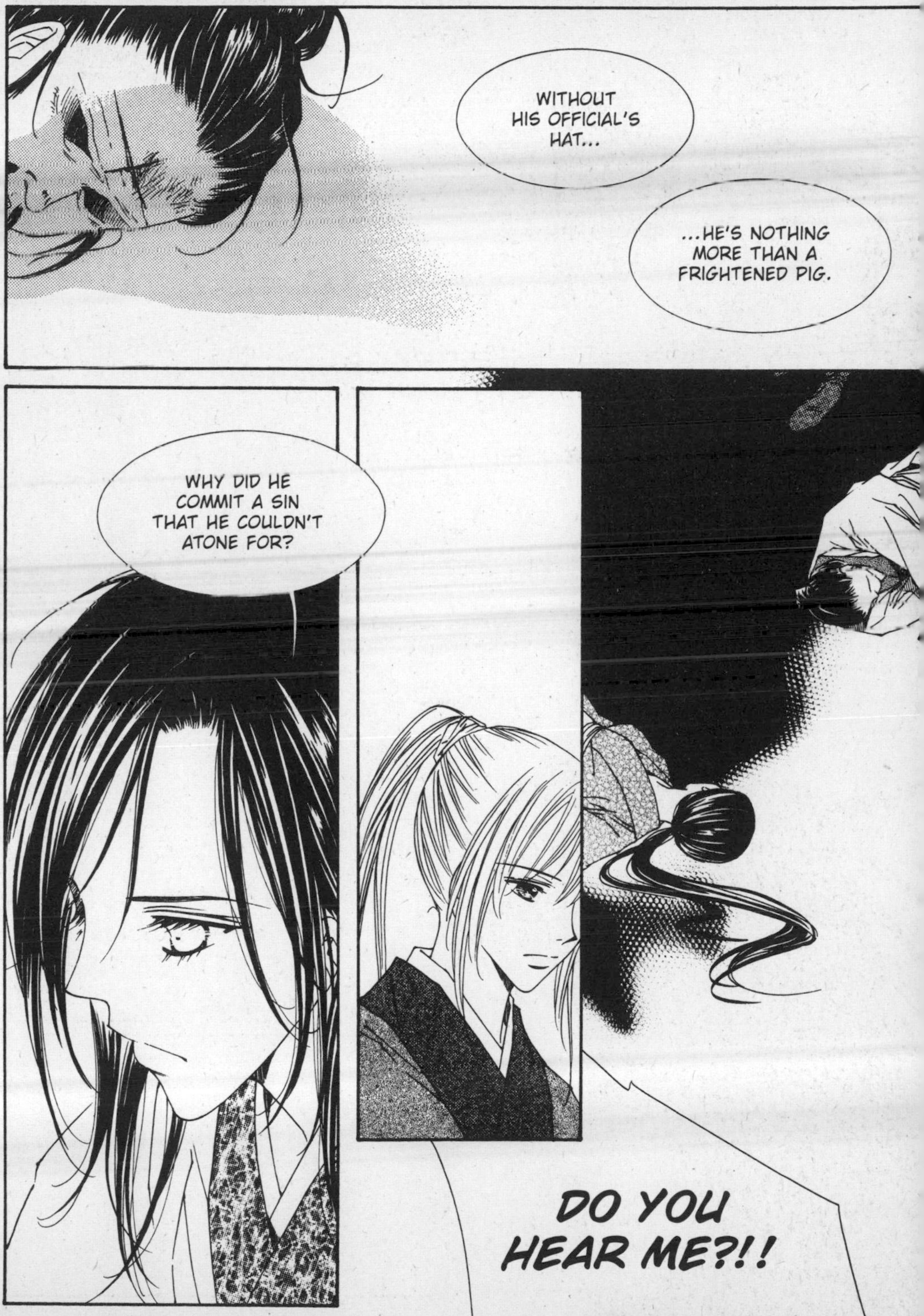
WITHOUT HIS OFFICIAL'S HAT...
...HE'S NOTHING MORE THAN A FRIGHTENED PIG.
WHY DID HE COMMIT A SIN THAT HE COULDN'T ATONE FOR?
DO YOU HEAR ME?!!

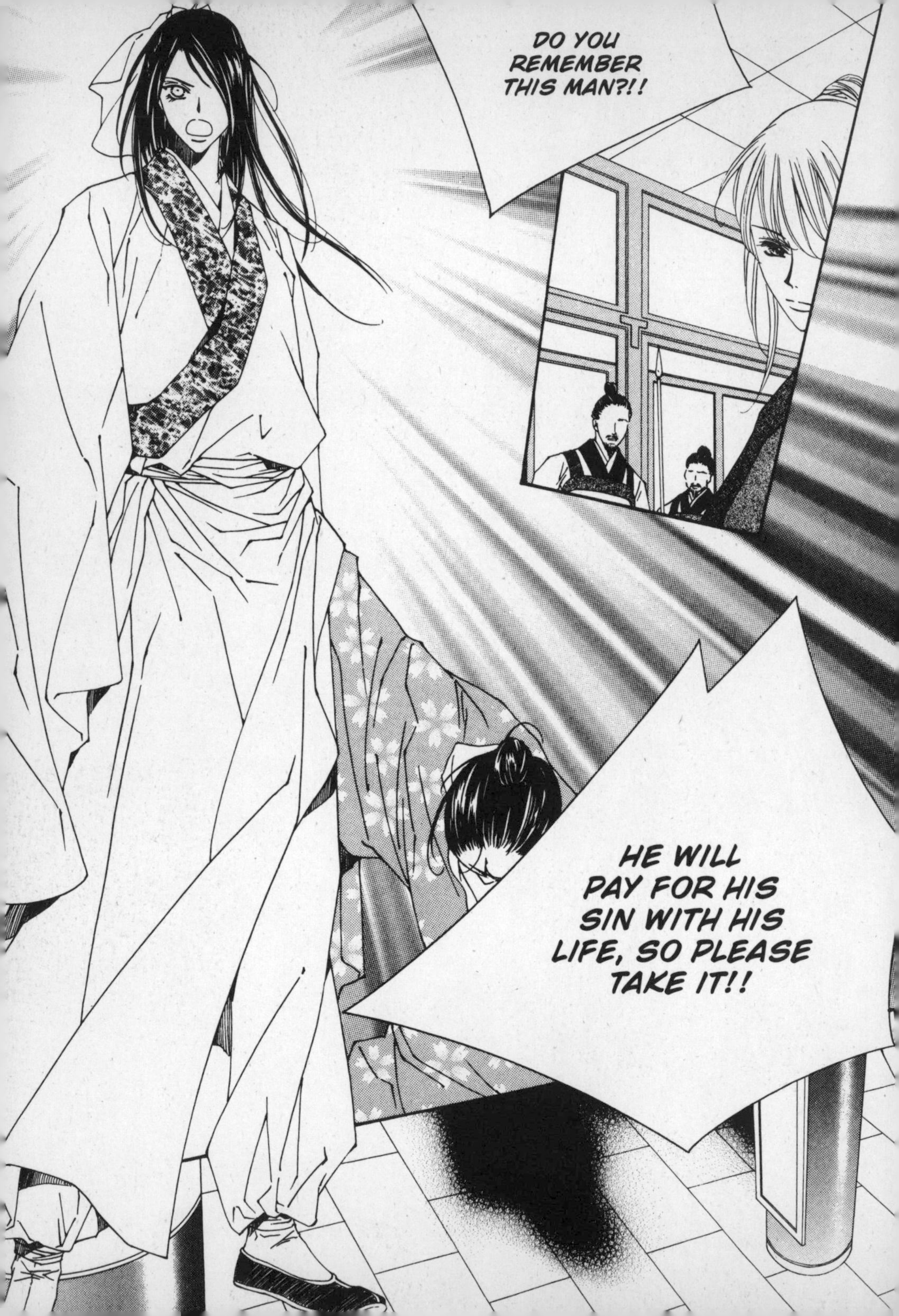
DO YOU REMEMBER THIS MAN?!!
HE WILL PAY FOR HIS SIN WITH HIS LIFE, SO PLEASE TAKE IT!!

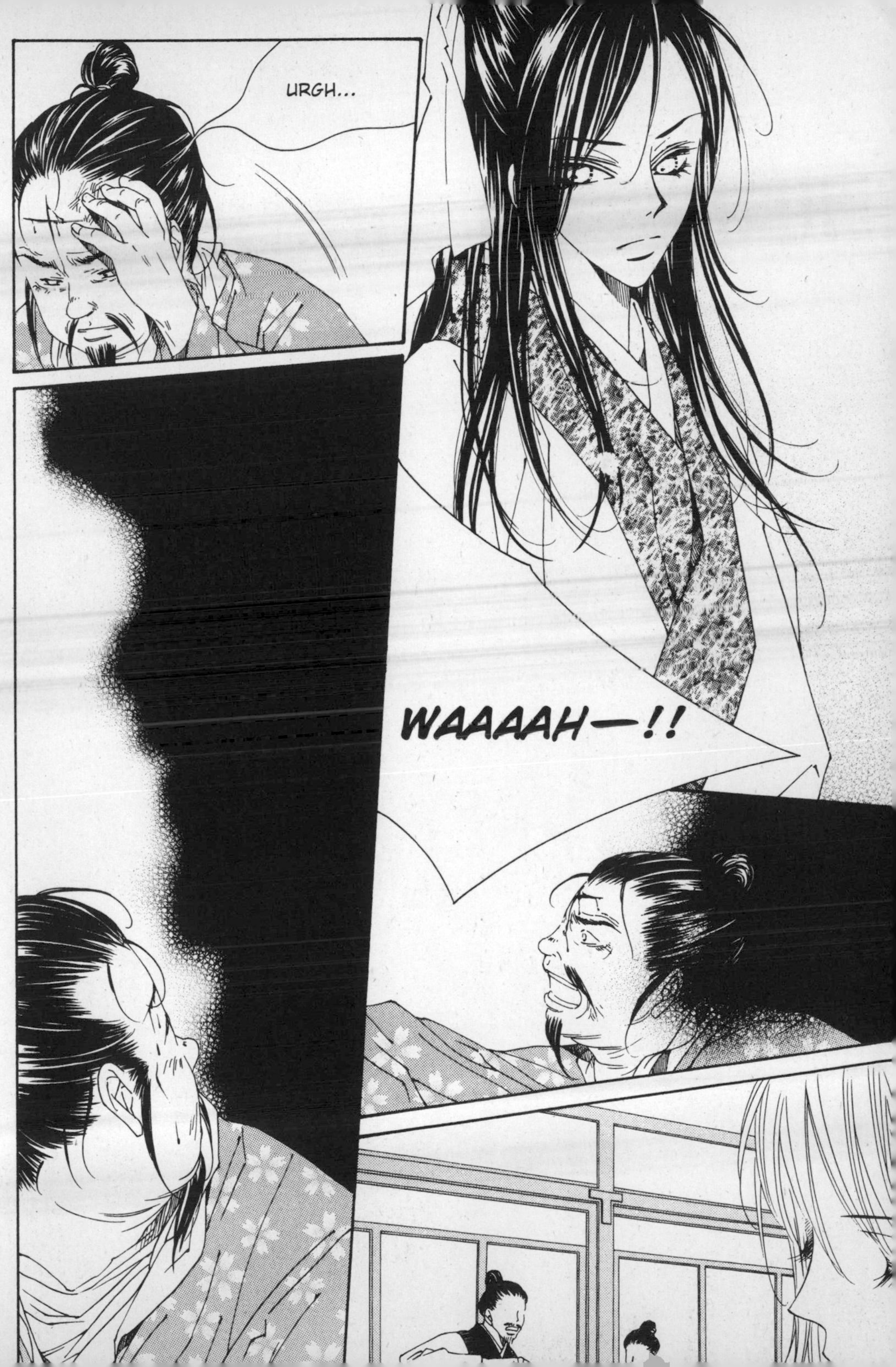
URGH...
WAAAAH—!!

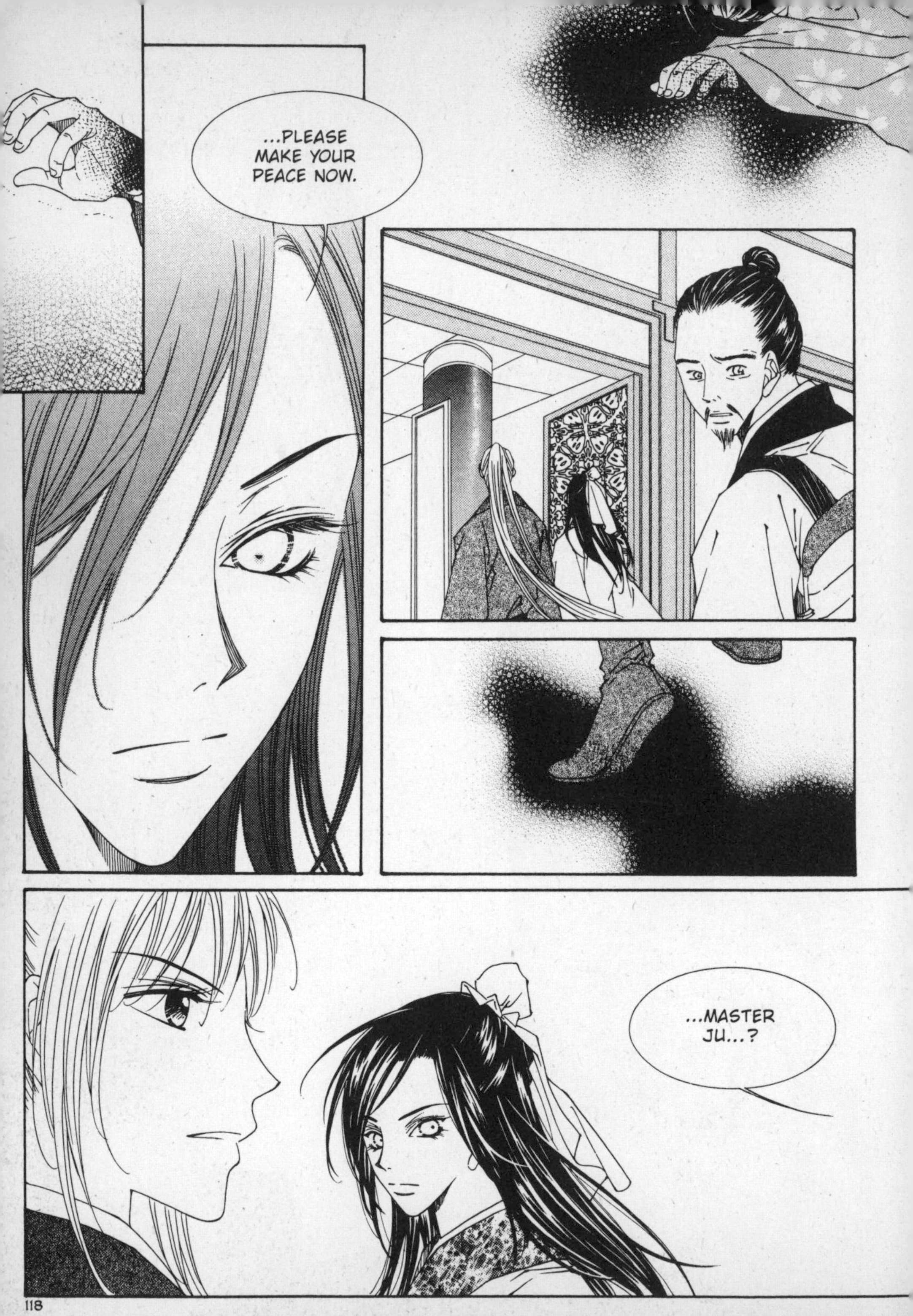
...PLEASE MAKE YOUR PEACE NOW.
...MASTER JU...?

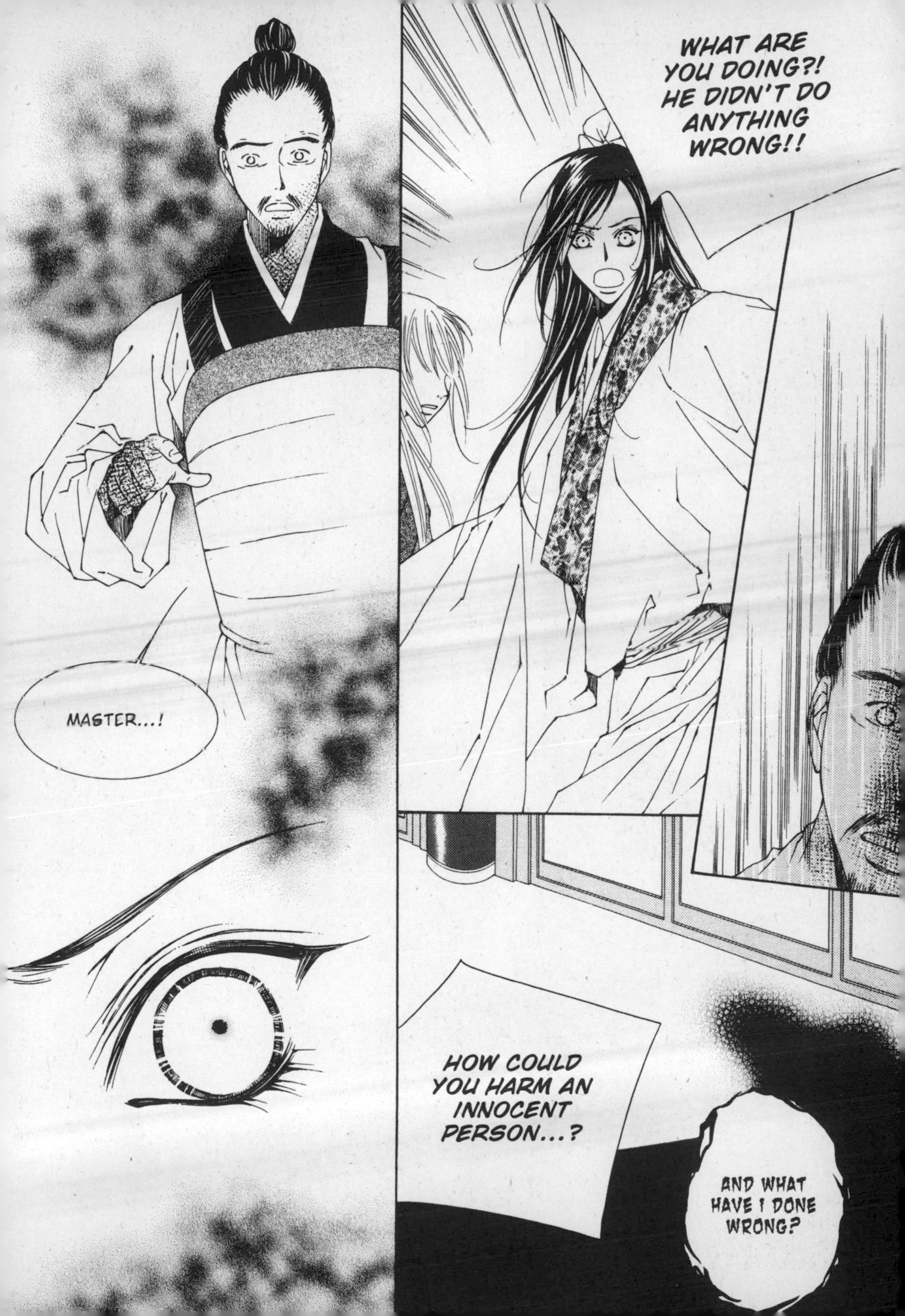
WHAT ARE YOU DOING?! HE DIDN'T DO ANYTHING WRONG!!
MASTER...!
HOW COULD YOU HARM AN INNOCENT PERSON...?
AND WHAT HAVE I DONE WRONG?

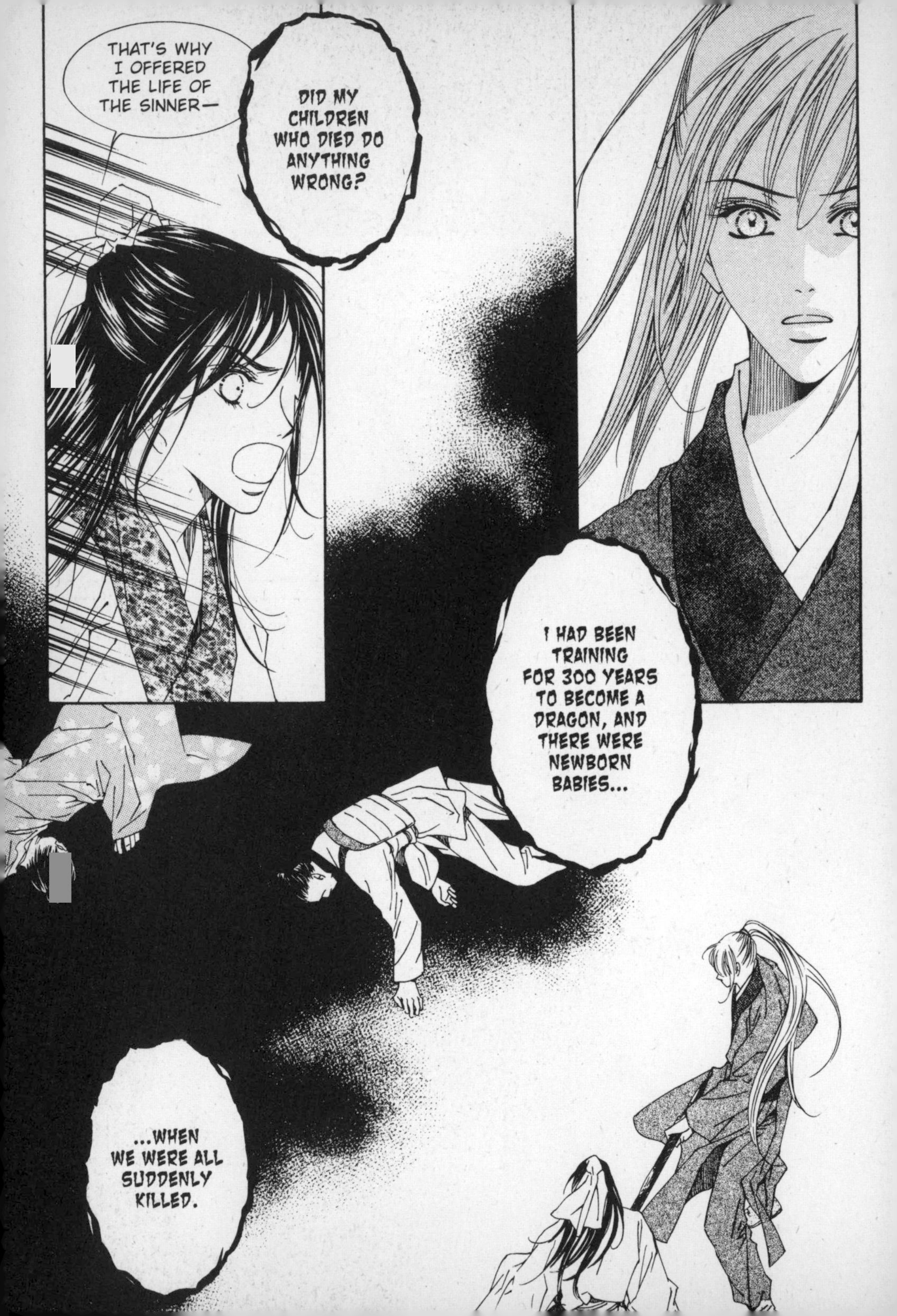
THAT'S WHY I OFFERED THE LIFE OF THE SINNER—
DID MY CHILDREN WHO DIED DO ANYTHING WRONG?
I HAD BEEN TRAINING FOR 300 YEARS TO BECOME A DRAGON, AND THERE WERE NEWBORN BABIES...
...WHEN WE WERE ALL SUDDENLY KILLED.

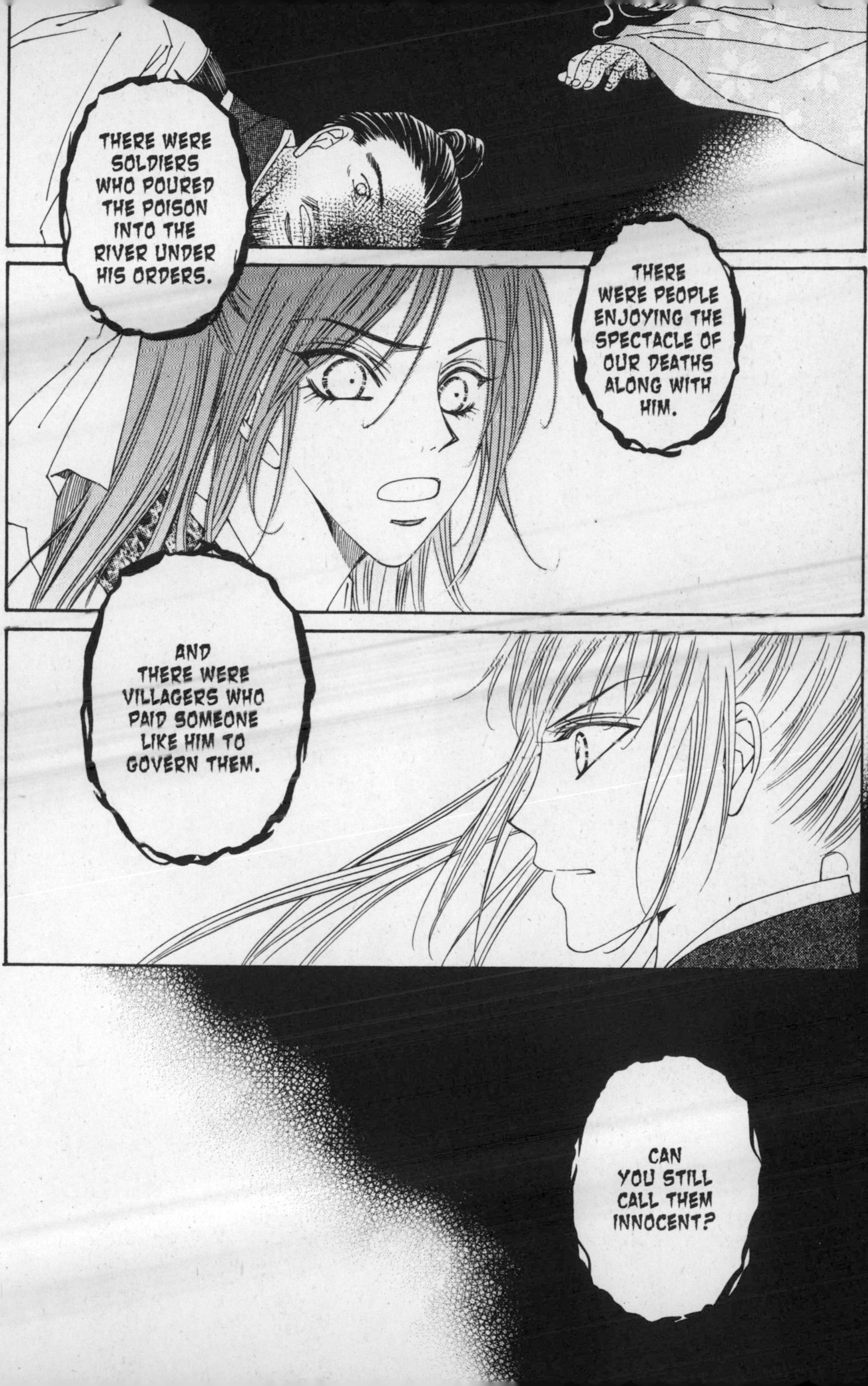
THERE WERE SOLDIERS WHO POURED THE POISON INTO THE RIVER UNDER HIS ORDERS.
THERE WERE PEOPLE ENJOYING THE SPECTACLE OF OUR DEATHS ALONG WITH HIM.
AND THERE WERE VILLAGERS WHO PAID SOMEONE LIKE HIM TO GOVERN THEM.
CAN YOU STILL CALL THEM INNOCENT?

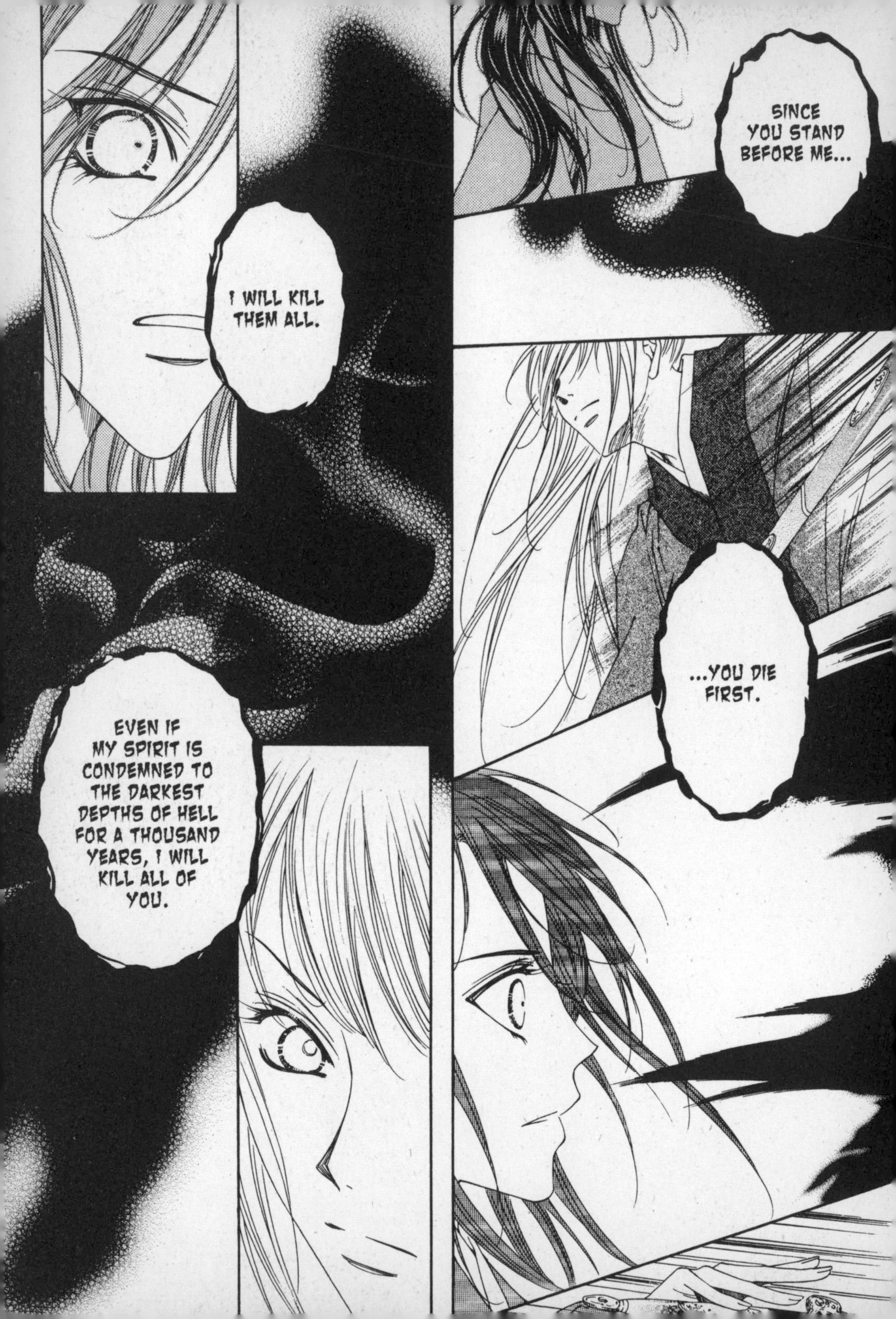
SINCE YOU STAND BEFORE ME...
...YOU DIE FIRST.
I WILL KILL THEM ALL.
EVEN IF MY SPIRIT IS CONDEMNED TO THE DARKEST DEPTHS OF HELL FOR A THOUSAND YEARS, I WILL KILL ALL OF YOU.

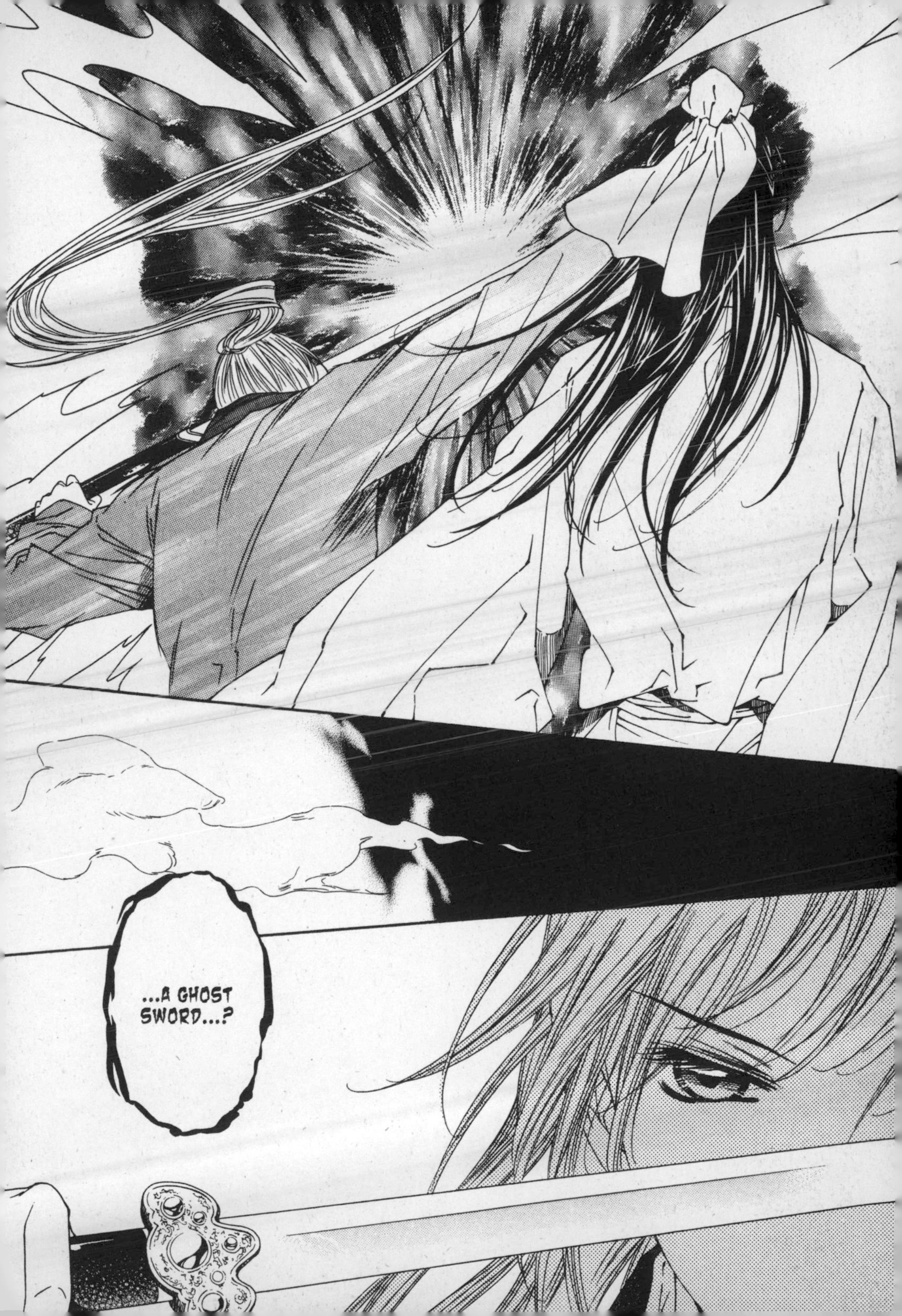
...A GHOST SWORD...?

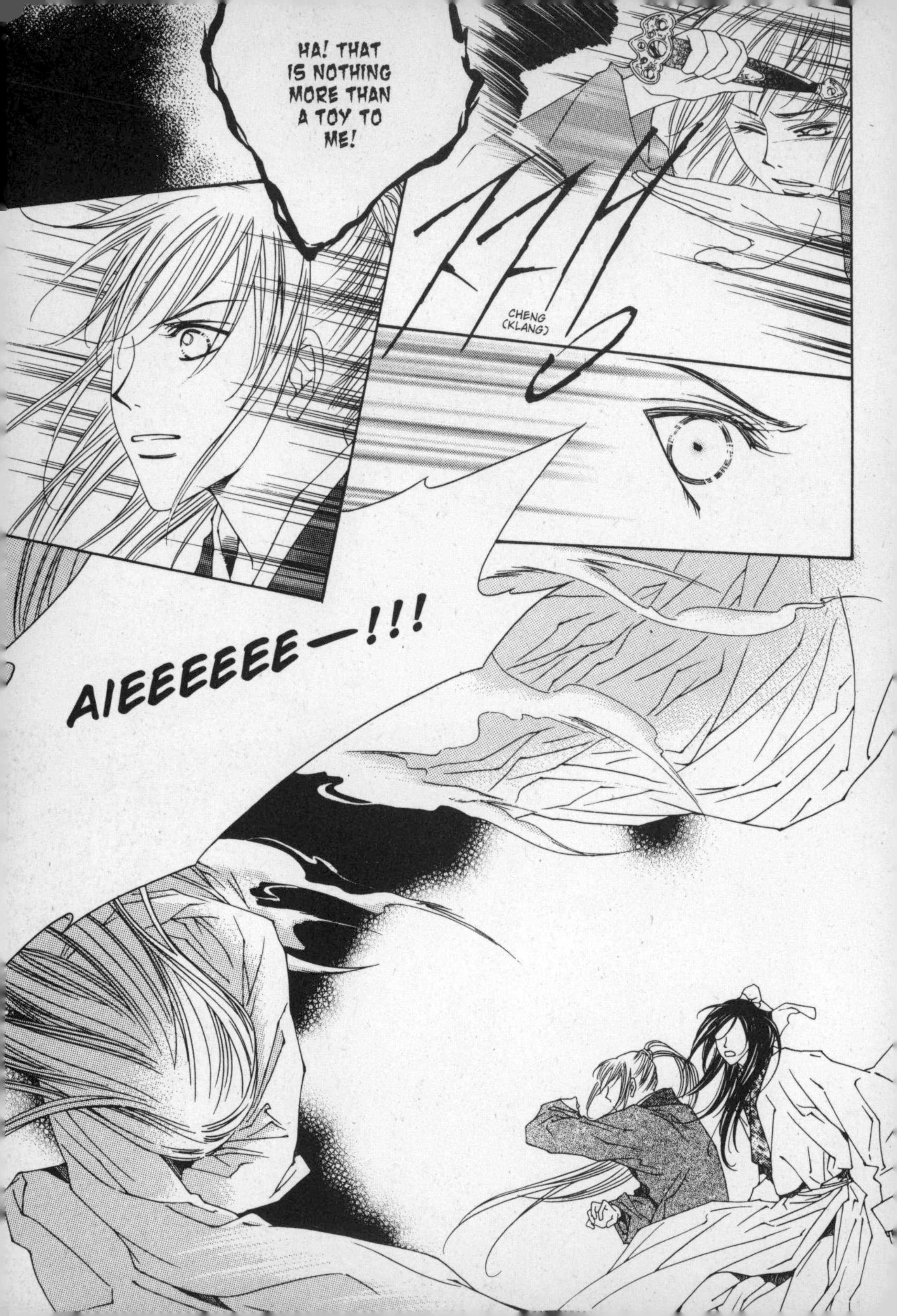
HA! THAT IS NOTHING MORE THAN A TOY TO ME!
CHENG (KLANG)
AIEEEEEEE—!!!

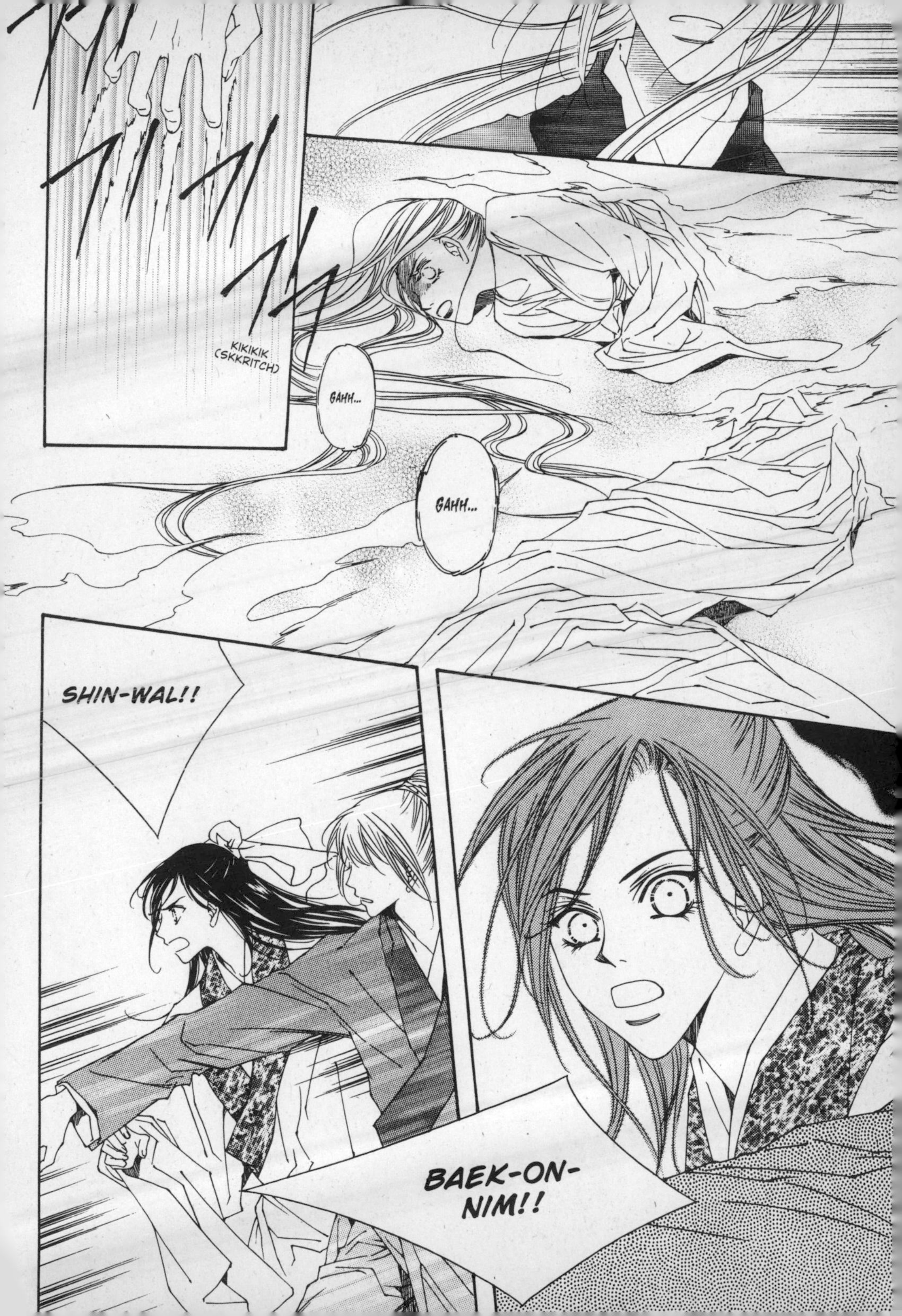
KIKIKIK (SKKRITCH)
GAHH...
GAHH...
SHIN-WAL!!
BAEK-ON-NIM!!

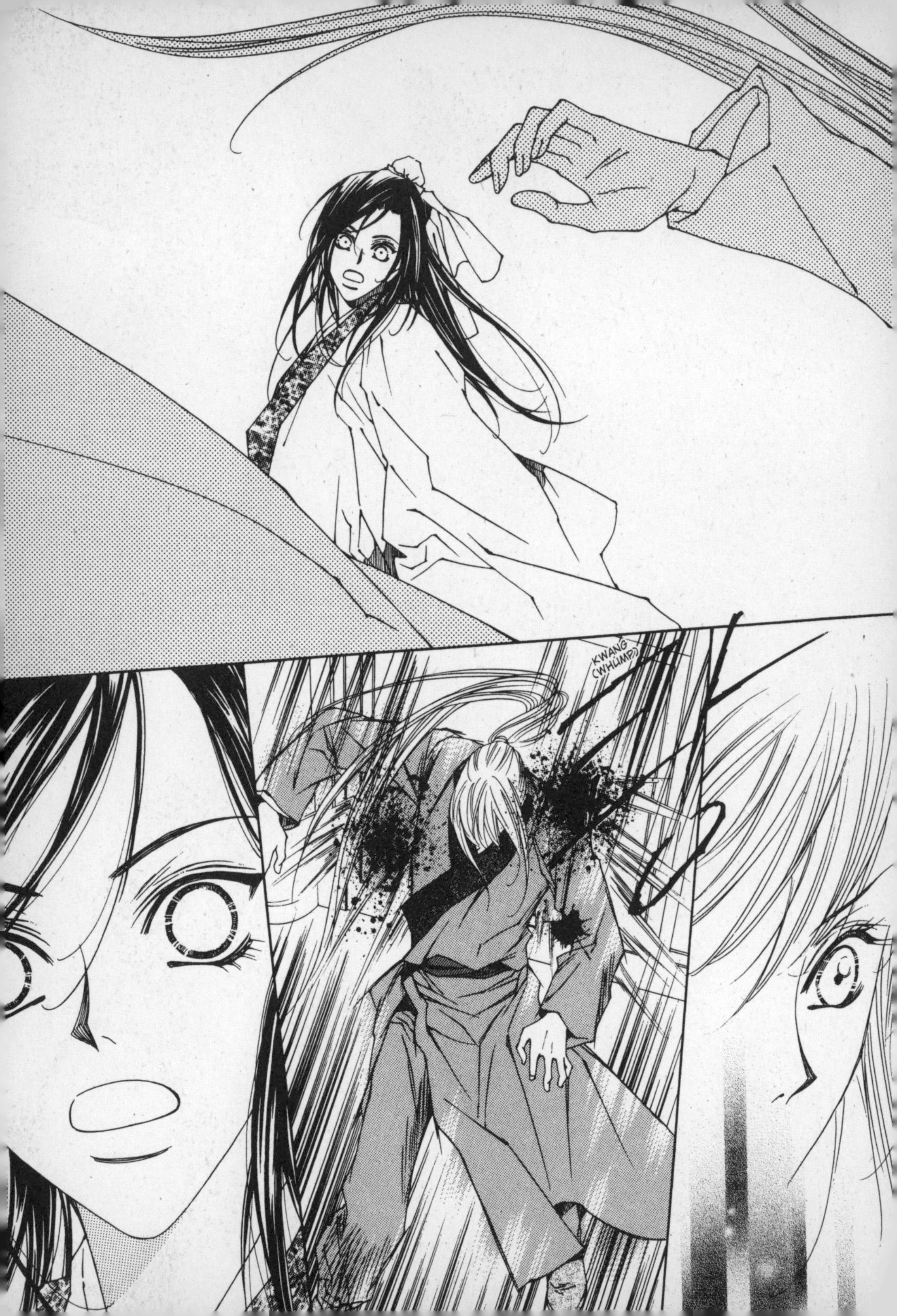
KWANG
(WHUMP)

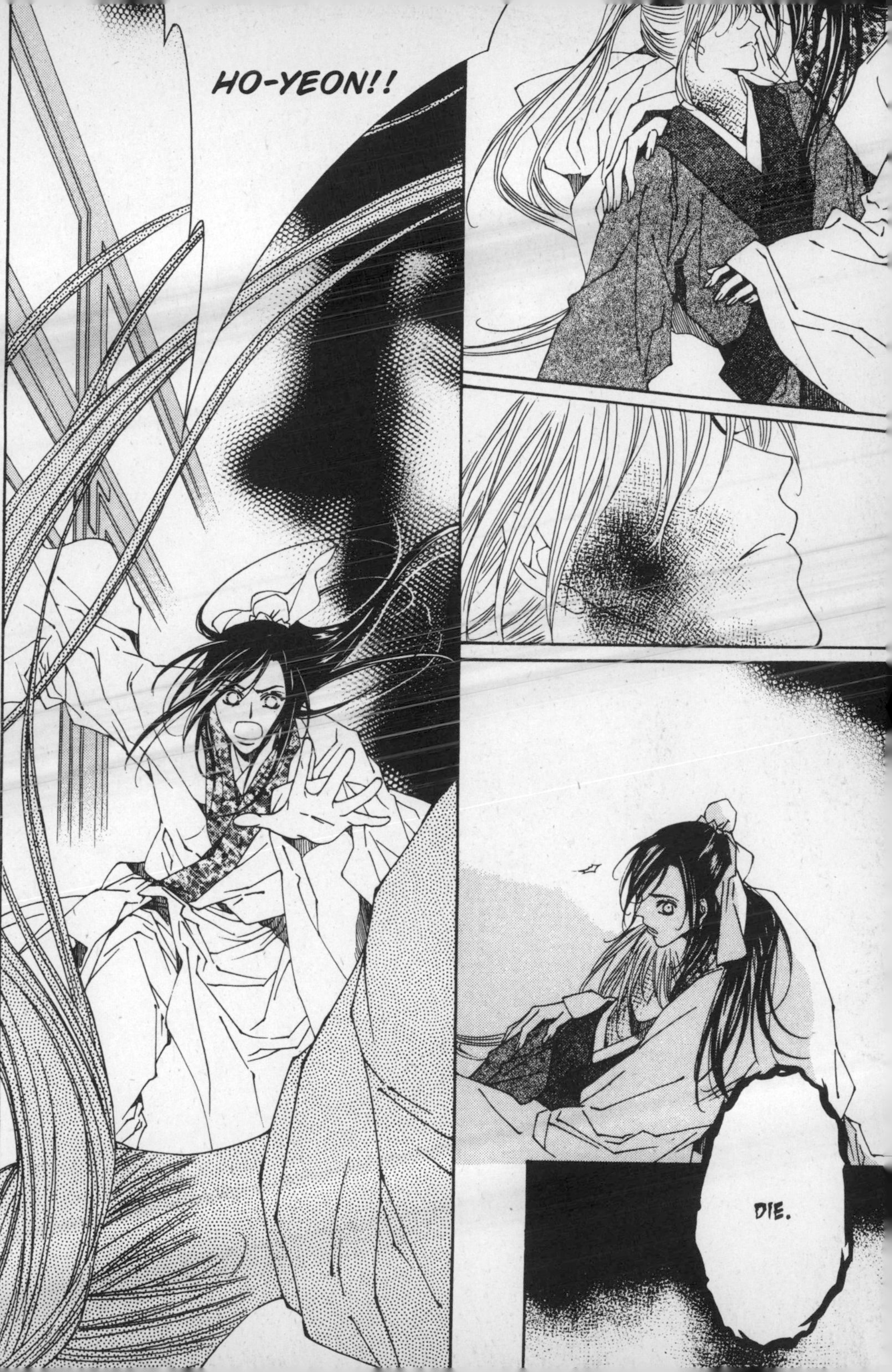
HO-YEON!!
DIE.

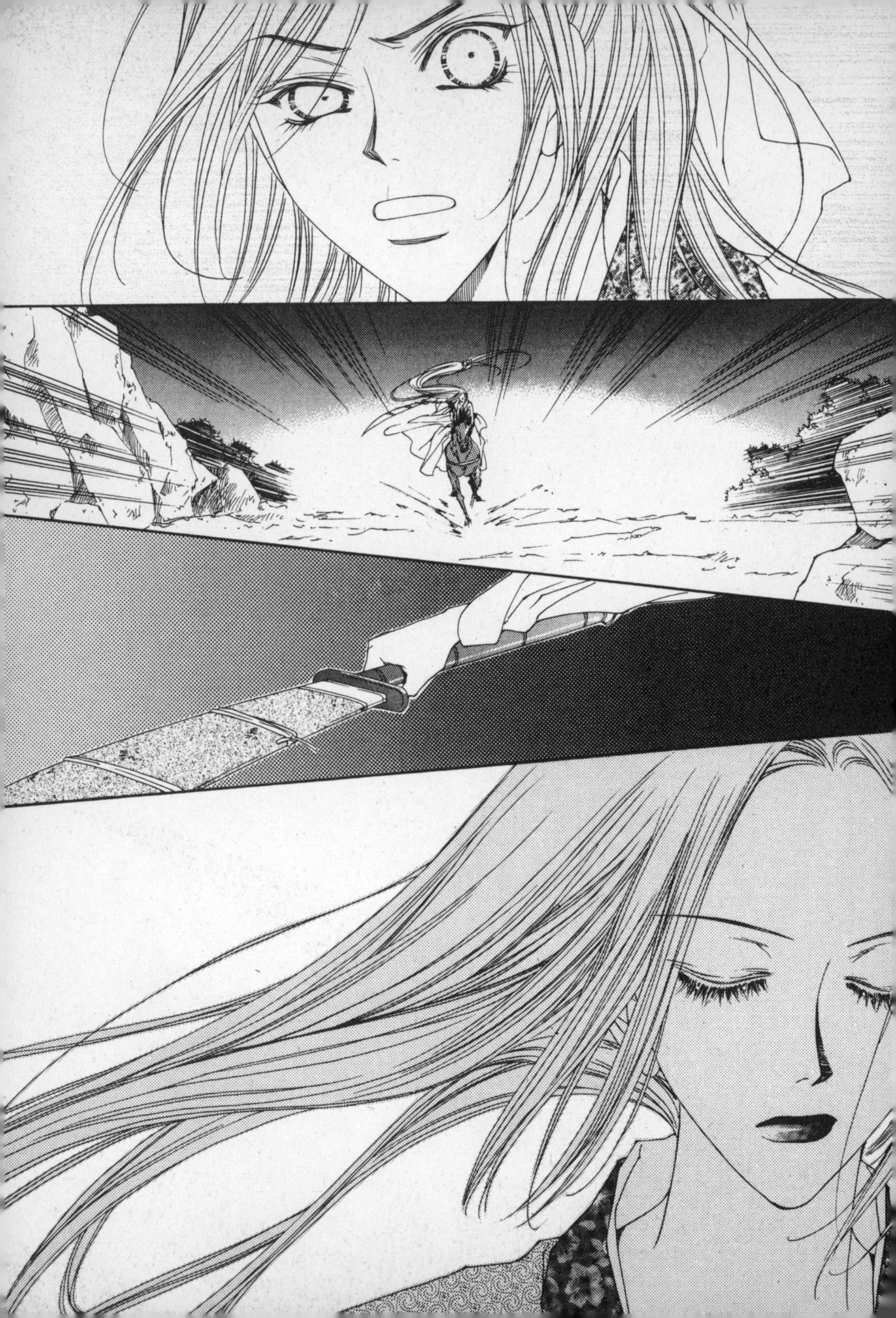

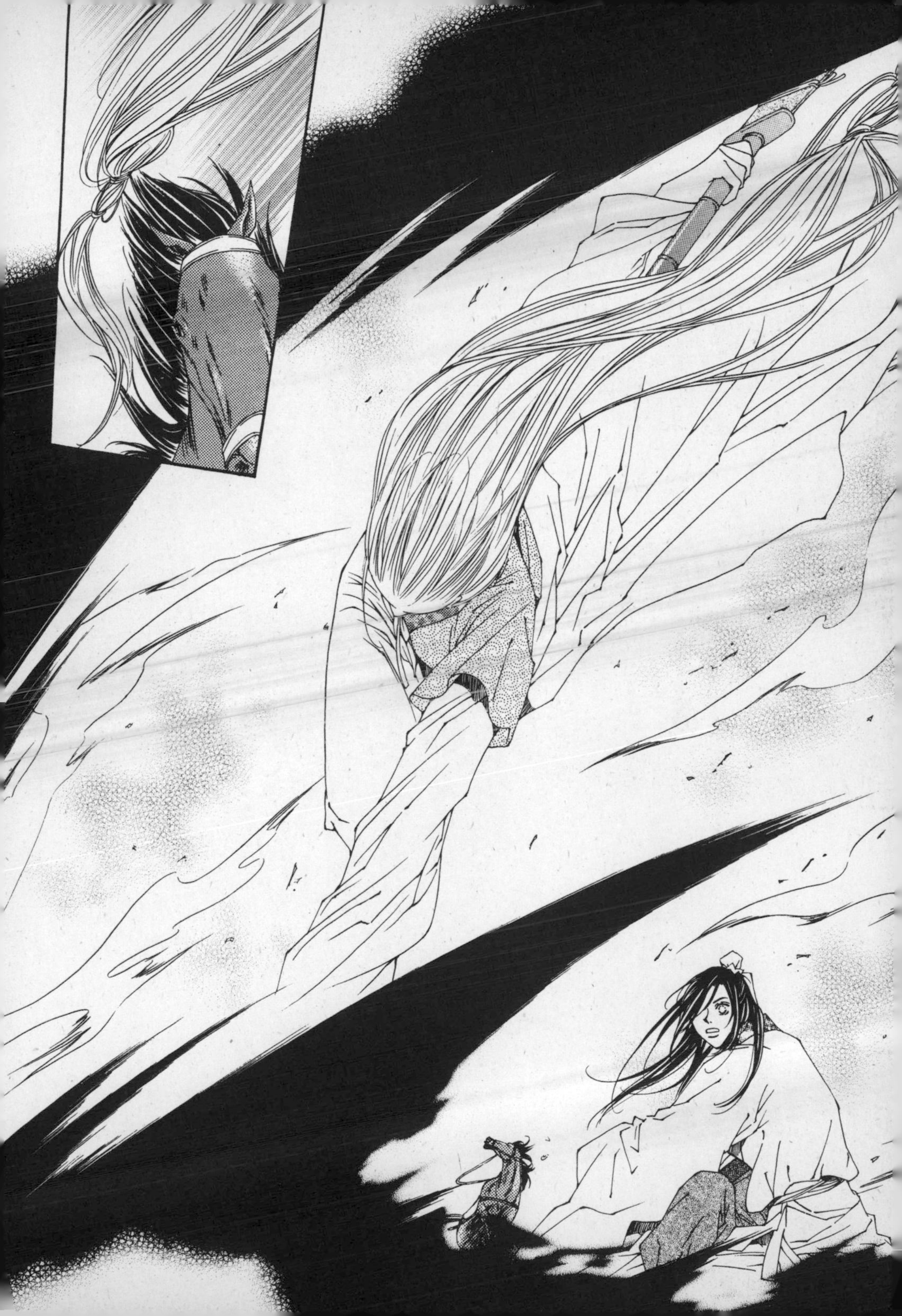

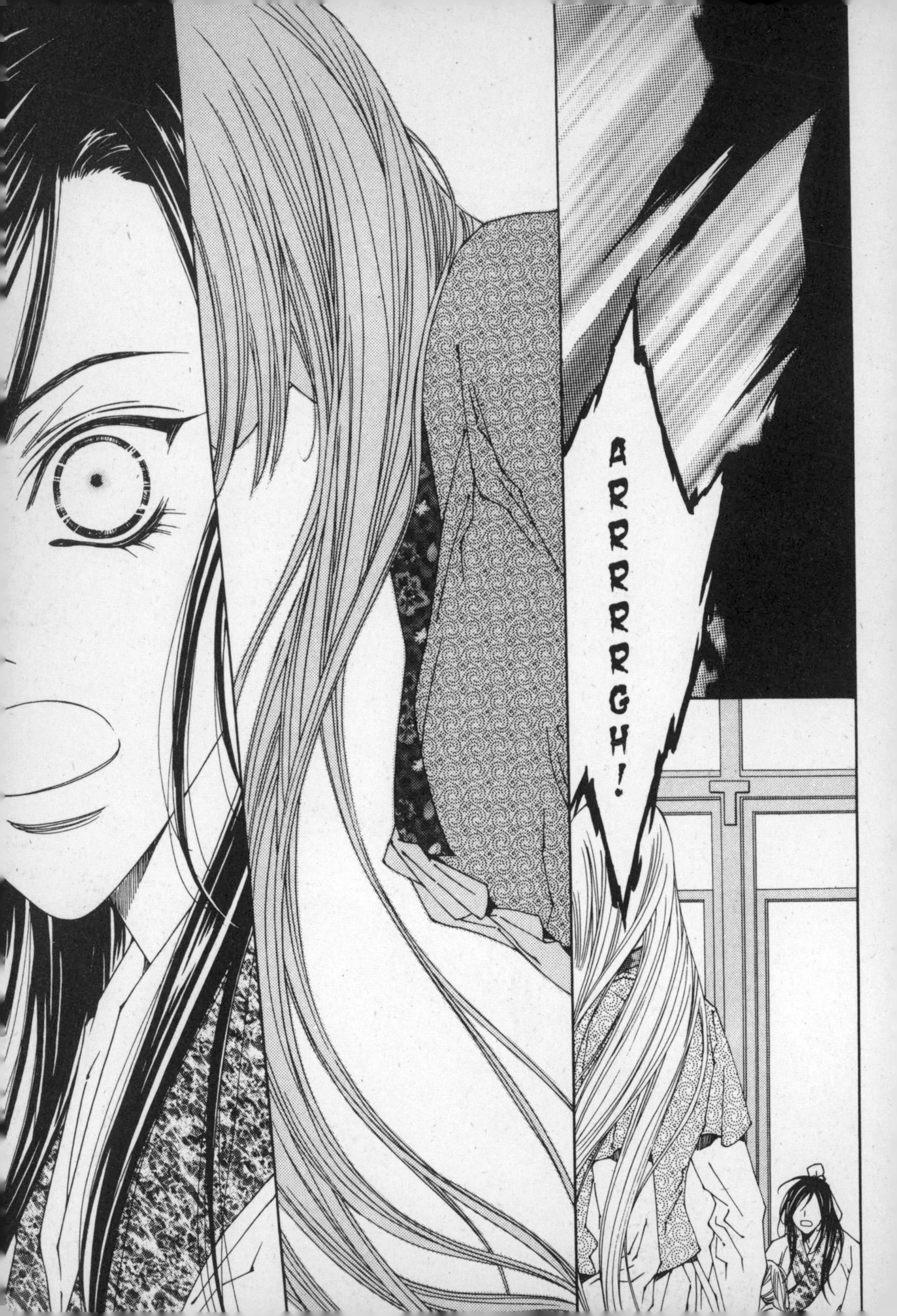
ARRRRRGH!

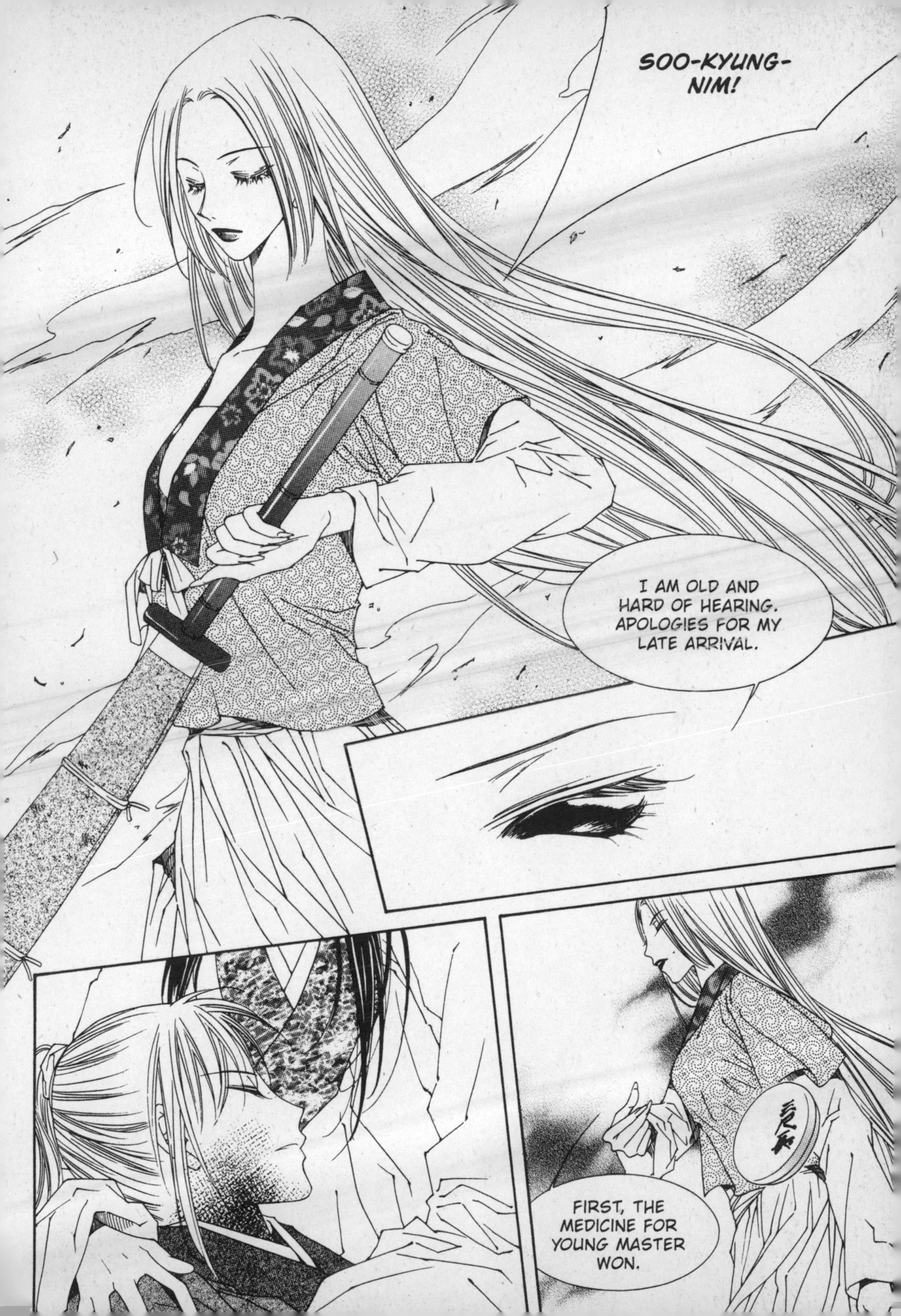
SOO-KYUNG-NIM!
I AM OLD AND HARD OF HEARING. APOLOGIES FOR MY LATE ARRIVAL.
FIRST, THE MEDICINE FOR YOUNG MASTER WON.

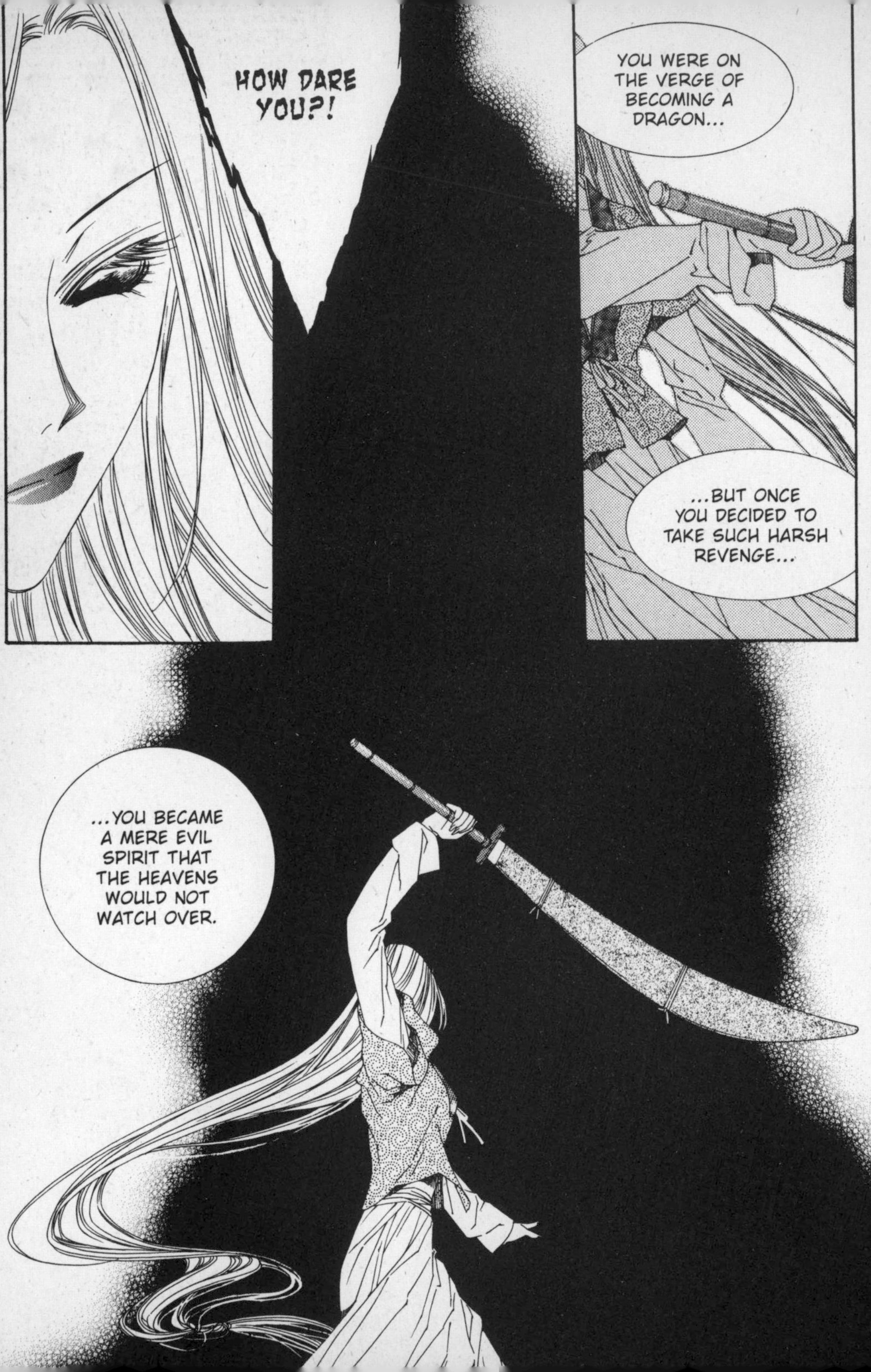
HOW DARE YOU?!
YOU WERE ON THE VERGE OF BECOMING A DRAGON...
...BUT ONCE YOU DECIDED TO TAKE SUCH HARSH REVENGE...
...YOU BECAME A MERE EVIL SPIRIT THAT THE HEAVENS WOULD NOT WATCH OVER.

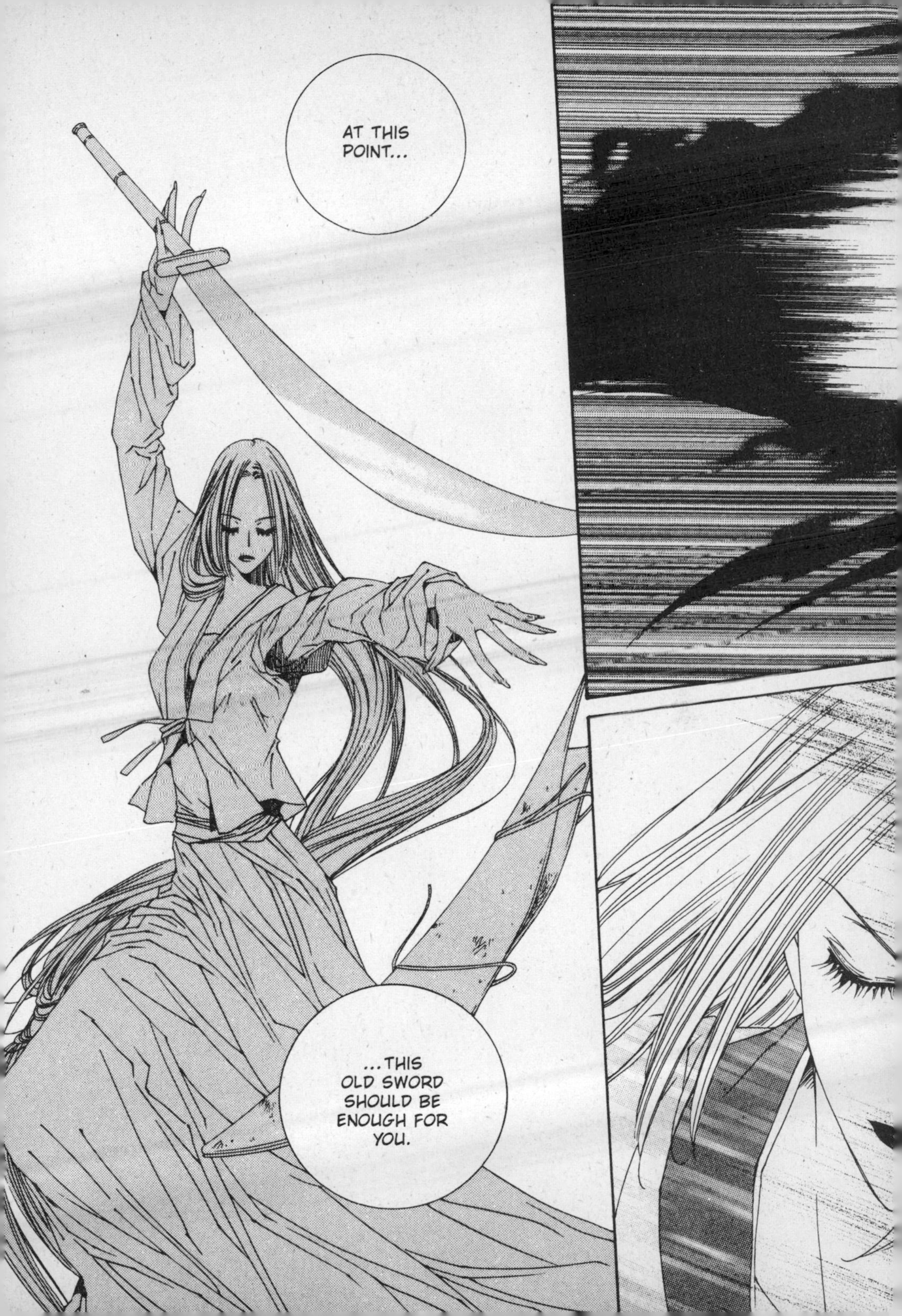
AT THIS POINT...
...THIS OLD SWORD SHOULD BE ENOUGH FOR YOU.

KYAAAAAAAA

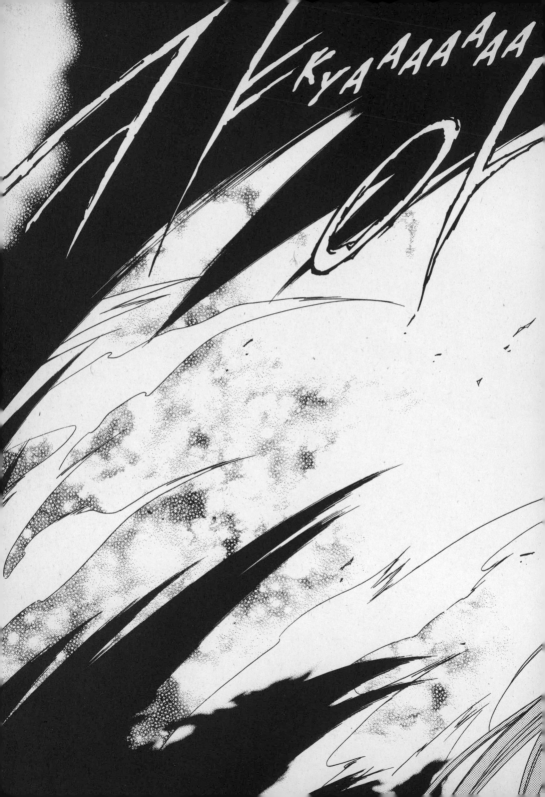

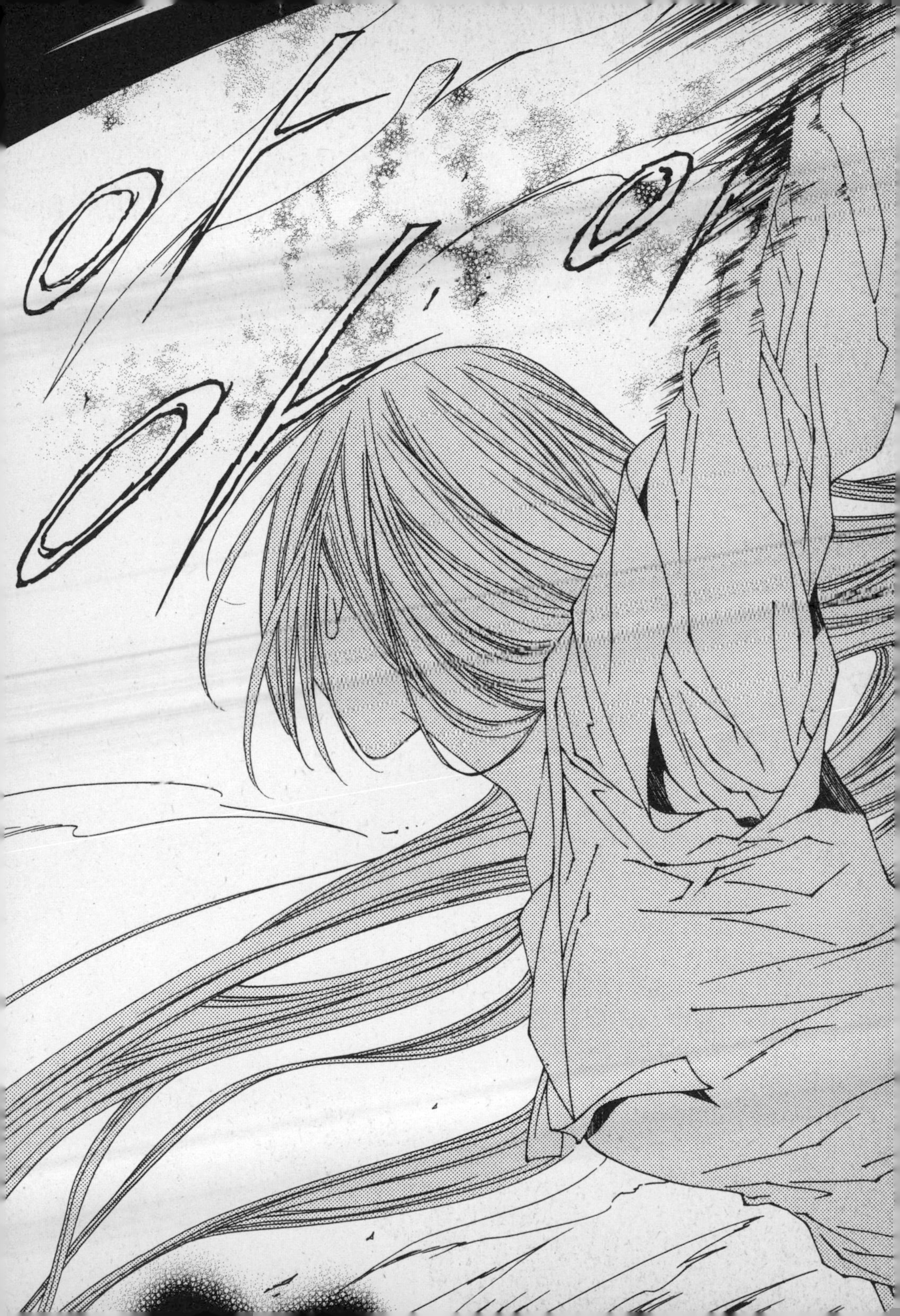

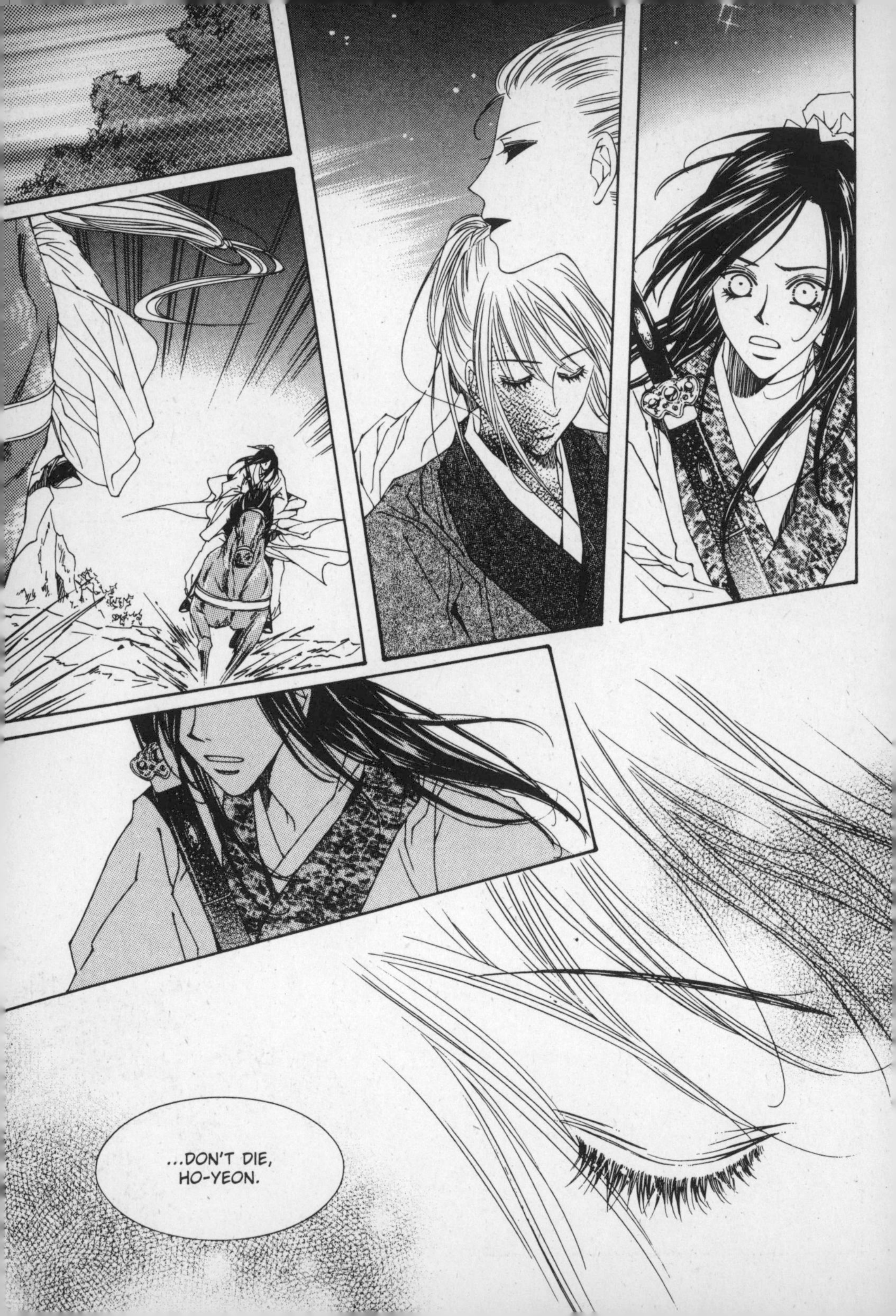
...DON'T DIE, HO-YEON.

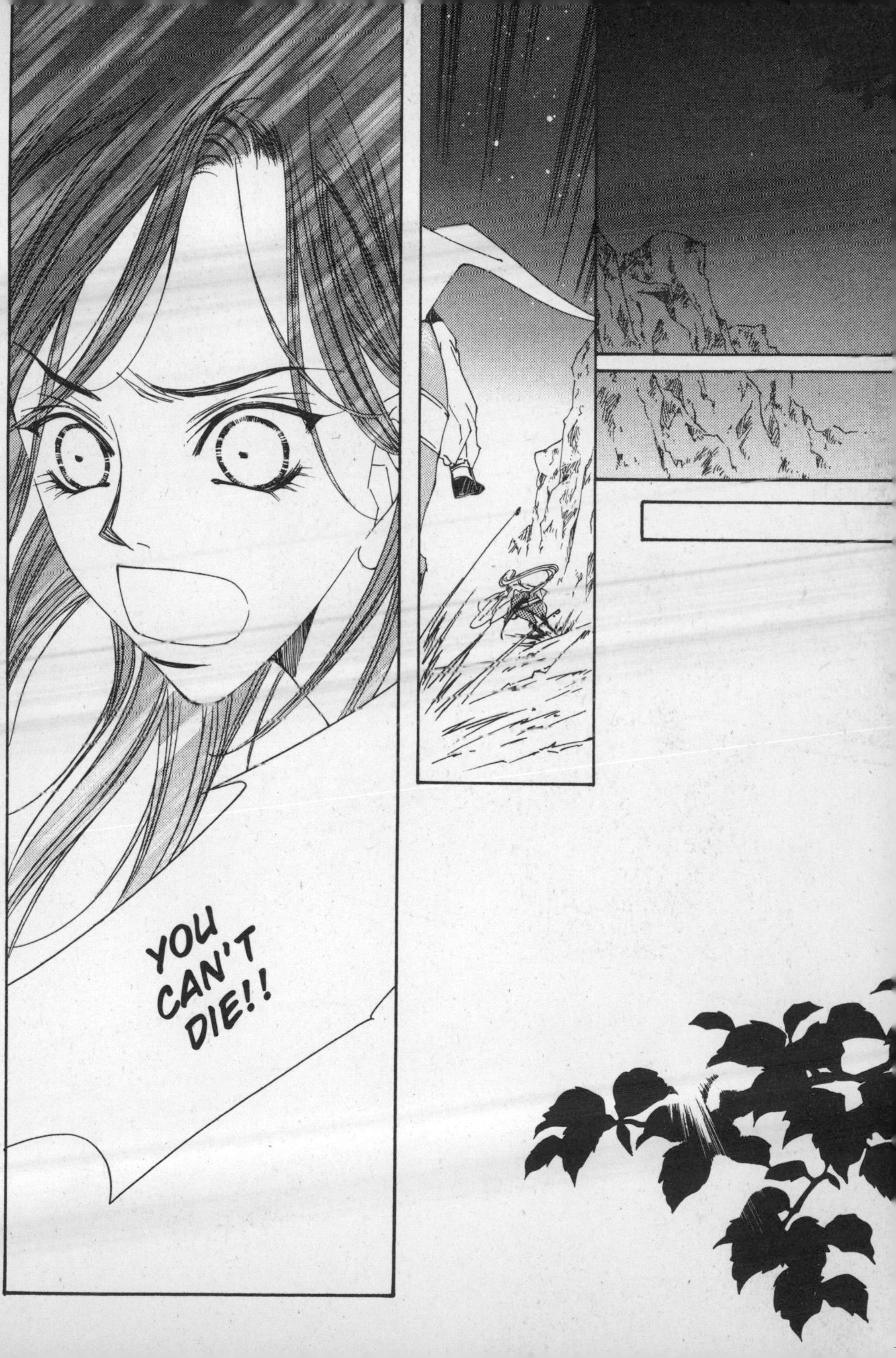
YOU CAN'T DIE!!

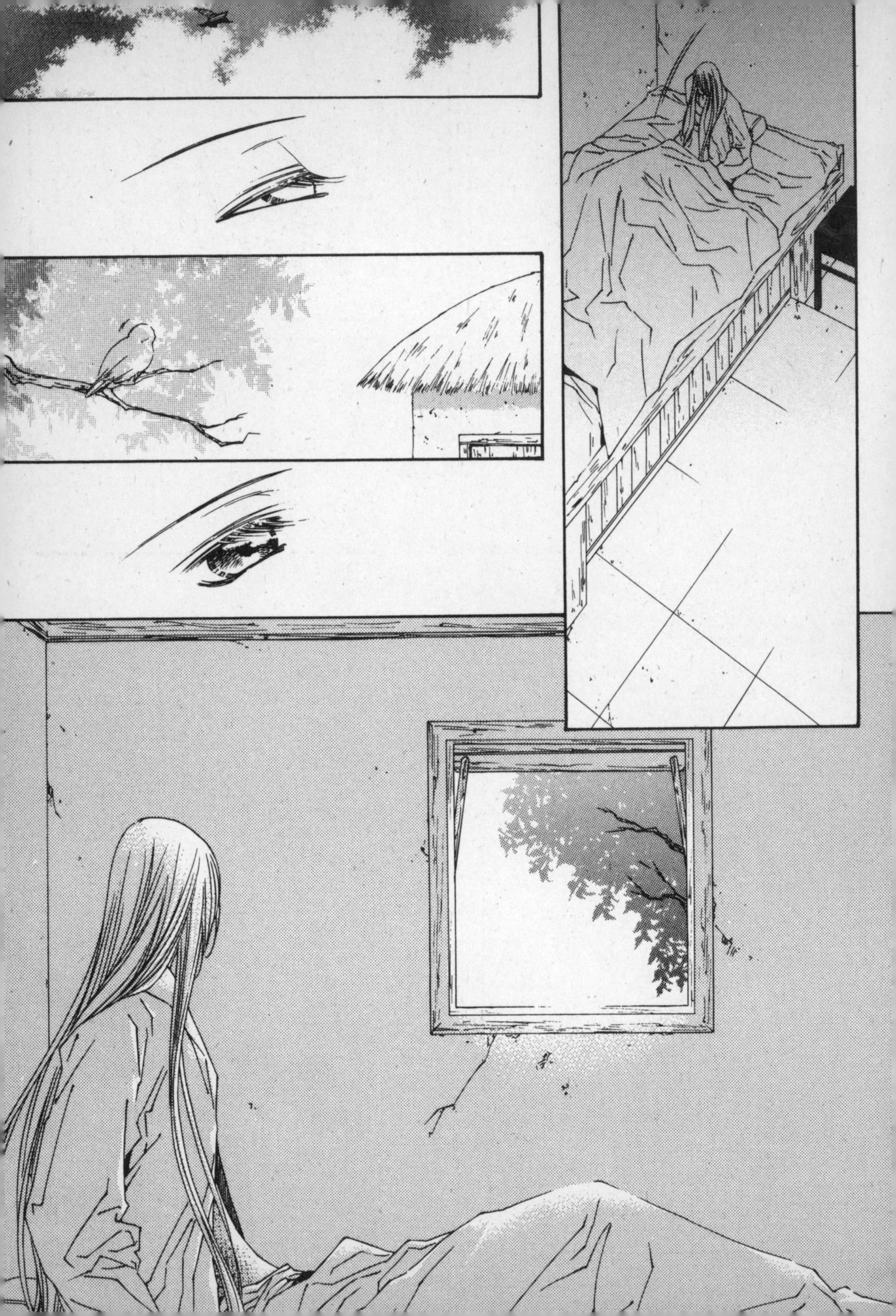

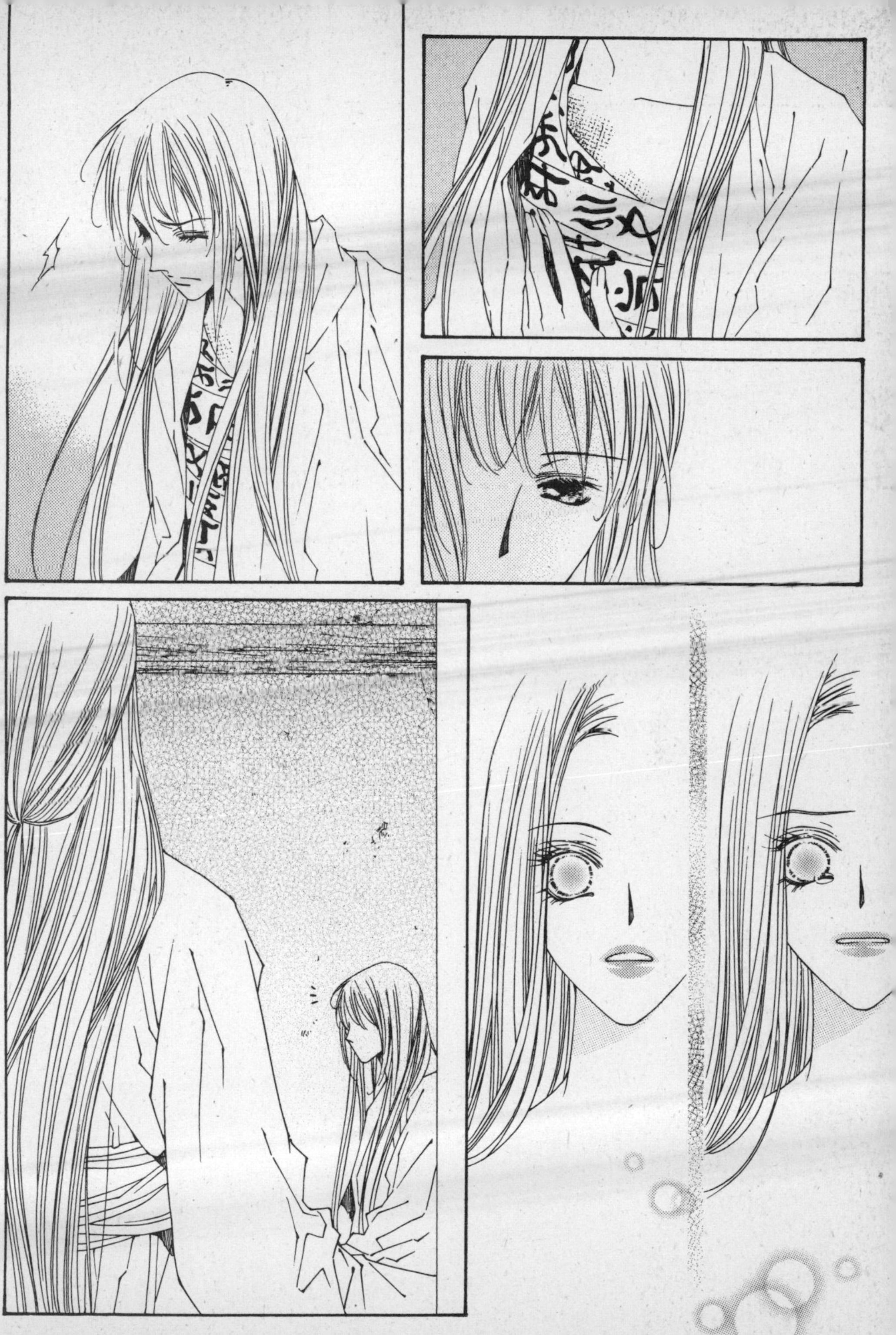

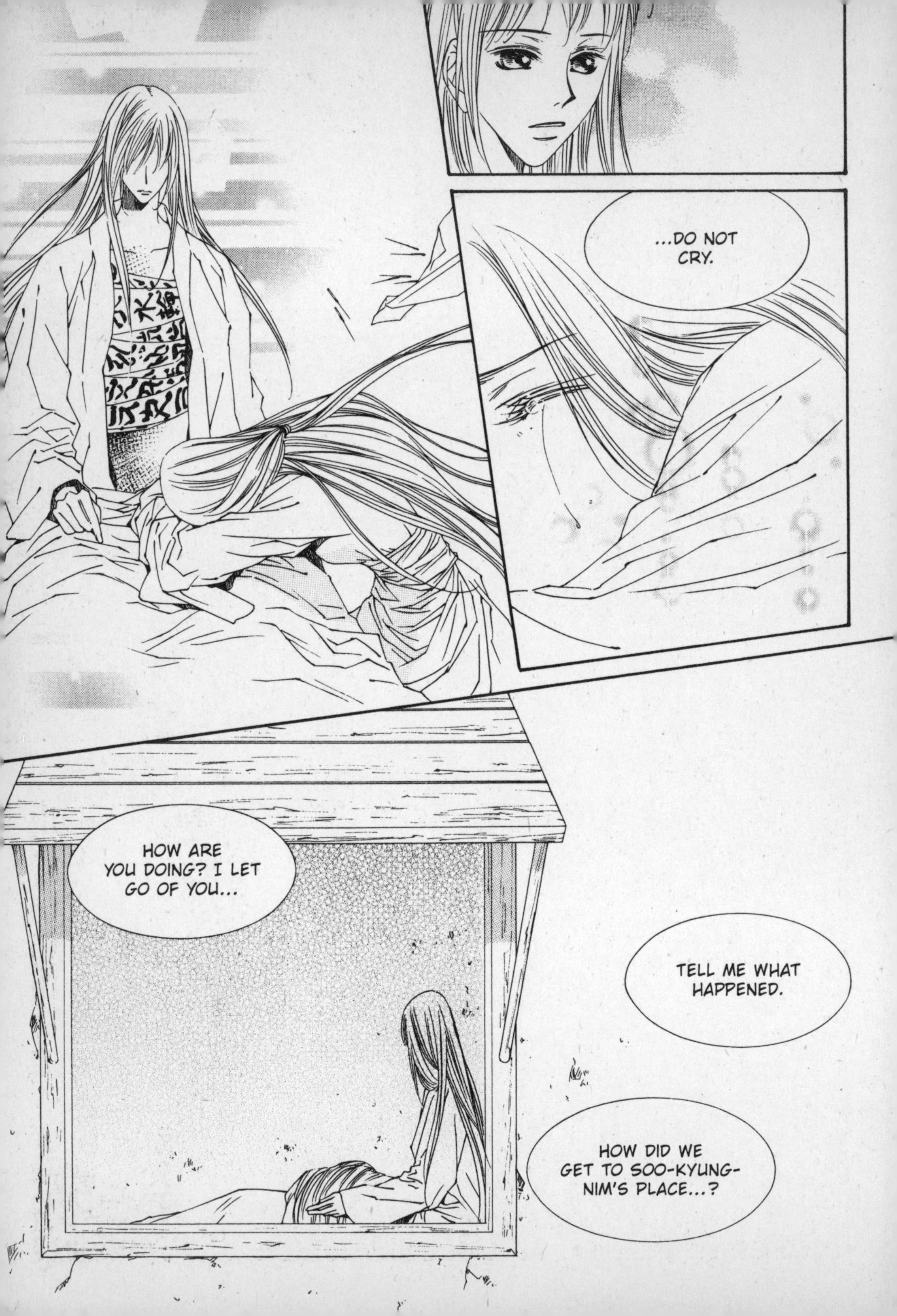
...DO NOT CRY.
HOW ARE YOU DOING? I LET GO OF YOU...
TELL ME WHAT HAPPENED.
HOW DID WE GET TO SOO-KYUNG-NIM'S PLACE...?

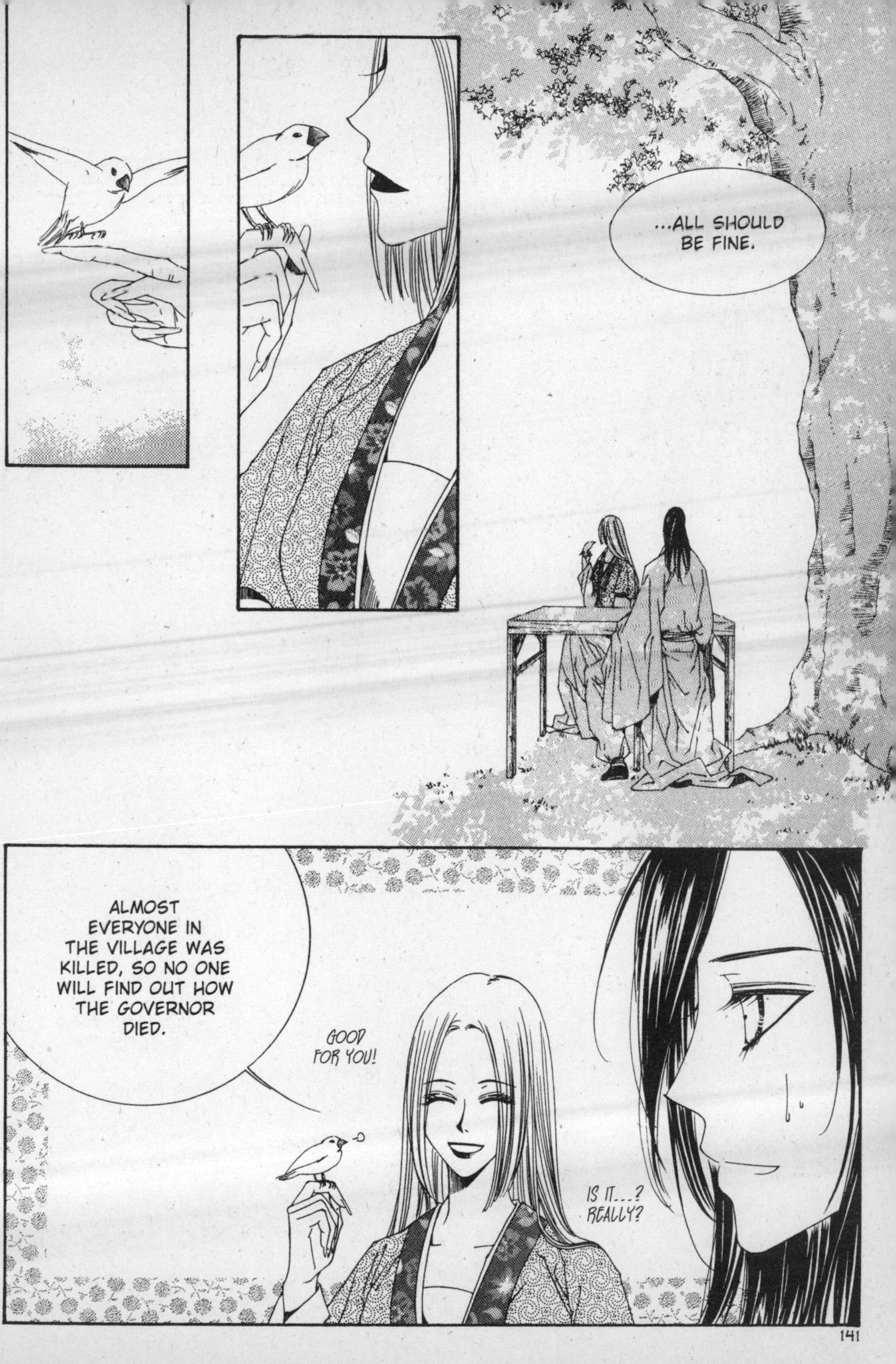

...ALL SHOULD BE FINE.
ALMOST EVERYONE IN THE VILLAGE WAS KILLED, SO NO ONE WILL FIND OUT HOW THE GOVERNOR DIED.
GOOD FOR YOU!
IS IT...? REALLY?

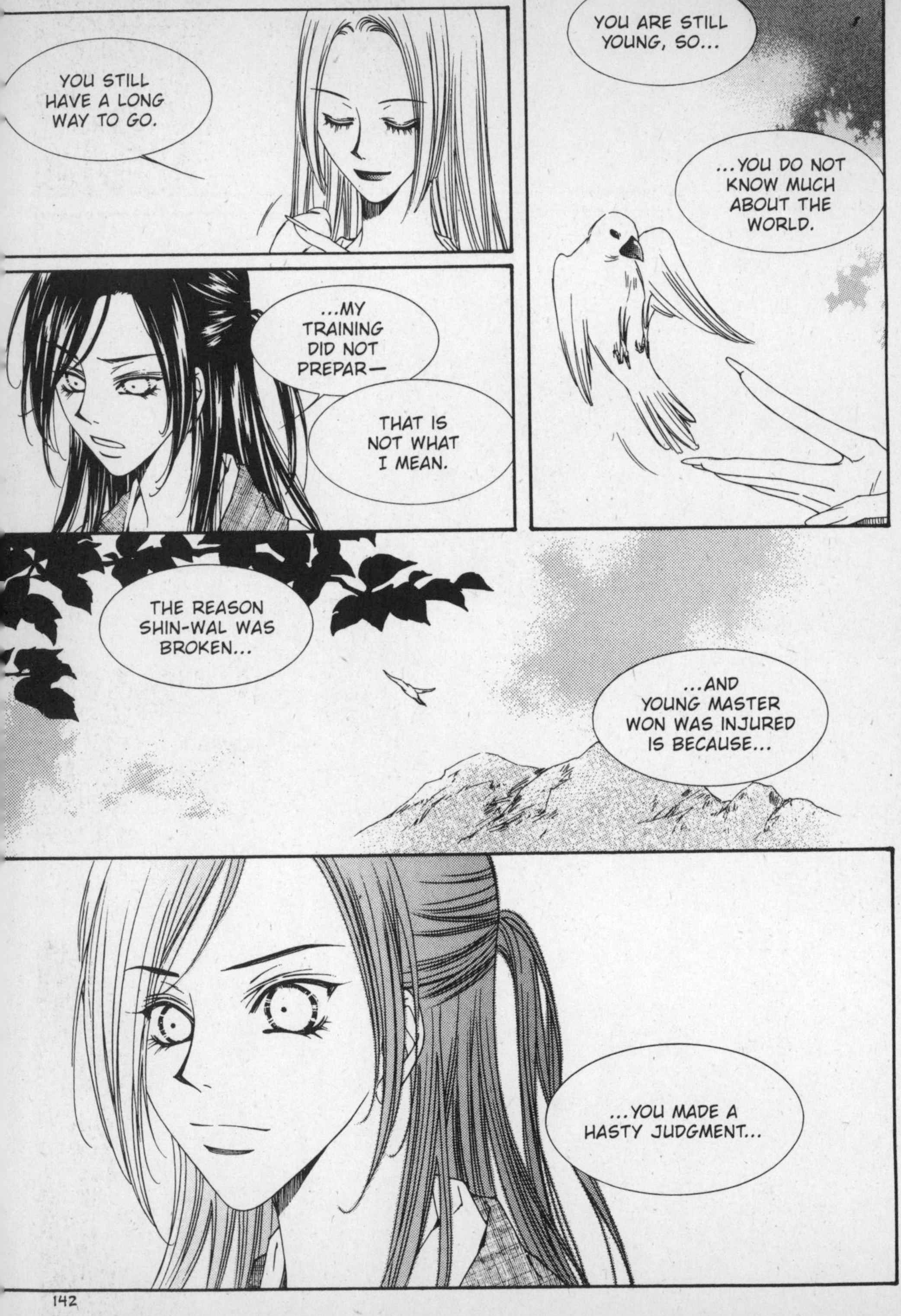
YOU STILL HAVE A LONG WAY TO GO.
YOU ARE STILL YOUNG, SO...
...YOU DO NOT KNOW MUCH ABOUT THE WORLD.
...MY TRAINING DID NOT PREPAR—
THAT IS NOT WHAT I MEAN.
THE REASON SHIN-WAL WAS BROKEN...
...AND YOUNG MASTER WON WAS INJURED IS BECAUSE...
...YOU MADE A HASTY JUDGMENT...

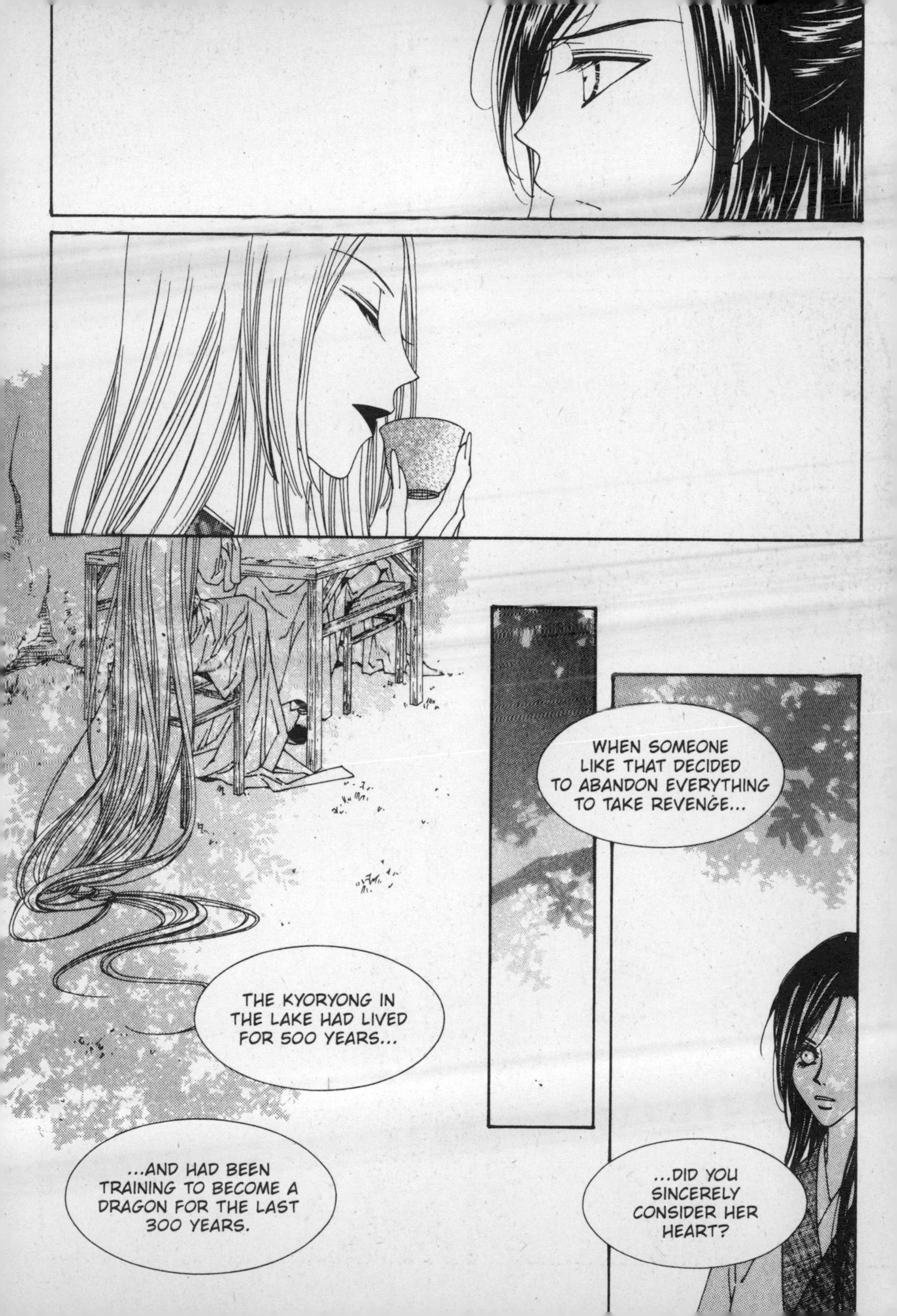
WHEN SOMEONE LIKE THAT DECIDED TO ABANDON EVERYTHING TO TAKE REVENGE...
...DID YOU SINCERELY CONSIDER HER HEART?
THE KYORYONG IN THE LAKE HAD LIVED FOR 500 YEARS...
...AND HAD BEEN TRAINING TO BECOME A DRAGON FOR THE LAST 300 YEARS.

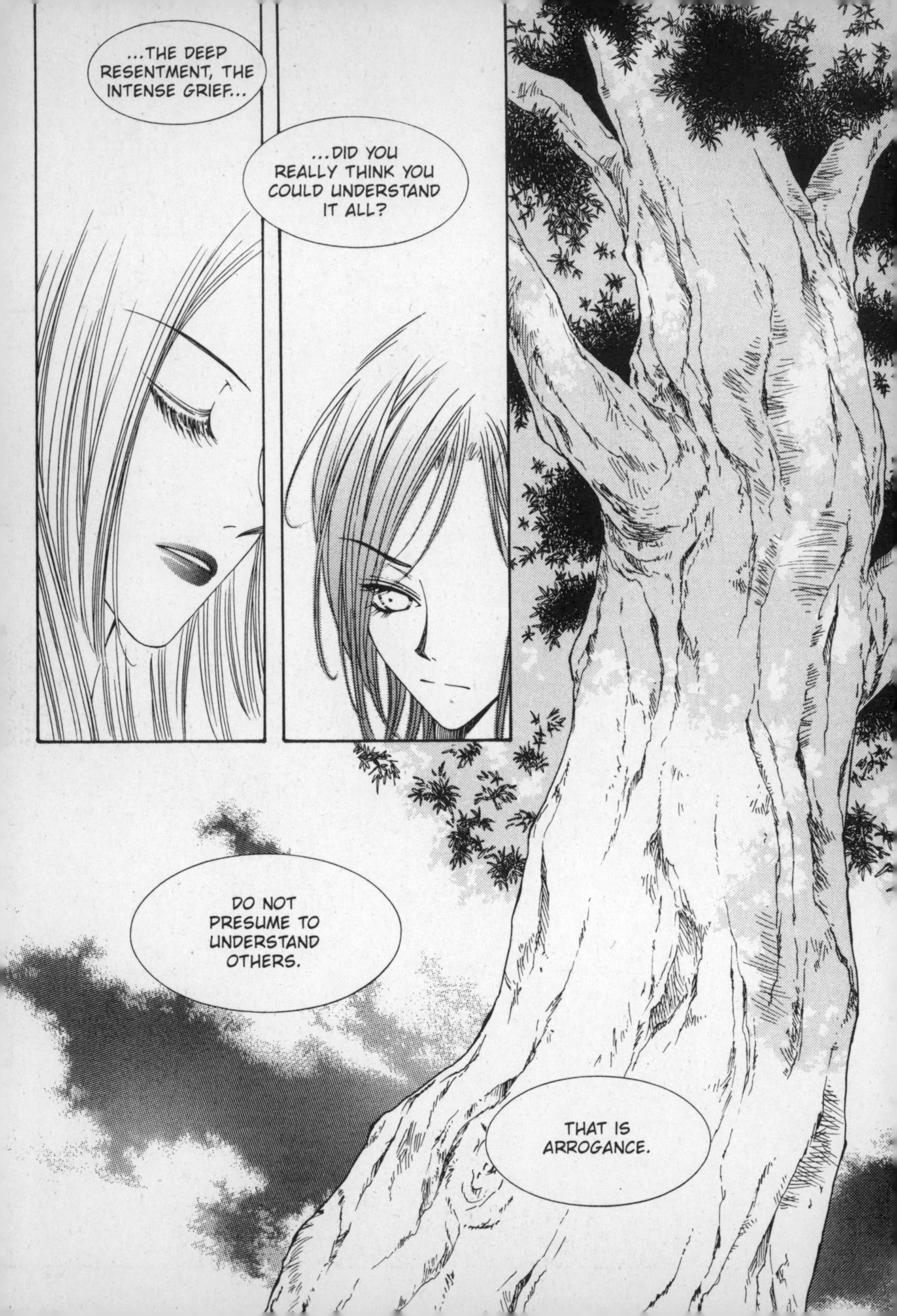
...THE DEEP RESENTMENT, THE INTENSE GRIEF...
...DID YOU REALLY THINK YOU COULD UNDERSTAND IT ALL?
DO NOT PRESUME TO UNDERSTAND OTHERS.
THAT IS ARROGANCE.

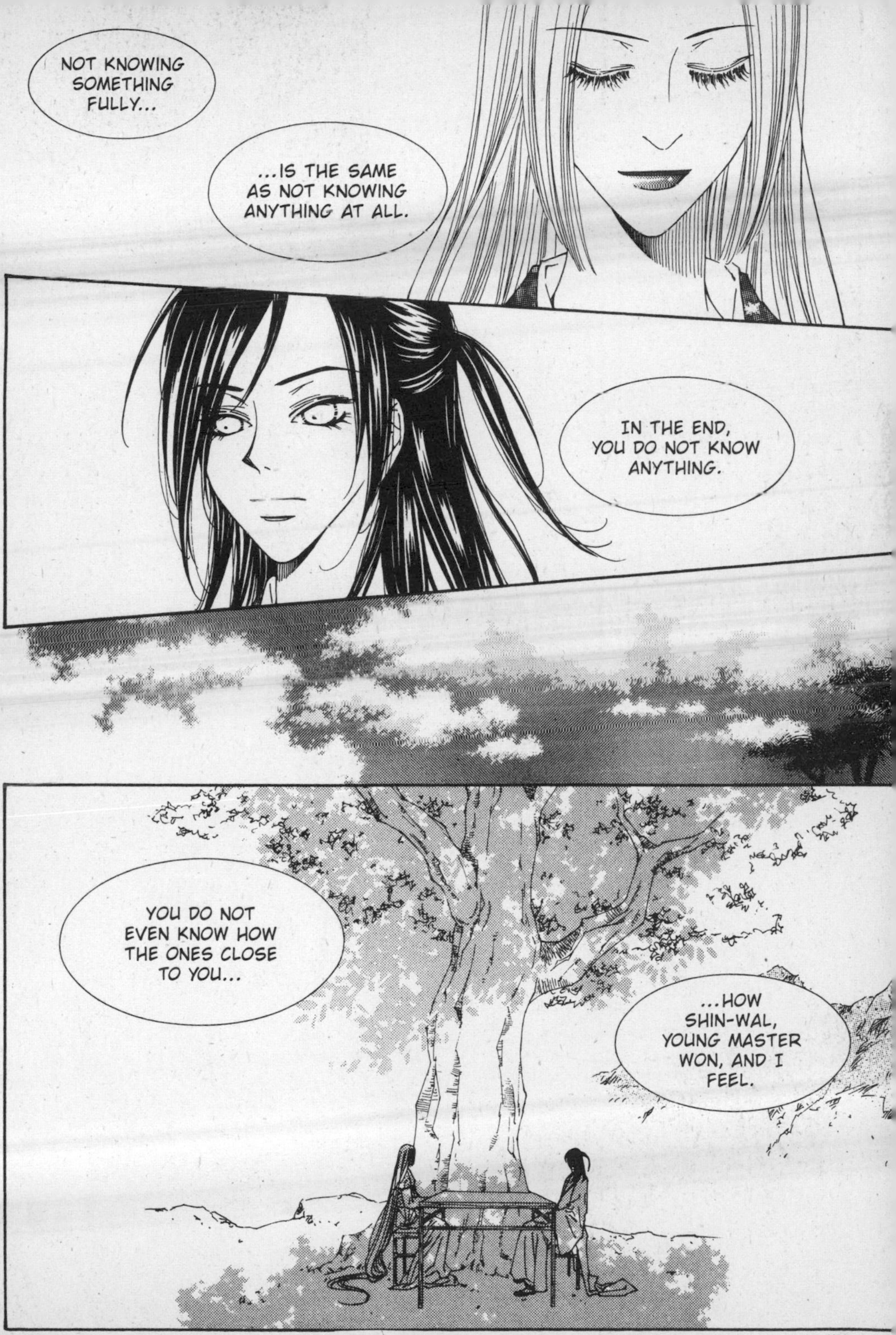
NOT KNOWING SOMETHING FULLY...
...IS THE SAME AS NOT KNOWING ANYTHING AT ALL.
IN THE END, YOU DO NOT KNOW ANYTHING.
YOU DO NOT EVEN KNOW HOW THE ONES CLOSE TO YOU...
...HOW SHIN-WAL, YOUNG MASTER WON, AND I FEEL.

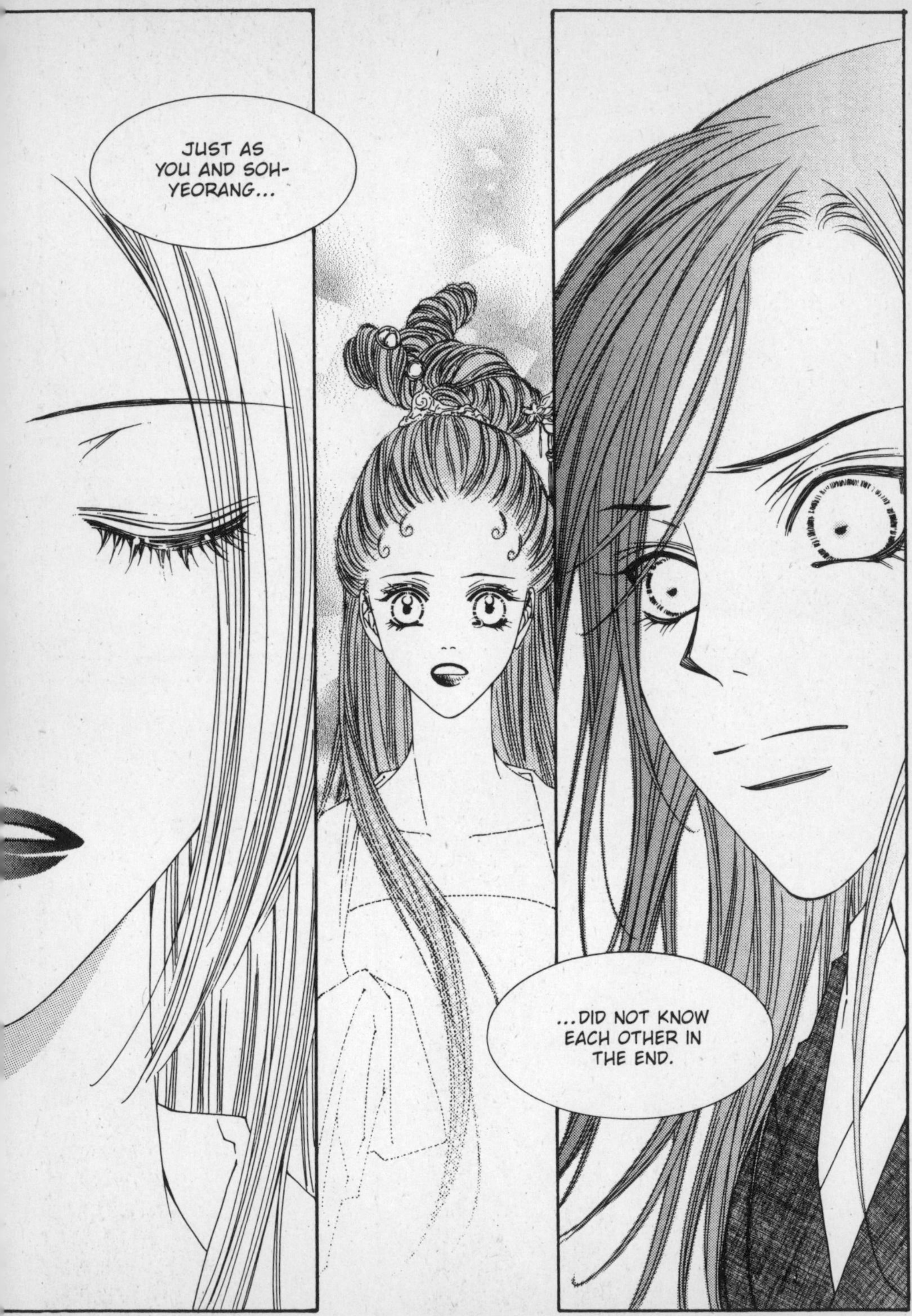
JUST AS YOU AND SOH-YEORANG...
...DID NOT KNOW EACH OTHER IN THE END.

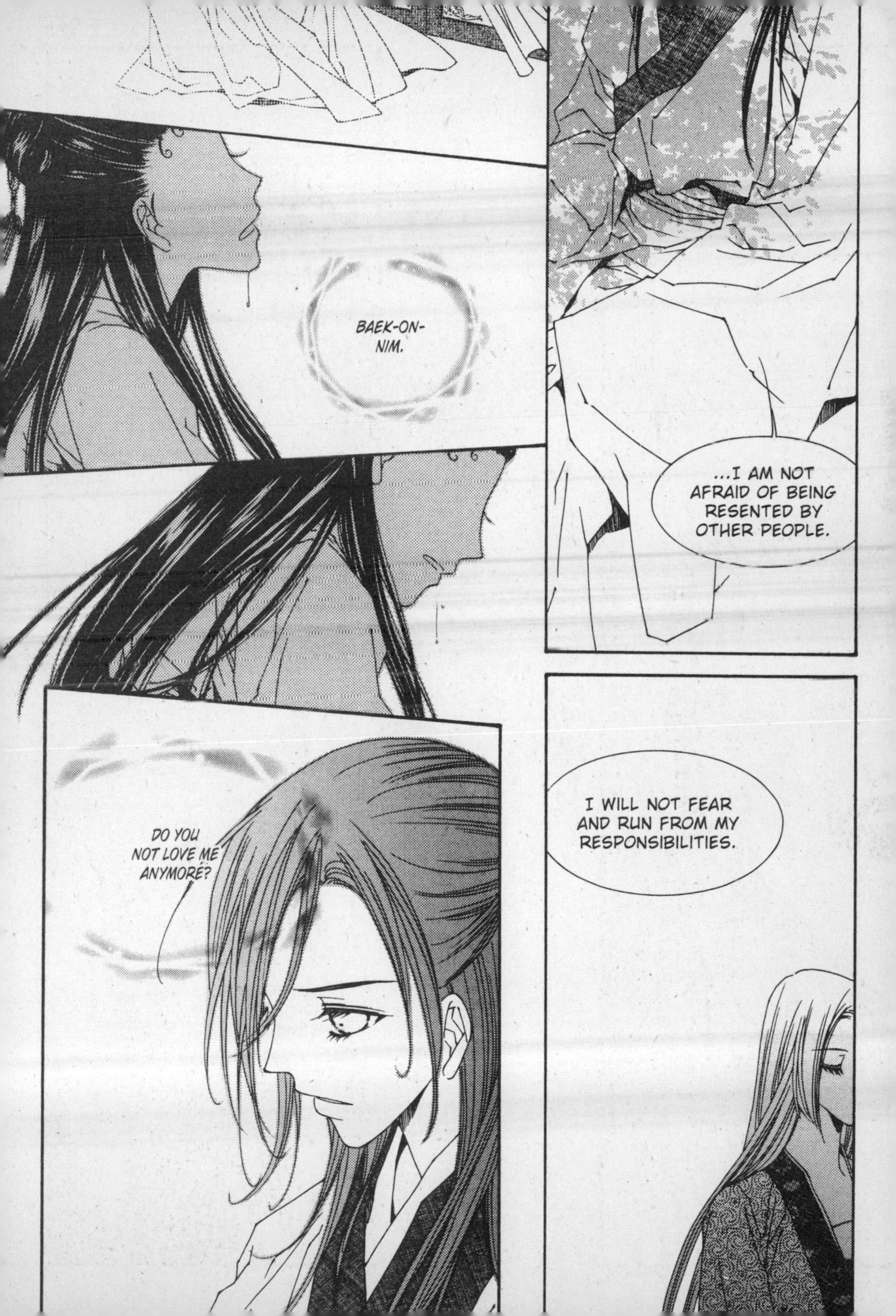
BAEK-ON-NIM.
...I AM NOT AFRAID OF BEING RESENTED BY OTHER PEOPLE.
DO YOU NOT LOVE ME ANYMORE?
I WILL NOT FEAR AND RUN FROM MY RESPONSIBILITIES.

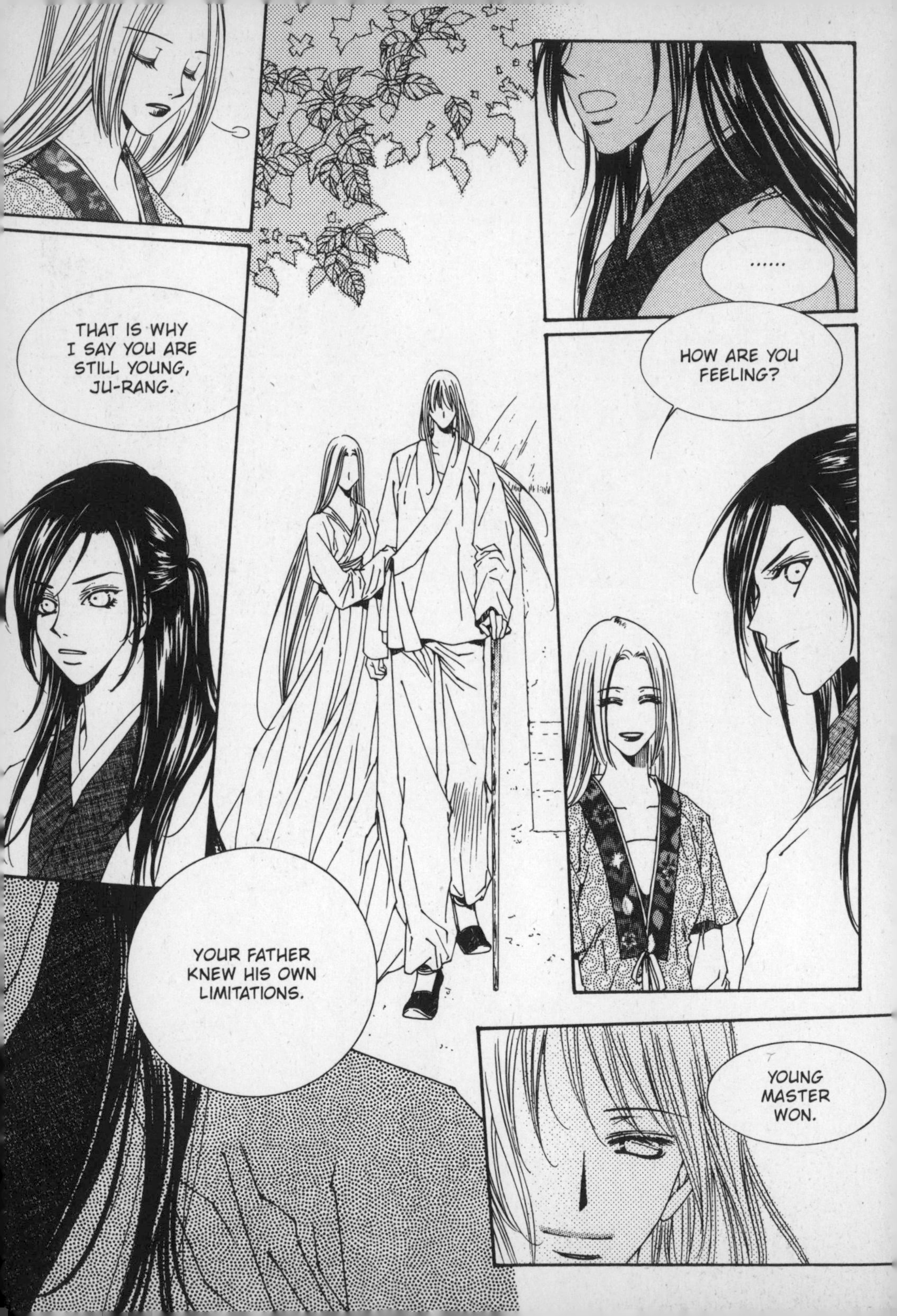
......
THAT IS WHY I SAY YOU ARE STILL YOUNG, JU-RANG.
HOW ARE YOU FEELING?
YOUR FATHER KNEW HIS OWN LIMITATIONS.
YOUNG MASTER WON.

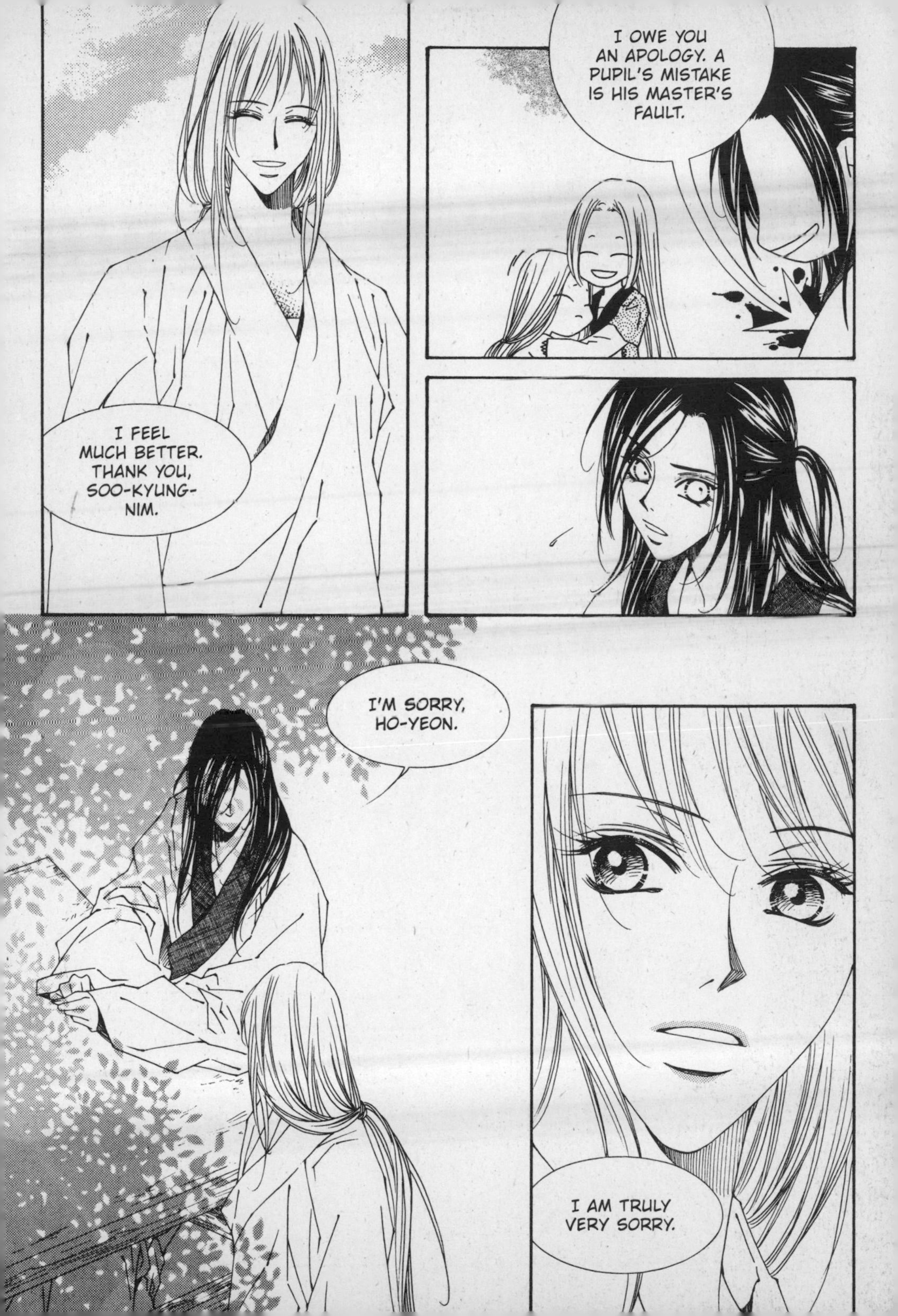
I OWE YOU AN APOLOGY. A PUPIL'S MISTAKE IS HIS MASTER'S FAULT.
I FEEL MUCH BETTER. THANK YOU, SOO-KYUNG-NIM.
I'M SORRY, HO-YEON.
I AM TRULY VERY SORRY.

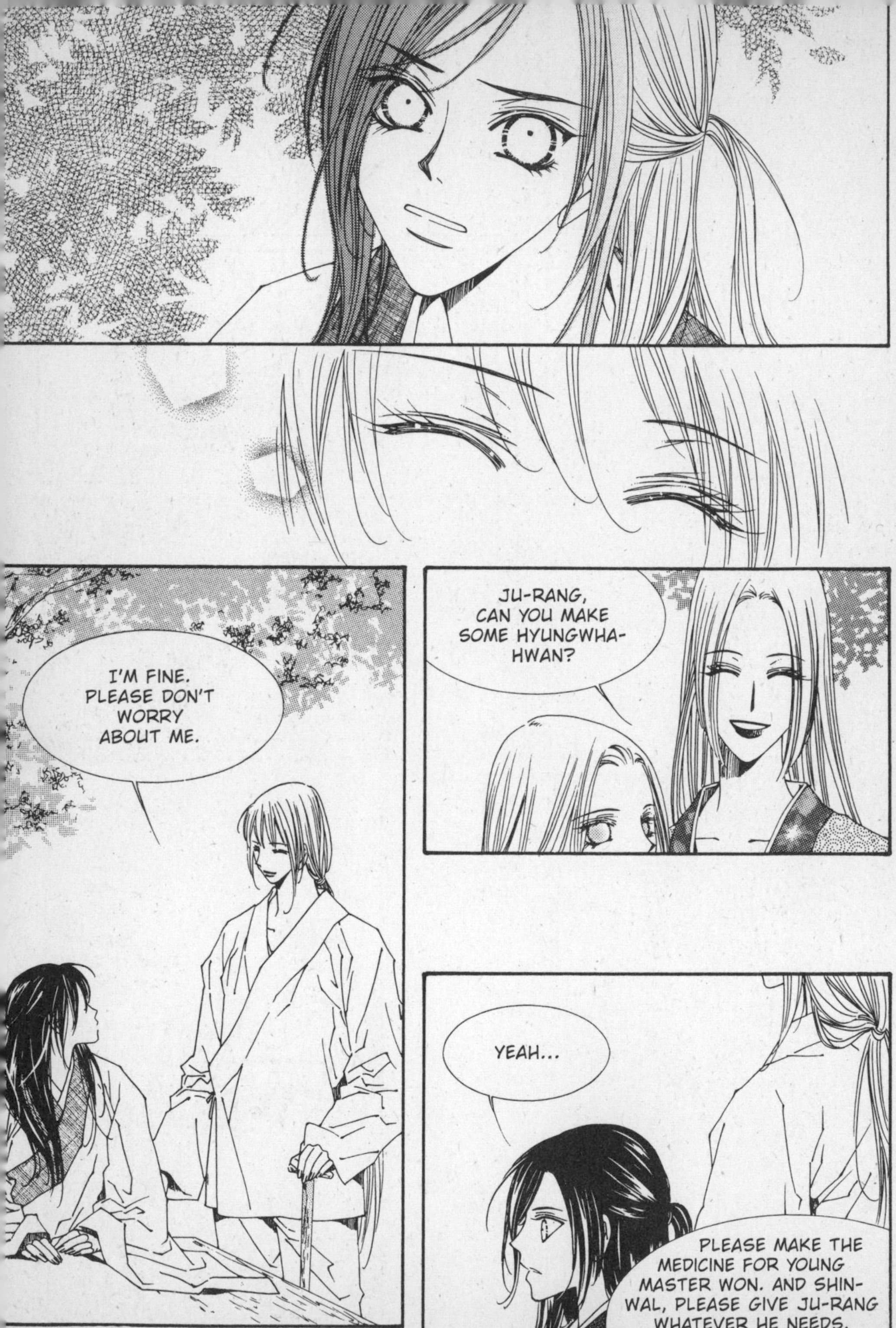
JU-RANG, CAN YOU MAKE SOME HYUNGWHA-HWAN?
I'M FINE. PLEASE DON'T WORRY ABOUT ME.
YEAH...
PLEASE MAKE THE MEDICINE FOR YOUNG MASTER WON. AND SHIN-WAL, PLEASE GIVE JU-RANG WHATEVER HE NEEDS.

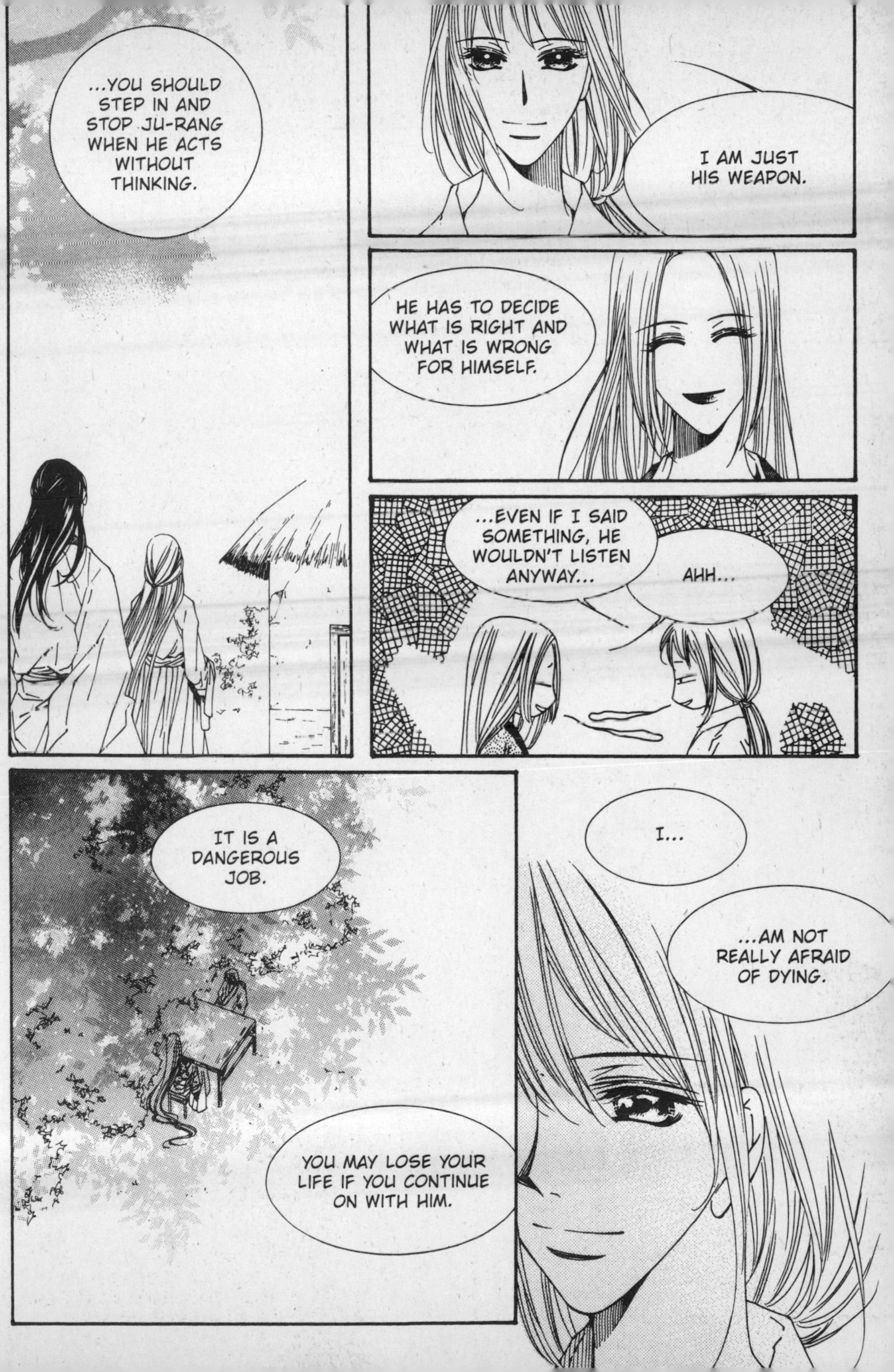
...YOU SHOULD STEP IN AND STOP JU-RANG WHEN HE ACTS WITHOUT THINKING.
I AM JUST HIS WEAPON.
HE HAS TO DECIDE WHAT IS RIGHT AND WHAT IS WRONG FOR HIMSELF.
...EVEN IF I SAID SOMETHING, HE WOULDN'T LISTEN ANYWAY...
AHH...
IT IS A DANGEROUS JOB.
YOU MAY LOSE YOUR LIFE IF YOU CONTINUE ON WITH HIM.
I...
...AM NOT REALLY AFRAID OF DYING.

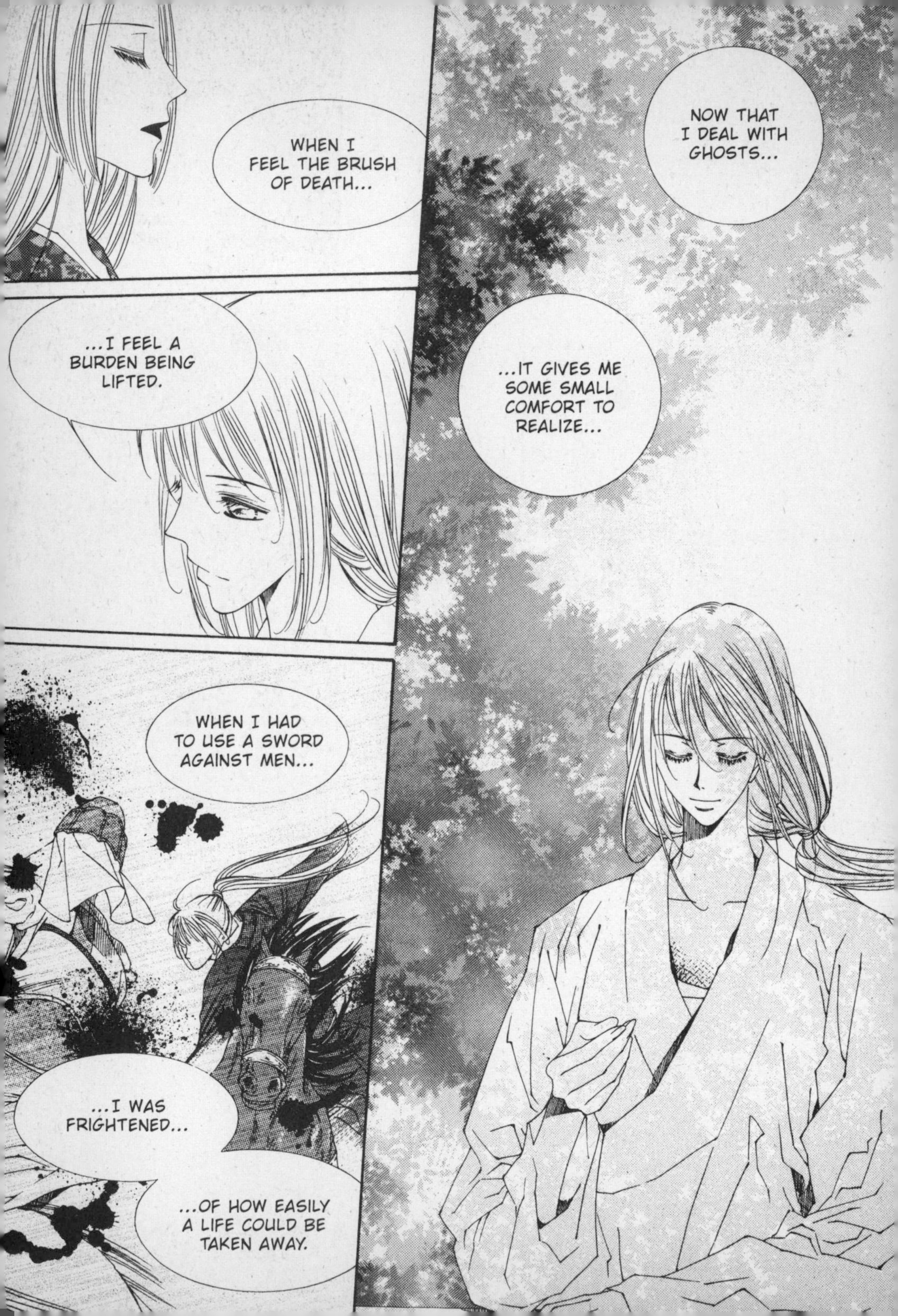
WHEN I FEEL THE BRUSH OF DEATH...
...I FEEL A BURDEN BEING LIFTED.
WHEN I HAD TO USE A SWORD AGAINST MEN...
...I WAS FRIGHTENED...
...OF HOW EASILY A LIFE COULD BE TAKEN AWAY.
NOW THAT I DEAL WITH GHOSTS...
...IT GIVES ME SOME SMALL COMFORT TO REALIZE...

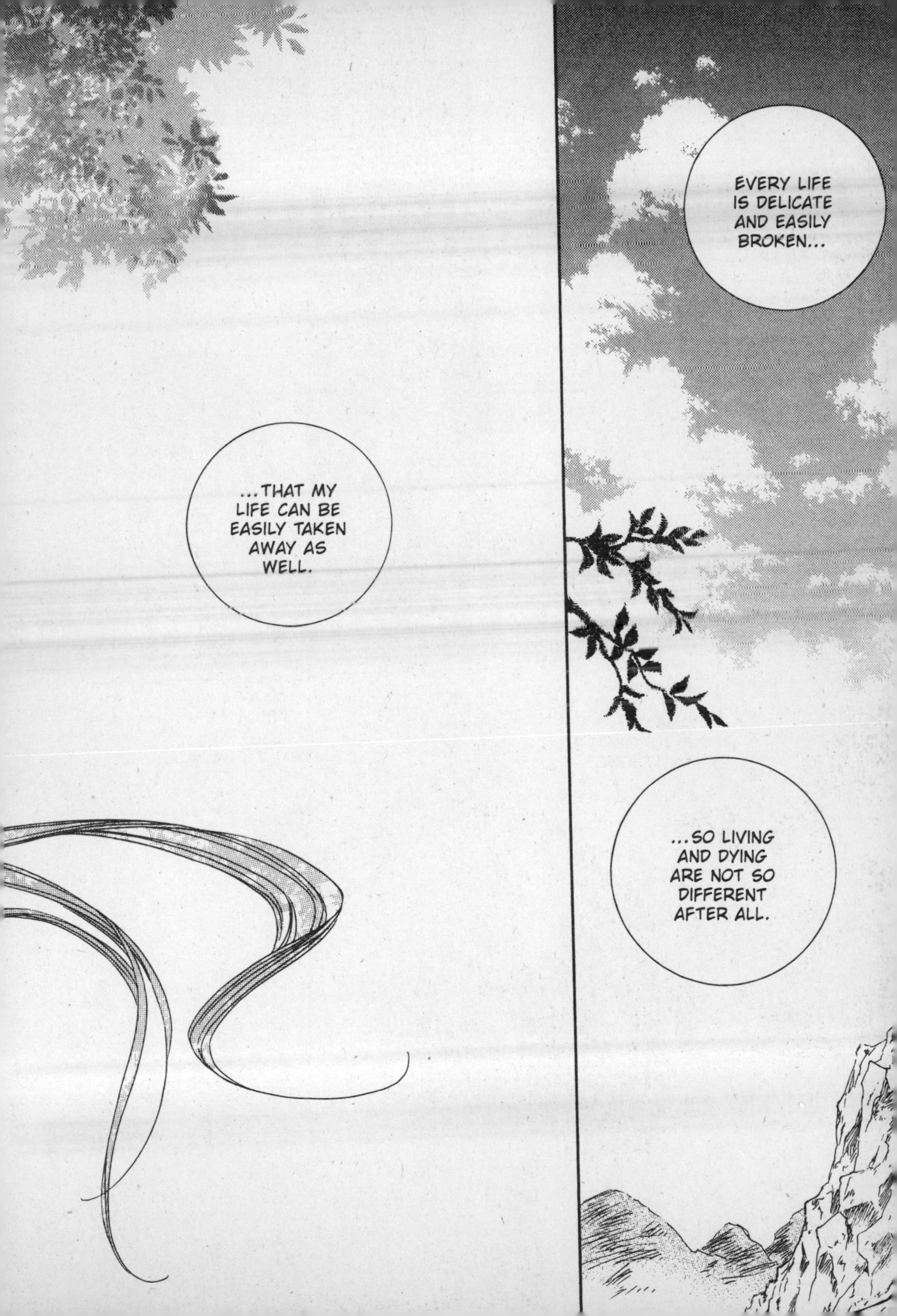
EVERY LIFE IS DELICATE AND EASILY BROKEN...
...SO LIVING AND DYING ARE NOT SO DIFFERENT AFTER ALL.
...THAT MY LIFE CAN BE EASILY TAKEN AWAY AS WELL.

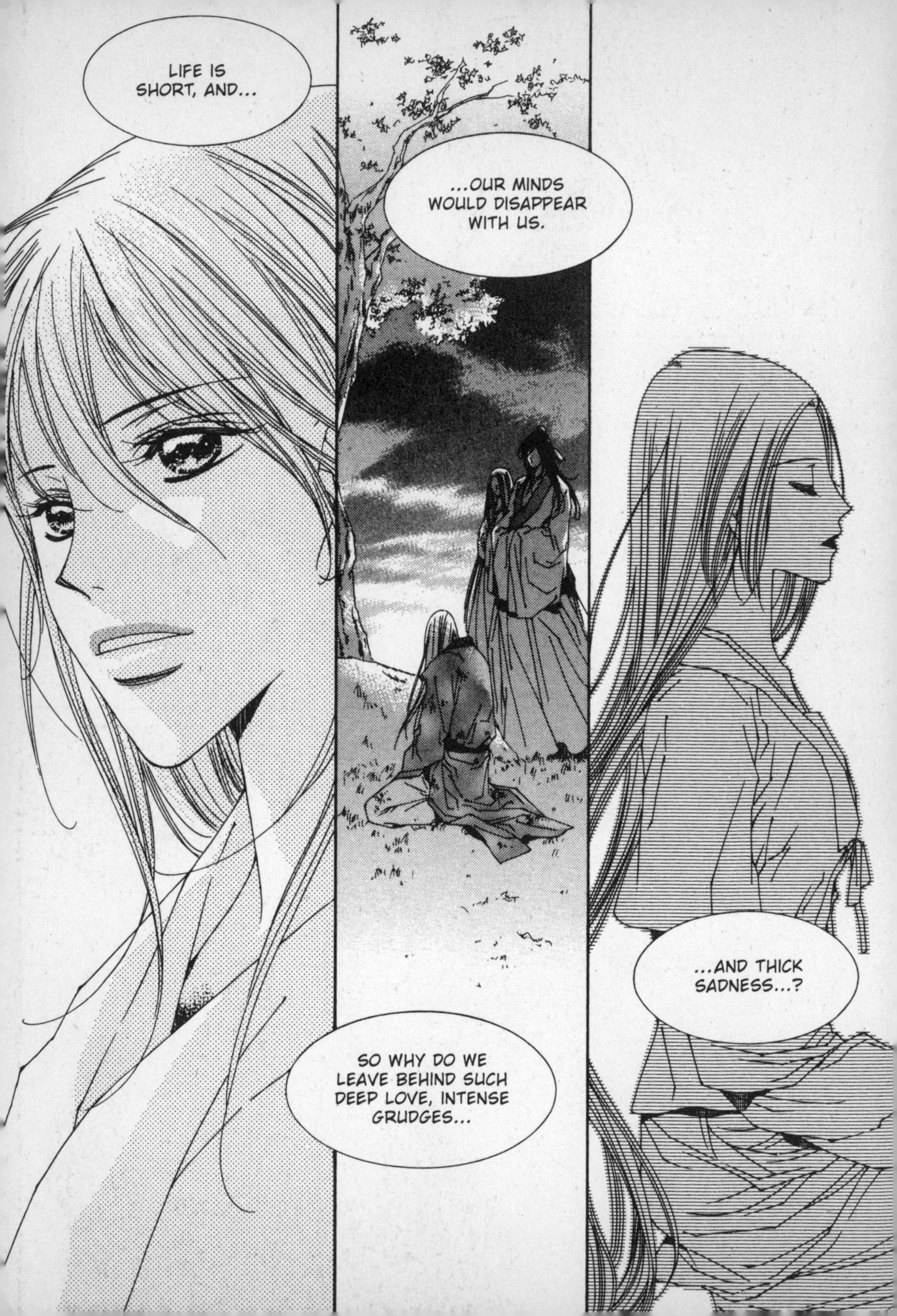
LIFE IS SHORT, AND...
...OUR MINDS WOULD DISAPPEAR WITH US.
SO WHY DO WE LEAVE BEHIND SUCH DEEP LOVE, INTENSE GRUDGES...
...AND THICK SADNESS...?

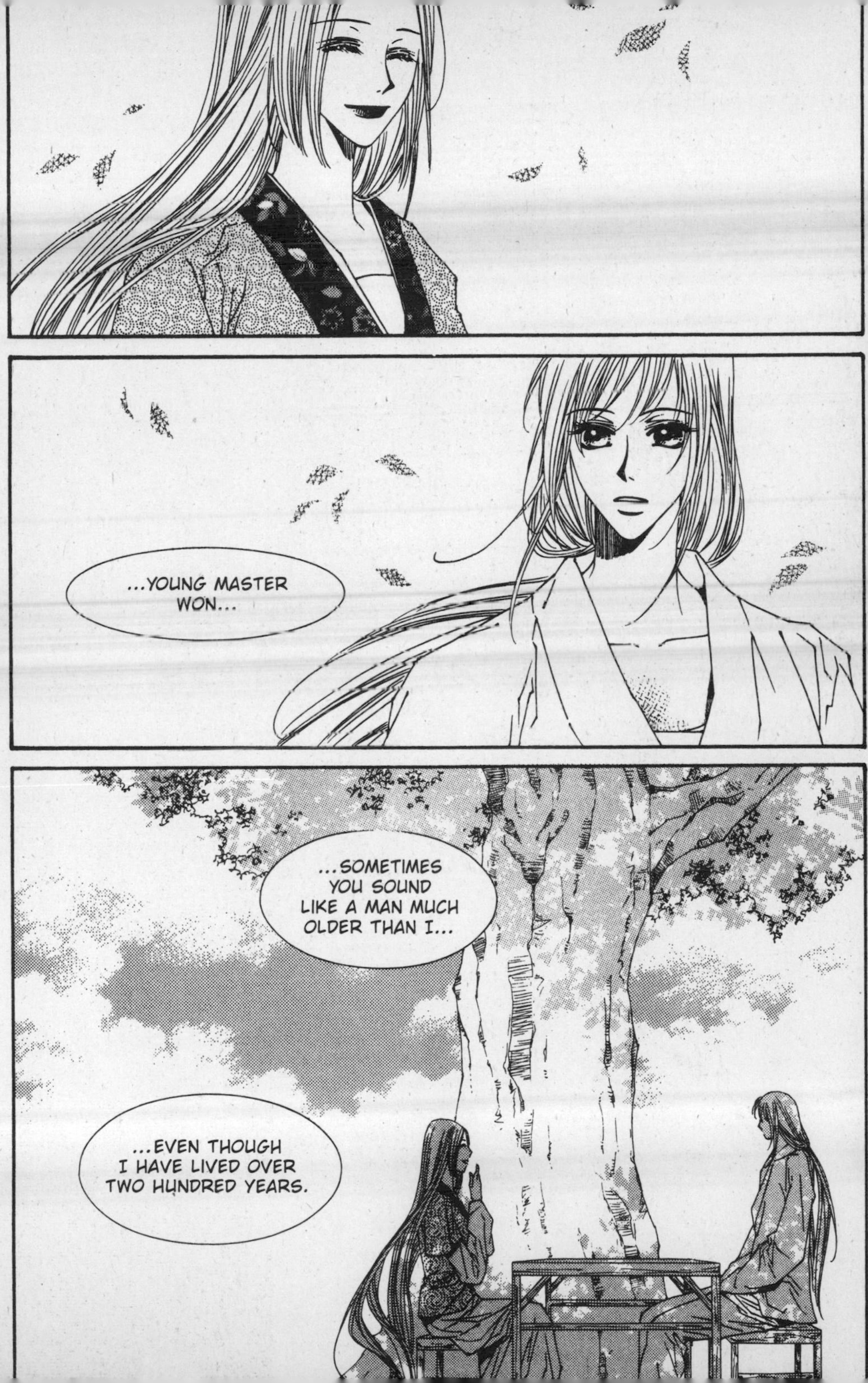
...YOUNG MASTER WON...
...SOMETIMES YOU SOUND LIKE A MAN MUCH OLDER THAN I...
...EVEN THOUGH I HAVE LIVED OVER TWO HUNDRED YEARS.

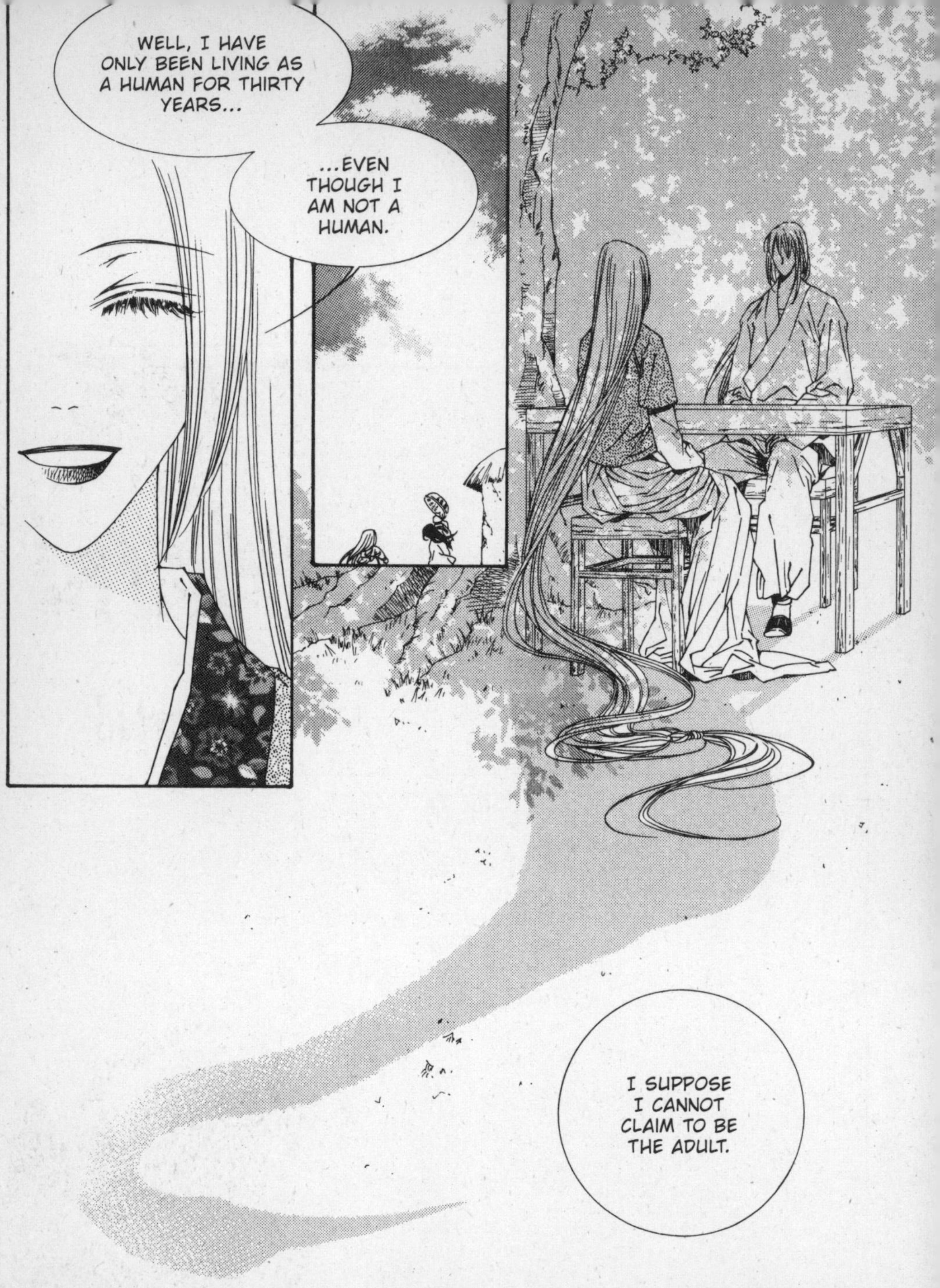
WELL, I HAVE ONLY BEEN LIVING AS A HUMAN FOR THIRTY YEARS...
...EVEN THOUGH I AM NOT A HUMAN.
I SUPPOSE I CANNOT CLAIM TO BE THE ADULT.

THE END OF CHAPTER SEVEN

TO BE CONTINUED IN VOLUME 3 . . .

TIME AND AGAIN

Afterword

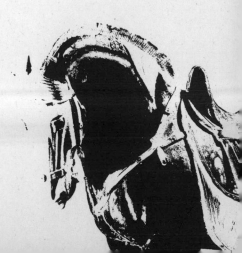

MONETARY VALUES DURING THE TANG DYNASTY

ACCORDING TO THE CHINESE BOOK JOYACHUMJAE, YOU COULD BUY THREE EGGS WITH ONE YUAN.

TODAY, ONE EGG IS WORTH ABOUT 20 CENTS.

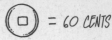 = 60 CENTS

1,000 YUAN = 600 U.S. DOLLARS

...SO 1,000 YUAN IS NOT ENOUGH THAT HE SHOULD MAKE SUCH A FUSS ABOUT IT.

I WANTED TO SAY 10,000 YUAN HERE TOO, BUT...

IS THAT WHY YOU WILL ONLY SPEND THE NIGHT WITH A 1,000-YUAN KINYU?

THE MOST COMMONLY-USED COIN DURING THE TANG DYNASTY WAS THE K'AI YUAN, AND IT WEIGHED 3.75 GRAMS. THAT MEANS 10,000 YUAN WOULD WEIGH 37.5 KG.

IT'S NOT SOMETHING A PERSON COULD CARRY AROUND EASILY!!

EVEN 1,000 YUAN WAS HEAVY.

THERE ARE A LOT OF STORIES IN CHINESE BOOKS ABOUT PEOPLE USING CARTS TO TRANSPORT MONEY.

I DIDN'T WANT TO DRAW HO-YEON CARTING AROUND MONEY (SINCE BAEK-ON WOULD NEVER DO IT) SO I TOOK ONE ZERO AWAY.

I'M SURE MY READERS WOULDN'T WANT TO SEE THAT EITHER.

PLEASE CONSIDER 1,000 YUAN THE SAME AS $5-6,000.

CHAPTER FIVE

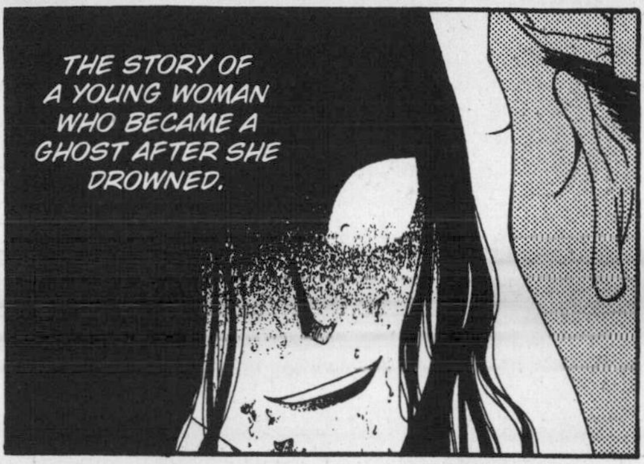
THE STORY OF A YOUNG WOMAN WHO BECAME A GHOST AFTER SHE DROWNED.

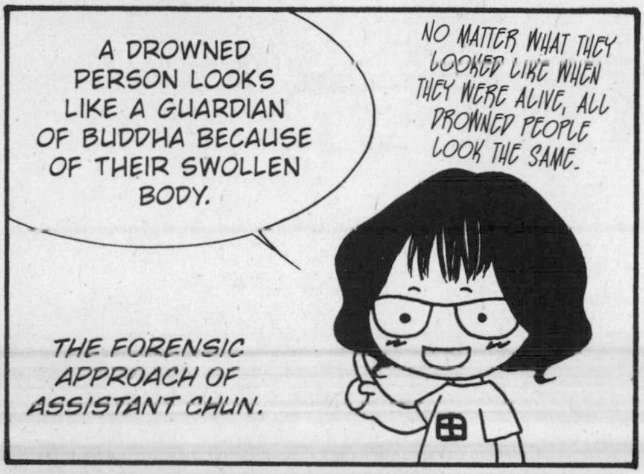
A DROWNED PERSON LOOKS LIKE A GUARDIAN OF BUDDHA BECAUSE OF THEIR SWOLLEN BODY.
NO MATTER WHAT THEY LOOKED LIKE WHEN THEY WERE ALIVE, ALL DROWNED PEOPLE LOOK THE SAME.
THE FORENSIC APPROACH OF ASSISTANT CHUN.

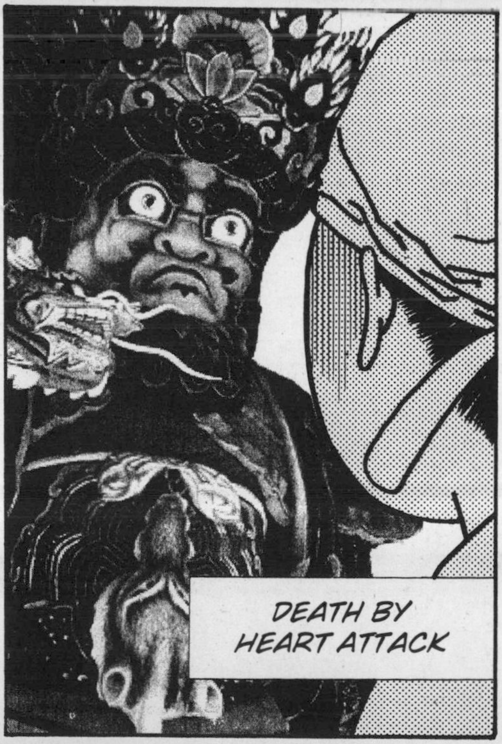
DEATH BY HEART ATTACK

CHANG'AN WAS THE FIRST AND LUOYANG WAS THE SECOND CAPITAL OF THE TANG DYNASTY. BUT COMPARED TO CHANG'AN, WHICH WAS A SPLENDID INTERNATIONAL CITY, LUOYANG WAS TREATED LIKE A RURAL COMMUNITY. EVEN THE BROTHELS WERE CONSIDERED TO BE ON A DIFFERENT LEVEL...

I DON'T BELIEVE THAT A SPIRIT STAYS BEHIND JUST BECAUSE HE OR SHE HAS A SAD STORY. I THINK IT DEPENDS ON THE PERSON'S POWER OF CONCENTRATION. WHAT DO YOU THINK?

CHAPTER SIX

BASTARD!

...WHY WOULDN'T I HAVE FOLLOWED YOU?

JUST WAIT! I WILL GET REVENGE FOR MY HUSBAND!

DO YOU THINK I'LL LET YOU BE HAPPY AFTER YOU'VE TAKEN MY LOVE AWAY FROM ME?

THIS LIFE IS...PRETTY GOOD...!

THAT IS HUMAN NATURE.

MY INSPIRATION FOR THIS STORY WAS THE TALES OF HANBING, WHICH IS ABOUT EXTREME LOVE TRIANGLES.

THREE "ON TOP,"
THREE "IN THE MIDDLE," AND
THREE "BELOW" ARE:

MASANG: A WOMAN ON TOP OF A HORSE
JANGSANG: A WOMAN PERCHED ATOP A WALL AND LOOKING OUTSIDE
NUSANG: A WOMAN ON TOP OF A PAVILION

YEOJOONG: A WOMAN IN THE MIDDLE OF AN INN
CHUIJOONG: A WOMAN IN THE MIDDLE OF DRINKING
ILJOONG: A WOMAN IN THE MIDDLE OF SUNSHINE

WALHA: A WOMAN BELOW THE MOONLIGHT
CHOKHA: A WOMAN BELOW CANDLELIGHT
YUMHA: A WOMAN BELOW A BEADED CURTAIN

...THE ABOVE CAN BE FOUND IN SUNGHO-SASUL BY IK LEE. NOW YOU CAN TRY OUT THESE POSES TODAY. ^^

YOU CAN FIND THE STORY OF A NOBLEMAN WHOSE HOBBY WAS ABUSING HIS SERVANT'S WIFE IN MYUNGYUP-JIHAE BY MAN-JONG HONG. IN THE CHOSUN DYNASTY, ADULTERY WITH A SERVANT'S WIFE WAS NOT PUNISHABLE BY LAW.

YOU SAY WHATEVER YOU WANT TO SAY, BUT YOU STILL GET SO UPSET WHEN SOMEONE TELLS YOU SOMETHING YOU DON'T WANT TO HEAR...

I'M SORRY THAT I'M STILL A CHILD.

THE STORY OF POISONING FISH IN A LAKE IS FROM GYESAN-DAMSOO. A GOVERNMENT OFFICIAL'S TYRANNY IS SCARIER THAN A SEXY VIDEO.

HERE'S HOW YOU CAN MAKE HYUNGHWA-HWAN:

MIX TOGETHER ARSENIC, IRON SULFIDE, GLOWWORMS, YELLOW VINE, WILD FLOWERS, THE BURNT HANDLE OF AN IRON HAMMER, ASHES FROM A FIREPLACE, THE CRUSHED HORN OF AN ANTELOPE, AN EGG YOLK, AND BLOOD FROM A ROOSTER'S COMB. THEN FORM MIXTURE INTO PILLS.

...I WONDER IF THIS MEDICINE WOULD REALLY WORK... (BURNT HANDLE OF AN IRON HAMMER?)

TRANSLATION NOTES

In Asian history and culture, a certain value was placed on a person's given name, so it was considered rude to use it too often. Thus, when a person married or reached a certain age, he or she would be given another name to be used more commonly. This is why Yoo Ju and Wee Won refer to each other as Baek-On Ju and Ho-Yeon Won respectively.

Page 14
The Lady of Guo was the sister of Yang Yuhuan, Emperor Xuanzong's favorite concubine. Like her sister, the Lady of Guo was reknowned for her beauty.

Page 17
The Butterfly Lovers is a Chinese legend often equated to *Romeo and Juliet*. The beautiful Yingtai Zhu disguises herself as a man so that she can attend classes at a distant school. For four years, she shares a room with Shanbo Liang, who is oblivious to the fact that his roommate is a woman. During that time, Yingtai falls in love with Shanbo, but before she gathers the courage to expose herself, her father calls her back home. Only when he visits the Zhu home months later does Shanbo discover his dear friend is a woman. They are devoted to each other, but their bliss is short-lived—Yingtai has already been promised to another. Heartbroken, Shanbo falls ill and eventually dies.
On the day of her wedding, Yingtai and her bridal party are hindered by a mysterious whirlwind that will not allow them to proceed beyond Shanbo's grave. With a clap of thunder, the grave opens, and Yingtai readily throws herself into the ground to join her beloved. Their spirits are transformed, and the lovers emerge from the grave as a pair of butterflies, never to be parted again.

Page 29
The Korean suffix *-nim* is used to convey respect, similar to *-san* or *-sama* in Japanese.

Page 50
Xi Shi is one of the legendary beauties of ancient China. Xi Shi was sent to King Fuchai of Wu by his enemies. Enthralled by her beauty, Fuchai neglected his duties and obeyed her every word. As a result, his palace was left vulnerable to attack and was eventually claimed by his enemies.

Page 94
A *kyoryong* is a mythical animal over eight feet long with the body of a snake with four bird-like legs, resembling a cross between a chicken and a dragon. It lives in water, but can eventually become a dragon and rise up into the sky.

A *kinyu* was similar to a Japanese *geisha*. These women would entertain their guests with dance, song, recitation, and conversation.

Page 99
Yuan was the ancient currency used in China and Korea.

Page 106
The curse of the three bastards refers to the incident involving Li Ying, Li Yao, and Li Yu, three princes from the reign of Emperor Xuanzong during the Tang Dynasty. One of the emperor's beloved concubines, Consort Wu, wished for her own son to be made crown prince, so she told the three princes there were intruders in the palace. As they prepared for battle, she then told Emperor Xuanzong that the princes were planning a hostile takeover. When the princes appeared dressed in armor, her false accusation seemed to be confirmed. The three were subsequently executed. At the time, people referred to the unfortunate princes as "the three bastards." When Consort Wu died not long after, they said it was the curse of the three.

Page 146
The suffix *-yeorang* was used to describe an unmarried woman during the Tang Dynasty.

Page 148
The suffix *-rang* is used to refer to someone else's son in a more familiar way.

Page 150
Hyungwha-hwan is a medicine that can be used to treat poisoning or wounds caused by illness, ghosts, or deadly animals.

TIME AND AGAIN ②

JIUN YUN

Translation: HyeYoung Im • English Adaptation: J. Torres

Lettering: Abigail Blackman

Time and Again, vol. 2 © 2006 by YUN Ji-un, DAEWON C.I. Inc. All rights reserved. First published in Korea in 2006 by DAEWON C.I. Inc. English translation rights in USA, Canada, UK and Commonwelth arranged by Daewon C.I. Inc. through TOPAZ Agency Inc.

Translation © 2010 by Hachette Book Group, Inc.

Yen Press
Hachette Book Group
237 Park Avenue, New York, NY 10017

www.HachetteBookGroup.com
www.YenPress.com

Yen Press is an imprint of Hachette Book Group, Inc. The Yen Press name and logo are trademarks of Hachette Book Group, Inc.

First Yen Press Edition: March 2010

ISBN: 978-0-7595-3059-1

10 9 8 7 6 5 4 3 2 1

BVG

Printed in the United States of America

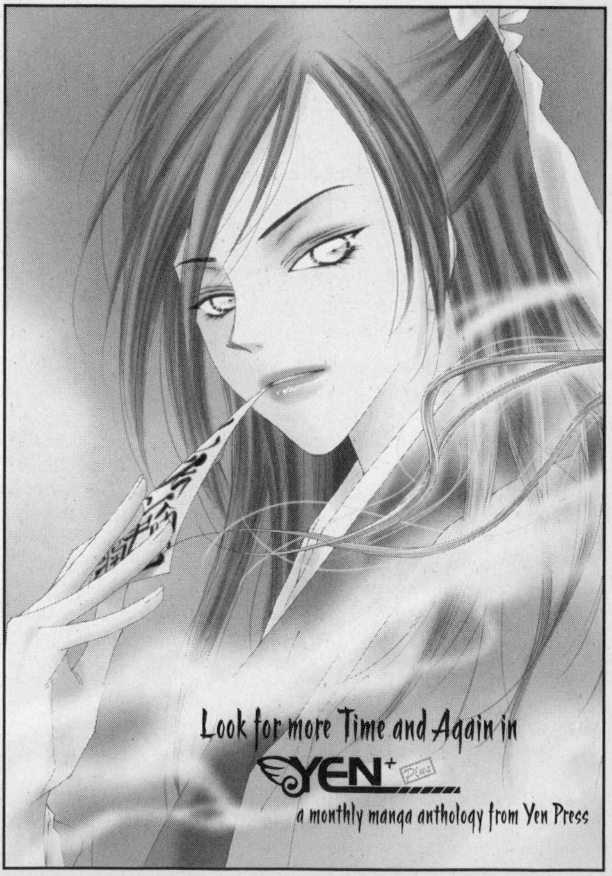
Look for more Time and Again in
YEN+ Plus
a monthly manga anthology from Yen Press